...amed because
...beach to
...and.

Congress years ago set aside land on the
beach for fish factories here. the factories
are all in ruins now but the land is still
called 'Promised Land'.

"An intrepid guide to native life in the fabled Long Island utopia offers a memoir of a half century spent tracking its inhabitants as proprietor of the Hamptons' newspaper of record ... redolent of saltwater and printers' ink—perfectly suited for comfortable days at the beach."

— *Kirkus Reviews*

"Rattiner knows his territory and shares a collection of charming early memories of the people among whom he lived and worked ... such as the lovely daughter of Harrison Tweed III, Babette; the drinkers at Jungle Pete's, tightlipped about their dead crony Jackson Pollock; artist Balcomb Greene; the sun-bathing lady proprietors of the Memory Motel; reclusive John Steinbeck."

— *Publishers Weekly*

"A folksy and often irreverent take on all points east of Riverhead. Some of Rattiner's East End exploits—from an ill-fated midnight rendezvous with an heiress to his temporary banishment by legendary barman Bobby Van—are chronicled in this book.

"Rattiner [finds] his way to the beach most every day, past the area cordoned off for the 'saber-tooth plovers,' to face the surf and type on his Dell laptop. The pristine sand, the sting of salt, the feeling that you are on the cusp of the world—that never changes."

— *Newsday*

"Rattiner's tales have the flavor of oral history, the passing along of stories from friend to friend—the time Rattiner shrugged off a chance to interview a young Richard Nixon, the day de Kooning toppled from his stool, that softball game where Bill 'Bubba' Clinton umpired with a silly grin. In these narratives, the evidence of a life well lived on a well-carved shore, Rattiner bottles the spirit of a rural enclave turned glamorous destination."

— *The Hampton Sheet*

"Now, bookshelves and beach bags alike must make room for Dan Rattiner's *In the Hamptons,* which is rich in both local anthropology and easy reading. This shouldn't come as a surprise. The author is, after all, the Dan of *Dan's Papers,* that ubiquitous, fine art covered, puckishly written, free, weekly, Truthiness and Advertising-filled newspaper-slash magazine you see blooming like flats of pansies wherever trades are plied on either Fork."

— *East Hampton Star*

"Whether Rattiner is writing about well-known people or local notables, he presents his material in entertaining fashion, holding the readers' interest. His unusual vantage point enables him to trace a half-century of changes 'In the Hamptons.'"

— *Jewish Journal*

"Dan Rattiner has been chronicling the people and events of the Hamptons for as long as I've been going there (since the sixties). If anyone wanted some insight into what made this area such an interesting place, all they'd need was a copy of *In the Hamptons.* It's as close to rubbing elbows as you can get. Enjoy!"

— Billy Joel

"If a guy says it happened in the Hamptons, and Dan Rattiner doesn't know about it, it didn't. Welcome to the high stool at the bar in the Memory Motel."

— Tom Wolfe

"Dan Rattiner, a first-rate observer of life, has been observing the life of the Hamptons for nearly fifty years. *In the Hamptons,* the result of all that clear-eyed observation, gives us every facet of the place—the strange and ridiculous, the artistic, the funny, the lovable and beautiful. Fifty years from now when people ask, 'What were the Hamptons?' they will need only to pick up this rich, sparkling book."

— Roger Rosenblatt, author of *Lapham Rising*

"If there was an honorary mayor of the Hamptons it would have to be Dan Rattiner ... a raconteur with a wicked sense of humor and an eye for detail."

— *Long Island History Journal*

In the Hamptons Too

In the Hamptons Too

FURTHER ENCOUNTERS WITH FARMERS, FISHERMEN, ARTISTS, BILLIONAIRES, *and* CELEBRITIES

DAN RATTINER

Foreword by
Alec Baldwin

excelsior editions

State University of New York Press
Albany, New York

Front cover image of the Hamptons street sign: © BlueMoonPics / iStockphoto.com

Back cover image of the beach and fence: © Hnin Khine / iStockphoto.com

Published by
State University of New York Press, Albany

For information, contact State University of New York Press, Albany, NY
www.sunypress.edu

Production by Diane Ganeles
Marketing by Fran Keneston

Excelsior Editions is an imprint of State University of New York Press

Library of Congress Cataloging-in-Publication Data
Rattiner, Dan
   In the Hamptons Too : Further Encounters with Farmers, Fishermen, Artists, Billionaires, and Celebrities / Dan Rattiner.
      p. cm.
   ISBN 978-1-4384-3263-2 (hardcover : alk. paper)
   1. Rattiner, Dan.   2. Journalists—United States—Biography.
3. Hamptons (N.Y.)—Social life and customs.   I. Title.

   PN4874.R29A3 2010
   974.7'25043092—dc22
   [B]   2009051681

10 9 8 7 6 5 4 3 2 1

To My Wife, Christine

CONTENTS

Contents

In June of 2002, I was staying in Los Angeles while shooting a film. My brother Billy was working out there as well, and one night we decided to make dinner at his place and gather with some friends around the television to watch Barbara Kopple's documentary *The Hamptons*. I had met with Kopple some time before and I had agreed to be interviewed for the project. A lot of other well-known East End locals agreed to appear, usual suspects like Billy Joel, Chevy Chase, Christie Brinkley, Jerry Seinfeld, and Russell Simmons.

Kopple's film played out and I was confused and angry. Eventually, a lot of people were angry. Kopple, presumably at the insistence of the producer, the ABC television network, portrayed the area in the way that nearly all long-term residents, seasonal or full-time, loathe and abjure. According to Kopple's piece, the Hamptons is the playground of young, drunken, fornicating rich punks whose lifestyles eclipse and even crush the cultures of the indigenous, more decent farmers, fishermen, and common folk. Kopple/ABC could not have gotten it more wrong.

I suppose the East End (only people who don't live here call it the Hamptons) is in the media so much because the media itself lives here. Newspaper and broadcast journalists and producers. Authors and editors of magazines, books, and television programs. A lot of those people have homes here. And, I suppose we get our share of immature, drug-addled, oversexed, and entitled visitors. However, if you think they define the community, you haven't read Dan Rattiner.

If you pick up the *East Hampton Star,* you'll learn the who, what, and where. The why and how are more likely found in the pages of *Dan's Papers.* Rattiner is a wonderfully odd bird. With his white hair and beard, his straw hats and wizened yet cherubic face, he looks like Santa Claus's kid brother who went off to yeshiva and retired on a thirty-one-foot Bertram in Montauk. Dan has been here a long time. And if you want to feel a more reliable pulse of the area, what's going on and what interesting things there are to do, see, and talk about (without the *New York Magazine* B.S.) read *Dan's Papers.* If you want to understand the crazy quilt of art, sand, money, farmland, literature, golf clubs, divorces, sea spray, and the area's remarkable blend of ego, generosity, and dedication to historic preservation, read Dan's book, *In the Hamptons,* and its sequel, *In the Hamptons Too,* which you hold in your hands.

You want history? East End history? Who else can give you authoritative takes on Pollack and de Kooning, Steinbeck and Vonnegut, Billy Joel and Steven Spielberg, Frank Mundus and Robert David Lion Gardiner? Rattiner's writing is so good that when he describes his encounters with Eleanor Leonard, Music Festival of the Hamptons doyenne, Eleanor is in the room with you. His description of his dinners at Bobby Van's with Vonnegut discussing Ruth Kligman and her pantheon of abstract expressionistic lovers is, itself, worth the price.

Now that's the East End I know and love! It's not about just anyone driving around here, drunk, lonely, looking for love. It's the ones who slept with greatness and who Kurt Vonnegut discusses over dinner with Dan at Bobby Van's. Now that's, well . . . *the Hamptons.*

—Alec Baldwin
Amagansett, October 2009

New York

New
Jersey

Long Isl

Long Island

Atlantic

Map created by Kelly Shelley

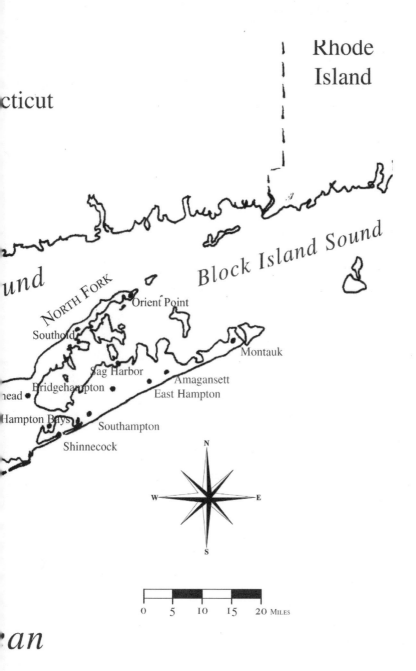

Richard T. Gilmartin

~~~~~~

The year my parents moved us out to the very tip of Long Island at Montauk in 1956, the Supervisor of the Town of East Hampton was Richard T. Gilmartin. It was apparently quite special for him to have won the election, and then the re-election, my father told us. Gilmartin was from Montauk, the most easterly of the six hamlets that constitute East Hampton Town, and no one from Montauk had ever been accorded this honor before. The other five communities were all three-hundred-year-old English hamlets with big white churches, windmills, great leafy elm trees, and a staunch bedrock Christian population whose ancestors went back all the way to colonial times. The land surrounding the towns was largely potato farms. There was a small colony of wealthy New Yorkers who came out to big oceanfront mansions in the summertime. But that was it. As for Montauk, far out at the end of a fifteen-mile-long peninsula, it was a raucous windswept tourist town consisting mostly of about forty motels with names like White Sands, the Atlantic Terrace, and the

RICHARD T. GILMARTIN AT HOME
(Courtesy of Timmy Gilmartin)

Surf and Sand, all lining the beaches in the center of town and all owned by "newcomers."

It had been a shock to the system when they were built, all at once, just a few years before, right after World War II. Certainly, there would never be anyone from Montauk running East Hampton. What did Montaukers know? And yet, there he was, this man Gilmartin, now in his second term.

I was sixteen years old, just turning seventeen the summer we moved to Montauk from New Jersey. The Hamptons meant nothing to me. They were just the sleepy little towns you had to drive through to get to all the activity at Montauk. You'd pass signs at the entrances to those towns that read FOUNDED 1644, or 1639, or 1648. One town, Southampton, had a sign at the entrance that read OBSERVE OUR VILLAGE DRESS CODES. I had no idea what that was all about.

In any case, we were certainly newcomers. In Millburn, New Jersey, where we had come from, all the houses were in neat little rows. All the dads went to work at eight in the morning. There were maple and elm trees everywhere and the summers were broiling hot.

Now our home was Montauk, where my dad had come to buy the only drugstore in town. There were rolling hills and dunes, beaches and ranches, a cooling wind almost every day, and a quaint little fishing village on a harbor about four miles away from downtown. Downtown featured as its centerpiece an abandoned seven-story skyscraper—everybody called it the White Elephant—facing an open, grassy plaza with a circle road around it that was the center of town. Our store was around the corner. The post office was on one side. The liquor store was on the other side. Across the street was a fishermen's tavern called the Shagwong, a bait-and-tackle store and a meat market. And that was about it, other than the dozens of motels and restaurants down by the beach a short walk away. Gilmartin must be quite a guy, I thought, to be supervisor of a town that wanted the village he lived in to just go away.

One day—just before the beginning of summer that first year, my dad called me back to the pharmacy to tell me I needed to go to the insurance office in the abandoned seven-story office building around the corner to sign some insurance papers.

"I thought nobody worked in the White Elephant," I said.

"Mr. Gilmartin does. And he's our new insurance broker."

"But if the building is abandoned, how do I find him?"

"You'll figure it out," dad said. He grinned. Apparently this was going to be some kind of test.

It was just a hundred-yard walk to the front door of the White Elephant. And of course it was locked. I banged on it. Peeling paint flew off.

"Over here," a man's voice said.

Just adjacent to and attached to the White Elephant was a small one-story building built out of the same white brick as the White Elephant. And out front, on a wooden post, was a small shingle that read RICHARD T. GILMARTIN, INSURANCE.

"Okay," I shouted back.

I walked over. There was an odd thing about the front entrance to this little building: it had a plywood ramp with a makeshift railing made out of plumbing pipes. The ramp went up only one step.

"Just push it open."

The voice had come from inside. I went in.

It was a single, large, dusty room, filled with bookcases, filing cabinets, paperwork, pictures on the walls, and this big wooden desk with a man in a wheelchair behind it. It brought me up short.

"Don't mind that I don't get up," the man said. "Just have yourself a seat."

Mr. Gilmartin was about sixty, hunched over, and had some kind of disease that gave him patches of white powder on his face and hands. He had a round face and a full head of salt-and-pepper hair in a crew cut. It all made him look like some strange overgrown teenager.

"People looking for me rattle the White Elephant all the time," he said. "I just shout through the window."

"My dad sent me over. I'm supposed to sign some paperwork."

He smiled. "Which dad? We've got a lot of dads."

"Al Rattiner."

"Ah yes."

He leaned forward, raised up a tall stack of papers on the left side of his desk with one hand, and then, when he found what he wanted, with the other slid out a single piece of paper. He looked down at it.

"Says here you're only sixteen years old. This is about a car. People who are sixteen don't drive cars in New York State."

"In New Jersey we get a learner's permit at sixteen and a driver's license at seventeen."

"Do you have a car?"

"I do. My dad gave my his old convertible."

"The local kids your age must love you. It's eighteen in New York. Everybody's gotta be asking you to give them a lift."

I fished out my learner's permit and handed it to him.

"Well, you have to sign this on the bottom. And I'll witness it. Either way you're underage so somebody's got to vouch for you. How do you like it out here?"

He slid the papers over to me with a pen and I signed.

"I like it a lot."

"Why?"

"My dad put me in charge of the soda fountain. It's a kid's dream. And also, as you said, I drive everybody."

"That'll do it."

I paused. "What's the story about the White Elephant? I've never seen an abandoned skyscraper before. Someone told me a businessman built it a long time ago and then the business failed."

"A millionaire named Carl Fisher built it. It was 1926. Then came the crash of 1929. Fisher went away and died of drink. He was going to build a city here. This was to be the first of many skyscrapers."

"Wow."

"You ought to go up to the top of it sometime."

"I should?"

"It's locked up. But if you ever want to," he leaned forward mischeviously, "I've got the key."

"I'd love to do that."

"Just let me know."

I left Mr. Gilmartin's office then, and walked back to the store. It sold everything. Jammed in everywhere were toys, toasters, kites, beach blankets, television sets, radios, swimwear, shorts and shirts, hats, cosmetics, magazines and newspapers. In the back, up two steps, was the prescription room. And along one whole wall, there was the soda fountain, with a marble counter and stools that spun around. At that moment, half the stools were taken by people slurping malteds and shakes and sodas and eating sundaes. Eileen Hewitt, behind the counter, was busy waiting on everybody.

"I signed the papers," I said when I got up to the prescription room. "And I met Mr. Gilmartin."

"We put everything on one policy," dad said. "And Mr. Gilmartin is quite something, isn't he?"

"How did he get sick?"

"He had polio when he was a boy. He's been paralyzed since."

"He sure doesn't seem to let it bother him," I said.

My job at the store was not only behind the ice cream counter, but also everywhere else in it, except, of course, the pharmacy. Some day, my mom said, this store will be yours. That is, if you are interested.

I stocked the shelves and with a plastic tag gun put the prices on the merchandise. I swept the floor. I waited on customers and worked the cash register, I unpacked deliveries in the stockroom and organized the shelves. I worked seven days a week.

"The business is only in the summertime," mom had said, explaining that. "It's now or never."

I loved my mom and dad, but I didn't enjoy working in the store. I daydreamed. I hope they don't make me become a pharmacist, I thought.

Sometimes I'd get time off. I loved the outdoors in that town—the sunshine and the wind from off the sea. I'd change into a bathing suit and go to the beach.

The kids my age were another matter. Unlike Millburn, where all my friends hoped to become lawyers or doctors or dentists, here the kids were different. One was a mate on a fishing boat. Another worked for his dad who owned a motel.

Another was a rich man's son out for the summer who did nothing. I met all these kids at night at one of four taverns in town where the guys went to meet girls.

One kid I befriended, two years older than me, was a private at the radar air force base out near Montauk Lighthouse. One day he asked me to lend him fifty bucks. Payday was in two days and he'd pay it right back. Two days later, he was gone, transferred to another base somewhere and I never saw him again. This sort of stuff did not happen to me in Millburn.

One morning, thinking about Gilmartin, I found some excuse to go back to see him. I felt drawn to him.

"I wanted you to see something," Mr. Gilmartin said when I came in. I hadn't even had a chance to say hello. "I know you've come here to go up to the top of the White Elephant, but I have someplace else I'd like you to see first."

"What's that?"

"Well, did you know that the United States Army, practically the whole thing, spent the month of August in tents here in Montauk? It was about sixty years ago. None of the town was as you see it now. As far as the eye could see, all there were were these white tents set up with soldiers in them. There were nearly ten thousand tents."

"Why were they here?"

"They'd fought and won the Spanish-American War in Cuba two months before. Then, for almost a month while surrender terms were worked out they had to wait in the hills overlooking Santiago. And they all got sick with tropical diseases. Dysentery. Small pox. Yellow fever. Malaria. In

America, President McKinley was afraid to bring them home. Everybody wanted them back in the States for homecoming parades and celebrations. He was afraid there'd be an epidemic. So he had them brought in troop ships to this isolated place—Montauk—to either recover or die. Said it was 'maneuvers.' "

He opened a drawer to his desk and pulled out a large piece of paper that had a site-plan drawing on it.

"Have a look," he said. "Last week a friend in a Washington museum traced this map of Montauk and mailed it to me. See all these squares? Each one is a tent. Here is Teddy Roosevelt's tent. The Roughriders were nearby. And over here, right behind where this building is now, right on Fort Pond itself, is a bigger square, which is a laundry. It's where all the soldiers had their clothes washed. I want to ask a favor of you."

"What do you want me to do?"

"I want you to walk over to where the laundry was, and I want you to look around in the weeds. I never knew there was a laundry there. So I've been wondering if there are any brass buckles or military buttons there. Could you have a look?"

He was a man in a wheelchair. "Of course I'll do that," I said.

The hike through the weeds to the shore of Fort Pond was a hundred yards from where we were sitting.

"I'll be right back."

"Take your time. Look good," Gilmartin said.

I spent twenty minutes combing through all the weeds and bushes. I got burrs stuck to my pants. I sank deep into mud at one point. But I found no brass buttons or buckles or anything else in there. I came back to the office.

"There's a big concrete pad of some sort next to where the laundry was," I said. "I think I found a wooden post that might have been one corner of it at one time. But no buttons."

"I know about the concrete pad. Try not to track in the mud," he said.

"What is it?"

"It was a launching ramp in the First World War for dirigibles. That was twenty years after Roosevelt was here. Some people tried to fly one to Paris. They failed."

"They did?"

"Crashed in Newfoundland."

"There is all this history here in Montauk."

"Yes there is."

"Did you ever meet Teddy Roosevelt?"

He laughed. "How old do you think I am? The wash room is right behind me. Get the mud off your shoes. I presume you are working the fountain this morning. You can't go back like that."

"I was in the stockroom."

"Wash them anyway. Then I'll give you the key to the White Elephant. It's best seen from up top at night."

Thus began a friendship between me and this wonderful older man that lasted for years. He'd tell me this astonishing story of the town. I had no idea there were places like this so full of history. And I was living in one!

SUPERVISOR GILMARTIN DEMONSTRATING NEED FOR DISABILITY
RAMP AT THE MONTAUK LIGHTHOUSE
(Courtesy of Timmy Gilmartin)

He had me drive to the huge cliffs on the south face of the Montauk Lighthouse, where there were rocks and boulders a hundred feet down on the stone beach. Gilmartin was interested in knowing whether or not I could get into the underground bunkers at the top of the cliff that served as ammunition dumps for the anti-aircraft guns that were mounted there during World War II.

"You'll easily find the concrete anti-aircraft pads they built there to fend off the Nazis," he said. "The guns are gone of course, but you'll see where they were bolted down on the pads."

I went out there in a strong wind later that day, and reported back that the underground ammunition dump, which

I had found by lifting the very heavy concrete hatch he told me about, had a steel ladder that went down only three feet before disappearing into filthy, oily black water.

"They're flooded," he said. "That's new. You want to get flippers and a mask and go diving?"

"No diving. The water's disgusting."

"I'll get somebody else. There's a guy I know on the police force. I want to get some anti-aircraft shells from down there."

"Would you like a dish of ice cream?"

"Sure."

"What flavor?"

"What have you got?"

He sent me to the Walking Dunes, a spot even windier than out at the Point, where three giant sand dunes were slowly being blown southward toward the Atlantic Ocean. He asked me about a particular silver tree top that he had been told was being slowly covered up, and I was able to tell him it was gone.

He showed me a drawing, published on the front page of the old *Brooklyn Eagle* newspaper, which included a small beach house in Napeague, almost to Amagansett, with an odd triple dormer on the roof. The artist had drawn a black X on the beach in front of it where four Nazi saboteurs came ashore one night from a submarine during World War II and where they buried explosives right in front of this house.

"I believe the house is still there, even after the hurricane last year. With the triple dormer, it should be easy to find."

It was still there. But there were no signs of Nazis or buried explosives. I did dig.

Another time, I brought him some news.

"There are two enormous buffalos in the pasture right out front of the entrance to the Deep Hollow Ranch," I told him. "They weren't there last week."

"That's got to be Hy Sobiloff. I'll talk to him. Hy writes books of romantic poetry. He's also very rich, with a house on the ocean. I bet he thought the ranch ought to have some buffalo to keep the cows company."

This caused Gilmartin to launch into the story of how the cattle from the two Montauk ranches were, for many years, driven at the end of each summer ten miles right through town to a corral at the railroad station to wait for the cattle cars to come.

"They'd been doing this since the railroad came through in 1895," he said. "But the very last one was last year. You missed it. They came right by here."

"Why did they stop having them?"

"Railroad stopped hauling freight. Now, big livestock trailers come to the ranch and take them right out of the pasture and down the highway, straight through town. The cattle drives were sure fun, though. You shoulda moved out here a year earlier."

"Do you have pictures?"

"Sure do."

He pulled one out of a drawer. It was an amazing thing, with the cars, the stores, the motels, and several hundred head of cattle charging down Main Street.

"See these tourists on the sidewalk watching the cows? Look at the expressions on their faces."

"Scared," I said.

"Yup."

"You take these pictures?" I asked. The angle was from right in front of the White Elephant.

"Yup," he said proudly.

Once, I ran into him on the front steps of the East Hampton Library, sixteen miles away, the nearest library to Montauk, and I helped his wife, Winnie, wrestle his wheelchair up the brick steps.

"He comes here every Tuesday after the Town Board meeting," she told me. "I make Tuesday my shopping day."

"Easy," he shouted as we hit a bump.

I offered to take him to see the gravesite of Stephen Talkhouse. Talkhouse was one of the last Montauk Indians. He was known for walking long distances. He could walk to East Hampton and back in a day, thirty-two miles round trip, and often did. People paid him to deliver messages along the way. He died in 1879 after having fought for the North in the Civil War.

"I can't get up there," Gilmartin said.

"You can now. They've paved the dirt track. The grave's got a white wooden fence around it with little American flags on the corners now. You want to go?"

"I'll have Winnie take me," he said.

I did go up to the top of the White Elephant. Each floor on the way up was filled with the desks, chairs, phones, wall calendars, and conference tables that had been there on

September 22, 1938, when everybody working in that huge building, as one, cleared out and just left it. Calendars on the walls displayed that month. Several had the day circled. Way up at the top was Carl Fisher's now wrecked penthouse apartment.

"It's a national treasure," Gilmartin said. "A giant historical filing cabinet."

"Did you know Carl Fisher?" I asked. "You must have been in your twenties."

"Of course I did. I worked for him. We all did."

Three years later, my friendship with Mr. Gilmartin ended. It involved just the most terrible tragedy imaginable.

The Gilmartins lived in a small house in the Shepherd's Neck section of Montauk where they had raised two children. One was Tommy Gilmartin, who at the time of the disaster was twenty-five. The other was Timmy Gilmartin, who was twenty.

When it happened, the whole town knew about it within hours.

On July 14, 1958, Tommy Gilmartin, alone in a brand new Austin-Healey sports car that his dad had bought for him, drove off the road halfway down the Montauk Parkway, the five–mile-long limited-access highway that Carl Fisher and Robert Moses, the Long Island State Park Commissioner, built as a joint venture in the 1920s.

Tommy skidded off the road and into the decorative wooden split-rail fence that lined the length of the parkway on both sides, demolishing the part he hit. One of the wooden railings, sixteen feet in length, came loose, got knocked into the air, and came over the hood to smash through the windshield and spear him. He died instantly.

The insurance office remained closed for a month after that. Also, it was announced that Mr. Gilmartin would not be running for re-election as he earlier had announced he would.

The town mourned. And, as a matter of fact, within a month, the wooden railings were all torn down and replaced by continuous steel corrugated railings so that could never, ever happen again.

I was nineteen when Tommy Gilmartin died. I was so upset I could not bring myself to go to the funeral. And I did not see Mr. Gilmartin until later when he briefly opened his office to wind up his business.

"I am just so sorry," I said, after summoning the courage to come over.

Tears welled in his eyes. "You have no idea."

With his office closed, I had no easy way of contacting Mr. Gilmartin. Indeed, according to my dad and other people in town, he and Winnie were now living in seclusion. I never saw him again.

I secretly believed, however, that Mr. Gilmartin had to know, and had to be very proud of my starting the town's first newspaper two years later. Many of the amazing stories that Mr. Gilmartin told me became the basis for the paper. I had never heard such remarkable stories about one single place. And I just thought that along with everything else in the paper, everybody would like reading them.

The birth of the newspaper had come from the fascinating and curious mind of Richard T. Gilmartin.

Taxi Wars

In late May of 1960, I went around Montauk with a pack under my arm explaining that beginning in July I would be publishing the town's first newspaper. I was twenty years old. The prior year, the year after Tommy Gilmartin died, I had come to the conclusion that the town needed a newspaper, in the summertime anyway, and that would fit the bill just fine with me, since I was now off at college from September to May. I got the blessing of my dad. He understood that I didn't like working in a retail store all day.

"If you can make as much money running a newspaper as you make working in the store in the summertime, it's fine with me," he said.

I was making twenty-five cents an hour, just like all the other clerks in the store at the time.

During my spring vacation prior to my starting the paper, I made a dummy of what I thought the newspaper ought to look like. I'd gotten magic markers, a pad of construction paper, a scissors, and some Scotch tape, and put it together on a table in our television room. I made various-sized boxes

AD FROM *MONTAUK PIONEER*, 1960
(Courtesy of the author)

on the different pages where the ads would go, and pieces of newsprint cut out from *Newsday* pasted in place to indicate where the stories would go. I drew the logo. I named it *The Montauk Pioneer.* I'd worked on newspapers in high school. I knew how to work with a printer. I knew what I had to do. I was very excited about my prospects.

Indeed, I had a wonderful time bringing this replica around to the different merchants during the last half of May, 1960, because what I found was that about three out of four of them wanted to be in it.

I sold ads up at the ranch, out at the fishing village, and, of course, downtown, where I'd go down one side of the street asking shop owners if they wanted to be in it, and then cross the street and go the other way getting yeses and nos. Of course, the owners were often not there. So I'd make a note of it. And I'd come back. There were no contracts to sign. If you wanted a particular spot in the paper for the summer, on page three on the top, or on the page where I would publish a map of the town, you just signed up by scribbling your name in the ad box itself. Each was marked with the exact price of what it would cost for each of the five issues I planned for the summer. $100. $200. $300. Take it or leave it.

One morning, I headed out from my dad's pharmacy, past the old Gilmartin Insurance building, then to the Pfund Hardware Store, the Pancake House, the Mobil station, the Montauk Diner, and then to the big Texaco station, which was owned by Marshall Prado, a World War II veteran who had lost his left hand in a battle somewhere. The Texaco station backed up to Fort Pond, directly behind it. It was an unusual thing to see a gas station in a resort that had its own little grassy beach. But there it was.

Next door to the gas station, there were two buildings under construction, also facing the highway. The buildings were both made of wood, both two stories high, and one larger than the other. And each of them, as with the gas station, backed up to its own beach on Fort Pond.

Out front, there was a thin, wiry little man with dark hair and leathery skin, banging nails into cedar shingles onto the side of one of these buildings.

I introduced myself, and told him what I was going to do. And he introduced himself as Joe Franzon, and what he was building was a taxi business.

"My wife is going to run the office in the big building. I'm going to fix my taxis in the smaller building. I've got three of them. I'm bringing real professional taxi service to Montauk."

This might be a problem, is what I thought. I knew the Windsors, who had been running the only taxi service in town for years and years. And the Windsors had already bought an ad on the back page.

"Here's the railroad schedule on the back page," I told Mr. Franzon. He could see the Windsor ad signed up for above the schedule. "You could have an ad right under it."

"Windsor's got the ad above it."

"I'm just going around seeing everybody. I got to him before I got to you. But the spot under it is available. And you could have it for the summer if you want."

"I can't believe you sold that ad on top to Windsor," he said, his temper rising.

"Well, I'm just doing the best I can," I said. "I hadn't seen you here before."

He signed his name across all three boxes under the railroad schedule. His ad would be three times that of Windsor. And three times as expensive.

"Next year, when you come around, see me first," he said, thumping his chest.

"Yes, sir," I said.

The summer was a big success for me. That first day, July 1, 1960, I excitedly drove through town delivering stacks and stacks of this free newspaper—no one had ever seen a free newspaper before—placing them in piles in each of the lobbies in the forty or so motels in town, and in just about every single store. The paper was even in the Franzon Taxi Company office, on a cigarette machine. I was so happy. I'd worked in my dad's drugstore for three summers. Now I was on my own, and if things worked out the way I planned, I'd earn about triple the amount of money I made working in the store. I wouldn't even need help with my college tuition.

Meanwhile, all through town, you saw the green WINDSOR taxicabs and you saw the blue FRANZON taxicabs. And I thought, well, competition is what America is all about. The next spring, however, I went to Franzon Taxi in the center of town first, just as he had asked me to, and his taxicabs were there, but nobody was around.

Then, just before the first issue of the newspaper—by this time I had signed up Windsor—practically on the last day I could accept advertising for it, I saw him there in front of his shop, with the three taxis all still lined up.

"Hi," I said, walking over to him.

"You want to see ME?" he shouted. I stopped in my tracks. He appeared very angry.

"You want to know what's going on with the taxi business? Windsor made a deal with the railroad, and he made a deal with THIS motel"—he pointed to the Sands Motel across the street—"and with THAT motel"—he pointed to the Memory Motel next to it—"and every other goddamn motel in this entire town. This town STINKS. I'm just here to pack up my stuff. And I am NEVER coming back to this godforsaken place. You're all a bunch of swindlers to do this. So just get off my property."

I turned around and headed back toward my car. I'm not a swindler, I had wanted to say. I'm just a kid.

"And as far as I'm concerned, these buildings are just going to ROT right here in the middle of this town," he shouted out at me. "Forever. A beach resort with an abandoned skyscraper, and now two more buildings. What do you think of that?"

I got in my car and drove off.

The man, as it turned out, was true to his word. The years went by. Jack Kennedy was assassinated, we landed on the moon, Richard Nixon resigned after Watergate, Elvis died, Ronald Reagan met Gorbachev in Iceland, and President Bush invaded Iraq and Afghanistan, and still these buildings stood, with the shingles falling off and the rain coming in through the roofs—a major, major eyesore right in the middle of downtown Montauk, with their backs to the pond and their entrances to the Montauk Highway.

Pretty soon, when I went through downtown Montauk, I didn't even notice them anymore. Occasionally, newcomers would mention them to me when I would take them through town.

"Oh yeah, those," I'd say, noticing them again as if for the first time. "Man got mad at the town. Left them like that."

"Well something ought to be done about them."

THE TAXI BUILDINGS, UNFINISHED, TODAY
(Courtesy of the author)

Sometime around 1970, somebody towed the three forlorn-looking taxicabs away. One day they were there, the next day gone. I had no idea how that had come about.

Then one day, in 2005—this was now forty-five years after the taxi wars days and I was sixty-five years old and a grandfather—I picked up a copy of the *East Hampton Star* newspaper and read a small article on the bottom of the third page that said a Mr. Carl Franzon has made an application to tear down these catastrophes and replace them with two new buildings.

It wasn't rocket science to assume that old Mr. Franzon had finally died. And that his son and heir wanted to make something of this fine waterfront and highway-front property right in the center of downtown Montauk.

The application, which included a set of plans, made its way through the various levels of bureaucracy that had to approve of them before the final vote. These would include, in East Hampton Town Hall, reviews by the Architectural Review Board, the Town Planning Board, the Zoning Board, the Zoning Board of Appeals, if necessary—and yes, it was necessary—and then finally the Suffolk County Board of Health and the Building Department.

It never made it.

The reason? Even now, the very proper villages and hamlets that comprise the Town of East Hampton *still* look down at all the motels and surfers and nightspots in Montauk. And now, with no Gilmartin or anybody else from that town in office, East Hampton was busting the Franzon family's chops once again.

East Hampton continues to decide what goes on in the unincorporated hamlet of Montauk. East Hampton says it cares about Montauk. Everybody in Montauk knows it doesn't.

I now publish what are called *Dan's Papers* in all the hamlets of East Hampton, plus about twenty other towns. Poor Franzon Jr. The requests for information, for plans and elevations, for preexisting sworn testimony, for zoning variances and Department of Health applications went on for years. The original plans called for a French mansard roof on each of the two buildings, but the Architectural Review Board said that would not be in keeping with the traditions of the historic Old English nature of East Hampton Town. This, said to an applicant in a motel town!

Carl Franzon took it back and made peaked roofs.

Next, the planning board said that because the property was so close to water, the new proposal would have to go through an elaborate environmental impact review that would take a year—even though the new buildings were situated on the preexisting foundations of the old. After that, the Suffolk County Health Department waded in with a decision that said the cesspool and well were not only too close to one another under present-day law, they were also too close to both the road and the water and, considering that the road and water could never be farther apart than they already were, the only solution would be to get approval from the Zoning Board of Appeals by pleading hardship.

I don't know many of the ensuing details, but today, five years after the application began, those two buildings, partially built now, replace the old, but the applicant has simply walked away again.

Fifty years from now, I swear, if I am still alive and they finally complete this project and open up a business on this property, I shall once again show up and try to sell the Franzons an ad.

Victor Syzmanski

~~~~~~

In the late spring of 1967, done with college and now twenty-seven years old, I left the family home to rent a small barracks house on the Montauk Highway in East Hampton. I had started a second edition of the paper there, so now there were two, one in Montauk and the new one in East Hampton, both published just in the summertime. I'd write for the Montaukers in one edition, and for the snooty East Hamptonites in the other.

I also opened my first office that year. I rented the front half of a barn in back of the Gay Amaden Real Estate Agency on Gay Lane in East Hampton. A furniture-maker built chairs and tables in the back half. It was hard to hear on the phone when he had his tools plugged in, and sometimes we had dust problems, but other than that we got along fine.

In the spring, I became friends with Victor Syzmanski and his wife Doris. They were constructing a small building they intended to make into a restaurant on the highway in Napeague, a narrow strip of sand five miles long separating the hamlets of Amagansett and Montauk. It would soon be open.

VICTOR AND
DORIS PLAYING
TOUCH
FOOTBALL AT
THE BEACH
FOR "NATIVES"

(Courtesy of *The Montauk Pioneer*)

Victor Syzmanski was about thirty-five, slender and tall, and usually had a tool belt strapped around his waist. He was a carpenter by trade from somewhere eighty miles away at the western end of Long Island. I met him one day, stopping to watch him build the restaurant, as I went out to Montauk for the afternoon. He and Doris and their three-year-old son Joe were on the premises.

"We're going to serve Italian food," he said when I met him there. "Italian food is big in the summertime. It'll be cool and breezy out on the deck. It'll be great."

Sometimes when I had a few hours free, I'd help Victor out by holding one end of the paneling against the wall as he nailed up the other. Doris would go to a deli with Joe and bring us lunch.

At other times, the three of them would come by my little barracks in East Hampton. One day about a week before they opened, we were sitting in my living room drinking coffee and playing cards. Joe was running around. Earlier that day, I had mentioned that the married couple who had rented me the barracks had both approached me, separately, about my buying the place.

"They're asking $10,000," I told them. "I'm told its worth $14,000. So it seems I won't be going wrong."

"Maybe something's wrong with it," Victor said. He got up and began tapping the walls and jumping up and down a little bit on the floor. He flipped a few of the light switches, then took out a screwdriver and removed a plate from one of the electrical outlets.

"Hmmm," he said. "Here's a problem. This wiring is really old. Come have a look."

I came over. The wiring looked like something from the 1930s. The strands were each made of thick copper wrapped in paper.

"I think you'll have to rewire the place," Victor said.

"Is that expensive?"

"Not really. I could do it for you."

"Well, not just yet. I haven't bought the place."

A month later, I *had* bought the place, and Victor Syzmanski was up on a ladder starting to snake wires through holes in the ceiling of my dining room. Meanwhile, the restaurant had opened with bunting and balloons and a big party a week before. It was called Junior's, after their son. It was busy right from opening day.

But now it was Tuesday, the day the restaurant was closed.

"I want to show you something," Victor said. "I have this new way I do electrical wiring."

He climbed down and showed me a new electrical outlet he had put in about waist high in the living room.

"I've just done this one," he said. "If you like it, I'll do them all like this."

Victor picked a lamp cord up off the floor and held it near the outlet.

"See? Look how easy it is to plug in right here. No bending down. You'll never have to bend down to plug something in again. Waist-high electric outlets. You'd think someone would have thought of this before. It's so obvious."

It sure looked that way to me.

"So what do you think?" Victor asked. "Should I do all of them this way?"

"Oh yeah," I said.

It was a small house, just twenty feet by forty feet all together, with six tiny rooms, some of them just big enough to walk into and then turn around. Victor finished doing the wiring as dusk fell.

As it got dark, we went around plugging in all the lamps in the house without bending down. We turned all of them on. The house was all lit up. Then we sat at the kitchen table and I poured him a glass of wine.

"Voilà," he said, raising his glass.

"What a job," I said, happily.

I had a girl friend at that time named Linda Liu, a tall woman who worked in the city as a model at Ford's. I'd go into town to see her, or she'd come out to see me. On Friday evening, three days after the job was done, I picked her up at the railroad station in East Hampton and told her I had a surprise to show her back at the house.

We went in and I showed her how I had these outlet switches where I could plug or unplug anything without having to bend down. I demonstrated.

"Dan, come sit with me on the sofa," she said.

We sat.

"Show me where, exactly, right now, the nearest electrical outlet is."

"It's right here," I said. "On the wall, right behind your ear."

"Dan, has it ever occurred to you that it is now virtually impossible to fashionably decorate this house? That on every wall, there are now electrical outlets right out where you can see them?"

"I hadn't really noticed that," I said.

She got up, sighed, and went into the kitchen and opened the refrigerator for a glass of milk. She did that every evening before she went to bed.

"Well, I just paid him to do it this way," I said.

From that point on, and for the rest of the summer, I could hardly help but notice that there were all these electrical wires and plugs everywhere on the walls. You couldn't cover them up either. There was electricity there where the plug met the outlet. It would be a fire hazard to cover them up.

I held lots of parties at the barracks. One Friday night, we had over the entire summer-stock crew of *How to Succeed in Business Without Really Trying*, in performance at the John Drew Theatre in East Hampton. It was an after-show party. There was lots of wine and nobody noticed the electrical wiring. About midnight, somebody persuaded the cast to perform the main number for the show right in the living room, a feat that included lots of stomping and dancing and leaps and catches. Everybody applauded. But there was something wrong. Now there was this weird trampoline feeling on the living room floor.

In the morning, after cleaning up the mess from the night before, I went outside and slid under the house between the cedar posts upon which the barracks rested. As I had suspected, the beam holding up the living room floor had banged the central cedar post below it so far into the dirt that with my flashlight you could see separation between the beam and post. Something would have to be wedged in there.

And then I saw that something *had* been wedged in there, but had been knocked free from all the stomping and banging. In the dirt next to the post, there was an old rusty axe head. I picked it up and slid it into the separation. Then I climbed out from under the house, got a hammer and a piece of wood, got back under the house and banged the axe handle in tight. End of problem.

Linda and I didn't make it through the summer. I was sad about that. She had found a guy named Harrison who lived in Greenwich Village. She told me she had fallen for him, and since she was an honorable person wouldn't be coming out anymore.

I briefly thought this might have something to do with axe handles, electrical outlets, and wiring, but then thought nah, that can't possibly be it.

Late in the summer, I drove down through Napeague and saw to my amazement that Junior's had, for some reason, closed. It wasn't even Labor Day yet. The building was still brand new, even still smelled new. What could have happened? I climbed the steps and knocked at the door. There was no answer. In the window, there was a sign listing all sorts of violations. This was not good.

Two weeks later, in Long Island's daily newspaper, *Newsday*, there was an article that said the Town of East Hampton Building Department had shut down Junior's because of a wide variety of illegal building practices. They also had never filed for a building permit. I had been there a couple of times during the summer to have dinner, but didn't notice any unusual outlet locations or any other oddity. What a shame that a restaurant, already very popular, had been closed like this. And where were the Syzmanskis? The only phone number I had for them was at the restaurant.

At five, I called the restaurant and as I suspected, there was no answer. The next day I drove out there, and I climbed the stairs again to the deck and the nice view and tried to look in. You couldn't look in. All the glass was covered from the inside with curtains.

I never did find out what had become of Doris and Victor Syzmanski. It was true they had closed with having paid only half of their bill for ads in the paper. But then Victor had done the rewiring at my house, which I had paid in full, but on the cheap. I just felt sad they were gone.

Every day for many years after that, I would think of the Syzmanskis as I would drive down the long, straight Napeague Highway through the dunes and past their now abandoned restaurant. And then, one day about ten years later, there was no more restaurant. I drove past where it had been, turned around, and drove past the other way. It was gone. All that remained was the foundation.

It was probably the only time in the history of the Hamptons that a building had been torn down like that. A blow for East Hampton against Montauk. I wrote about it from the two perspectives in the two different editions, chastising East Hampton in that edition, and expressing outrage in the pages of the Montauk edition.

As for my little barracks building, just three years after I bought it, I sold it for $22,500. This seemed quite a tidy little profit for me at the time. It was last sold for about $1.1 million. This was two years ago. I had seen the OPEN HOUSE sign out front driving by and had stopped in to have a look around. It was all remodeled and fixed up, and the high-up electrical outlets were gone. They were now back down on the baseboards. Somebody must have been shocked when they saw them at waist height. Who did that anyway?

Anonymous

~~~~~~

On August 22, 1983, a small item appeared in one of our local weekly newspapers.

PLAQUE MISSING

The man who walks around the huge, abandoned hotel high on the hill overlooking Montauk every morning, Rex Addison, noticed on Thursday that the plaque on the big boulder in the old courtyard of that place had been stolen. He called the police and reported it. Somebody had cut the bolts that attached it to the boulder. The broken bolts were found on the ground. If anybody knows where it has gone, please call 668-5000, the offices of the real estate company in downtown Montauk that owns the Montauk Manor building. It had considerable value.

I read this item sitting in the living room of my home overlooking Three Mile Harbor. I was a married man by that time. I had three kids, ages twelve, ten, and two, with

MONTAUK MANOR, 1928
(Courtesy of the Montauk Library)

another one on the way. I had just come home from a busy day at work at the newspaper office in Bridgehampton. I was publishing editions of the paper in six different communities in the Hamptons, not only in Montauk and East Hampton, but also in South and Westhampton and the North Fork of Long Island. The corporate name for all of them was now *Dan's Papers*.

A plaque stolen? I thought. I know that plaque. And what a sad story that was.

During the booming 1920s, after the wealthy land developer Carl Fisher bought the tip of Long Island, Montauk, from end to end, he built the seven-story building, a golf course, a polo field, a yacht club, a surf club, and this huge, stately 230-room English Tudor hotel high on a hill. On

June 1, 1927, he held a great grand opening. With hundreds of people in attendance, many of whom had come from Miami Beach and New York City for the occasion, Fisher announced there would be two more hotels of a similar size built during the next three years in other locations around Montauk. Montauk was on its way. The slogan was "Miami Beach in the Winter. Montauk in the Summer." And he did own Miami Beach. What could go wrong?

Two years later, the Great Crash of 1929 brought about the economic collapse of the entire United States. No further hotel was built in Montauk after this first one. And this hotel, through the 1930s, struggled along in receivership. Carl Fisher died of drink in 1939.

The plaque? In 1938, at the very bottom of the depression, some marketing people working for what remained of Fisher's organization tried to create a little interest in this still-new and little-used hotel in the middle of nowhere. That year would mark the fortieth anniversary of the time when Teddy Roosevelt, his two hundred Rough Riders, and the thirty-two-thousand–man American army had arrived in Montauk's Fort Pond Bay aboard a troop ship from Cuba. Why not have a reunion?

And so the word went out, an attempt was made to round up some of the surviving Rough Riders, and about forty of them were brought out from Manhatttan on a Long Island Railroad train to be honored at the Montauk Manor, all expenses paid. Not many other guests were in attendance, but just being at the Manor, with its splendid views all the way to the horizon in every direction, made for a wonderful time. Photographers and press people were there, and at the end, small trophies honoring these old soldiers were handed out, and a heavy bronze plaque about three feet by four was wheeled out on a cart and unveiled. It would soon be bolted to a large rock at the entrance to the Manor to celebrate this occasion, the hotel manager told the men. Everyone applauded. It would be there for all to see forever.

> Erected by the Montauk Historical Society in commemoration of the return to Montauk from the war with Spain, August 14th, 1898, of Colonel Theodore Roosevelt and his gallant Rough Riders (First U.S. Volunteer Cavalry).

> —Montauk Manor. August 22–29, 1938

I had seen it many times in the 1950s as a teenager sneaking around up there with friends. Though the hotel was now abandoned, there were ways you could get in.

We had admired the trashed elevators, the medieval-style lobby with the big stone fireplaces and the slate floors, the giant dining room with the chandeliers and tables and chairs still there, the enormous writing room all paneled in mahogany and teak with desks and inkwells. We also took note of the bolted-down plaque on the boulder out front, with moss now growing on those words. What would become of this place, anyway? Nobody was going to be tearing it down, that was for sure. The stone walls of the place were four feet thick.

And then one day, in 1983, forty-five years later, there was this phone call.

"There's a man on the phone who insists on talking to you," my secretary said.

"Name?"

"Wouldn't give it. But he said it was important. About the Montauk Manor."

"I'll take it."

We now had a lot of advertising from the Montauk Manor. It still was not open, but some new company had bought it and was looking to turn it into condominiums. They had built five model apartments on the ground floor, and you could get to them without having to walk through the rest of this trashed five-story building. To make that possible, they had built models in the former magnificent spaces that had once been the dining room and drawing rooms. They'd have probably gutted the medieval-looking lobby too, if it hadn't been necessary to walk through it to get to the models' entrances.

About six months earlier, one of the partners had taken me through to have a look at them under construction. It had really upset me. Such a treasure, lost this way. And who knew? The place looked exactly as it always did from the outside. Who could have stopped them anyway?

"The hotel rooms were very small. We're going to combine three of them for each condominium unit. So there will be eighty-eight units."

I'd been up in those little rooms, sometimes with girl friends. But I didn't tell him that.

What could you do? I took their ads.

"Here he is," the secretary said. And now this mystery person was on my phone.

"You're Dan Rattiner?" he asked.

"Yes."

"Look, I don't want to tell you who I am, is that okay?"

"Okay."

"One night, a long time ago, me and some of my buddies went up to the Montauk Manor and we stole a big, heavy bronze plaque bolted to a rock out front. We didn't mean anything bad by it. The place was a wreck. And it was just a prank."

"I remember that plaque."

"Well, the thing is, I'm married now. I have two kids. I'm a responsible citizen. But I still have the plaque. And I feel really badly about that. I want to return it."

"Then why don't you?"

"Well, I don't know how to do that. I read where they're reopening the place soon. If I go there, maybe they'll arrest me. And I can't risk that. I need an intermediary."

"So you thought of me," I said.

"Yes. I'd give this to you, and then you'd give it to them."

I didn't miss a beat. "I can do that," I said. I was thinking how special I must be for him to have chosen me for this task. It would be a badge of honor for me. LOCAL NEWSPAPERMAN BROKERS RETURN OF HISTORIC PLAQUE TO MONTAUK.

"You can?"

"Sure. Just bring it by the newspaper office."

"I can't do that. Somebody would see me there."

"Nobody would ask your name. You tell me when, I'll tell the staff that. I promise."

"Could we just meet, say, on a street corner?"

The first indication that maybe this wasn't going to be handled as easily as I thought came when I got home.

"Guess what?" I said to my wife. I told her what had happened.

"You're getting involved with stolen goods?"

"No. Not at all. I'm *returning* stolen goods. This is a *good* thing."

She looked at me blankly. "Sounds like you're getting involved with stolen goods."

"Really," I said. I smiled. "He chose ME to get this thing returned."

She shrugged. Then walked out of the room.

"This really is a good thing," I shouted after her.

One week later, at four in the afternoon of a hot August day, I stood at the appointed place, which was on the south-west corner of School Street and the Montauk Highway in Bridgehampton and waited. It was a cloudy day.

Four turned to five after four, then ten after. Was I being set up? Was there something else going on? I looked at my watch.

A policeman I knew drove by. I waved. I was thinking it is really important to get this plaque back to the Montauk Manor. I hope the guy doesn't get scared off seeing me wave to the policeman.

At about twenty past four, he showed. There was no mistaking him. Here was this man about five foot six, about thirty years old, slightly balding and heavyset, wearing sneakers, white socks, and shorts, and walking toward me down the sidewalk toting a heavy canvas bag.

Plop. He set it at my feet.

"Here it is," he said, looking up.

You could see in the top. The plaque had been wrapped in newspaper and then Scotch-taped tight.

"What do you think it weighs?" I asked.

"It weighs thirty-four-and-a-half pounds," he said.

There are two park benches on the corner of School Street and the Montauk Highway and I motioned for him to come over to them with me and set himself down.

"No thanks," he said. "Can't stay."

"Well, tell me about how you got this? How many guys were you?"

"Oh, four. We'd been drinking. It was late."

"Where are you from?"

"I can't tell you that."

"Just the town." I was thinking about writing this story.

"Oh, Floral Park. Look. I really have to go. Thanks for doing this. Do you need any help carrying this thing?"

"No."

And then he turned and he was gone, leaving me with this canvas bag at my feet.

I looked around. Across the street was the Candy Kitchen ice cream parlor. Two kids were coming out eating ice cream cones. Across the highway was the Bridgehampton Historical

Society mansion. There was a couple looking at a big rusty ship's anchor on the front lawn. Behind me on this corner was the Bridgehampton Community House with the park benches on the front lawn. And right next door, there was the Bridgehampton Fire Department, with the garage doors open and the red shiny trucks all lined up inside. It was just a normal day. Except that I had this canvas bag at my feet and in it, stolen goods.

I picked up the bag and, tipped over to one side with the weight, walked as quickly as I could toward my car without attracting attention. I'm the Leaning Tower of Pisa is what I thought. And here comes the police car back. Wave again. Everything is fine, officer. Now I am at the car. And I've bundled the bag safely inside it on the floor behind the front seat.

It seemed to take an interminable amount of time for me to arrange to get this plaque back to the Manor. I called up there, but the office was closed for the weekend. Please call on Monday.

On Monday, I called and was told I'd have to get in touch with the main office in New York City in order to return such a thing. I did that and got an answering machine that said leave a message and someone would call me back. I did and they didn't.

During the entire time, I kept the plaque in its bag in the mudroom closet in the back hall at my house. I covered it with some blankets. It was probably the first place the police would look for a valuable stolen plaque if they came by my house with a search warrant.

I did, of course, at one point, rip open a little corner of the newspaper to make sure there was a plaque inside. There was. I taped it back up.

Finally, the big day came. Would the police have a welcoming committee there for me? I drove up the long gravel driveway to the top of the hill, thinking, well, this could go really well or it could go really badly. I had been told that a man named Park would meet me there that day. That was a good sign. I parked in front of the hotel—the façade was all fixed up—and by the grand front door there was a wooden sign that read MONTAUK MANOR CONDOMINIUMS. I went into the front lobby.

There was only one person in this magnificent, medieval space, a middle-aged woman sitting at a makeshift desk covered with brochures about the time-share condominiums. She looked up at me and raised her eyebrows inquisitively.

I looked all around. There was nobody else.

"Is Mr. Park here?" I asked her. "My name is Dan Rattiner and I have an appointment with him."

"Oh yes," the woman said. "Well, Mr. Park had to go out. But he told me about your plaque. So just leave it right here." She pointed to a leg of the desk.

"Right there?"

"Yes."

"Okay," I said. "But I have to go get it. It's locked up in my car outside."

"I'll be right here," she said.

And so I lugged in the canvas bag, and set it, with a loud thump, on the slate floor by the leg of her desk.

"Do you want my name and address?" I asked bravely.

She sighed. Now *she* had to deal with this plaque. "That won't be necessary," she said. "Mr. Park said he'd have us find a spot for it." She paused. "Somewhere."

Betty Friedan

~~~~~~

One night in late June of 1967, my friend Jim Lytton was over at my barracks house in East Hampton. We'd had spaghetti and now we were playing poker. The conversation was about women, largely because here it was a Friday night and neither of us had a date.

"You know there's a big party tonight near here," Jim said. "My parents are going. Maybe we could crash it. It's at the home of a very rich couple named Scull. Robert and Ethel Scull. I think there are going to be lots of women there."

"What makes you say that?"

"My mother told me."

"So why is she going?"

"It's something new. They call it the Women's Movement. It's right on Cove Hollow Road, right here behind your house."

I'd heard of the Sculls. They had a very valuable art collection. But I'd never met them. And I wouldn't normally think of crashing a party, except all we'd have to do is walk

BETTY FRIEDAN AT 40

down this dirt road through the woods to get to Cove Hollow Road. It was right there.

"Okay," I said.

About ten o'clock, we slipped out the back door and across the yard to the dirt driveway that connected Mrs. Collins's house next door to Cove Hollow Road way in the back. And then I thought of something.

"I have to get something," I whispered.

"What?"

"I want to bring maybe twenty copies of *Dan's Papers* with me. I've brought papers to parties before. That's another way of getting them around."

"Okay."

"I'll be right back."

I ran back to the house and got them out of the back of my station wagon, then returned with them under my arm. Jim was still where I had left him.

"Okay," I whispered again.

Soon, after poking through some brambles and bushes, we emerged onto Cove Hollow Road.

"Which way?" I asked.

Jim shrugged. We looked up and down Cove Hollow Road, which is pretty straight at this point, and sure enough, just a short walk down to the right was this white modern house, all lit up, with several dozen cars out front parked every which way.

"No doubt about it," Jim said.

"Maybe I'll get to meet your mother," I said. Now that I had an excuse to go to the party, I was feeling more comfortable about all of this.

We walked up the road, and then very gently knocked at the front door. Someone opened it.

"We're here for the party," I said. "And we brought the current issue of *Dan's Papers*."

The man who opened the front door was a butler in a white shirt and bowtie. "Just put them right there," he said. He pointed to a small side table in the front vestibule. Seemed like a good spot to me. People could pick them up coming or going. I set them down. And Jim and I just stared at this crowd. There were indeed a lot of women.

The place was, inside, like a modern museum. The walls were dazzlingly white, there were vases and other objets d'art placed on pedestals here and there, and huge glass sliders led out to a wooden deck surrounding a swimming pool.

Looming over all the people at the back of the pool was a giant steel sculpture that could only have been brought there by a forklift. There was a string quartet playing Mozart outdoors. Everybody was talking, smoking, drinking, all at the same time. Altogether there were about two hundred people in this house. Waiters and waitresses in white moved among them bearing trays of nibbles and wine. But there was a very strange ambiance at this party.

"A lot of these people seem really angry about something," I said.

"It's just they're all talking at once," Jim said. "I'm going to try to meet some babes." And he walked off. He actually went through the crowd and out to stand by the pool where there were several particularly attractive females.

A man came over to me. We hadn't been in there even five minutes.

"Are you the guy who left the newspaper in the front hall?" he asked.

"Yes."

"Ethel Scull asked me to ask you to remove them. She says you have no business leaving things in somebody's home without asking."

"I'll move them," I said. But I felt lousy about it. I went and picked them up, then turned. The man had followed me. "I have to tell my friend I'm going out," I said, nodding back toward the pool deck.

"Okay," he said.

At this point, carrying the newspapers, I took my first foray, which also turned out to be my last, across the living room and out to the pool. The women *were* angry about something. They were angry at *men*.

Jim was talking to two tall, slender women who appeared to be ten years older than he was. He was being his charming and delightful self. But the women just stared at him. He was all of twenty-five years old and he was quite shabbily dressed for a fancy dress party. As a matter of fact, so was I. Twenty minutes earlier we had been playing poker. I motioned to the newspapers under my arm.

"Jim, they want me to take these back to the house. So I'm going to go."

"Glenda and Irene, this is my friend Dan," Jim said, indicating me.

"I'll see you later," I said. "Nice to meet you, ladies."

"Nice to see you," one of them said.

Back at the house, I suddenly felt tired. I turned on the black-and-white TV and watched the end of a James Bond movie, then the eleven o'clock news. There was a demonstration against the Vietnam War by some students at a college in the midwest. Dozens of people had been arrested.

And I was just dozing off on the sofa when, Jim, breathless, came banging in through the screen door. It made me sit straight up.

"You won't believe this," he said. "There was a woman at the party who just took off all her clothes and jumped into the swimming pool. *I was right there!*"

I turned off the TV. I rubbed my eyes. "A *naked* woman?" I asked. "Was she *nice?*"

"I don't know. The whole thing was over in a second. And then she was in the water."

"What about when she got *out?*" I asked.

"They had a towel for her." He paused. Then he smiled. "Dan. You missed it!"

A week later, *Time* magazine had an article about this party at the Sculls. "It was like the shot heard round the world," the reporter wrote. "The Women's Movement is for *real.*"

The woman who jumped into the pool naked was a writer named Jill Johnston. The act of her jumping in, she told a lot of assembled commentators and reporters who had shown up for the party, was to make a political statement. There had been a congresswoman there, Patsy Mink, who was supposed to make a speech chastising a physician who said that women were too hormonally imbalanced to have positions of power. But loud hoots from the crowd prevented her from doing that. And then Jill Johnston had jumped into the pool naked.

A lot of confusion followed and Patsy Mink quickly left. Gloria Steinem followed her out, trying to bring her back. Feminist Betty Friedan, one of the leaders of the movement, who was now living full time in Sag Harbor, got in front of the microphone and tried to calm everybody down.

One month later, the phone rang at my office. I picked it up.

"Hello?"

"You have an ad in the paper for a delivery boy?" It sounded like a girl on the phone.

"Yes," I said. "Are you applying?"

"Yes, I am."

"Well, I'll tell you about the work. The job is to work on the delivery crew delivering *Dan's Papers* to all the stores. You put them on the cigarette machines or by the cash registers in stacks. It's heavy work. Maybe two hundred stores on a route and you do one route a day. If you're still interested we could set up an interview."

"But you say this is for a delivery *boy.*"

"Yes, it is."

"Not a *girl.*"

"We've had girls take the job. They say they can do the work. But they try it and they only last a few days."

"So all girls can't?"

"Not that I can find. I really think it's a job for delivery *boys.* But if you want to try it, whoever you are, I'll give it a try again. But you seem to have quite an attitude."

Click.

Still holding the phone, I turned to face my staff, a total of four people, all women, who were all staring at me, wide eyed.

"What's the matter with people?" I said.

I hung up.

The 1970s came and went. For a long time, Betty Friedan seemed to be in the center of things. Her book *The Feminine Mystique,* published in 1963, had sparked the movement. This was four years before the shot heard around the world at the Sculls.

My own view of things was, as time went on, that in addition to sparking the women's movement, the book essentially wrecked half the marriages in America. Before that book, more than nine in ten marriages lasted forever. Husbands and wives were even buried next to one another for eternity. Now there were men, women, and children all over the country so many turned into refugees because marriages broke apart. I had even become one of them.

I would occasionally see Betty Friedan at gallery openings or dinner parties from time to time. She was a small, not particularly attractive woman very determined to change the world. And early on, she would show up with her husband Carl, who told me he approved and was proud of what she was doing. But by 1970, Carl had divorced her and she was attending events alone. Once, I had dinner with her and art gallery owner Elaine Benson at the very fancy American Hotel in Sag Harbor. All of us were newly single by this time. Finding a mate was on the menu. Also, we all had too much to drink.

In 1980, she was selected by the *Atlantic* magazine as one of the one hundred most influential people in history. She was right up there with Einstein.

On a warm Friday afternoon in August, 1988, the two of us got into a lively discussion about the women's movement at an Andy Warhol opening at the Elaine Benson Art Gallery in Bridgehampton. As a result, Betty invited me to come over to her house for lunch the following day. She was about seventy at this time.

When I arrived at her little house on Garden Street in Sag Harbor, I found it swarming with carpenters and painters and electricians. The front door was wide open. I stood by it and looked for the bell. There didn't seem to be any.

"She's out back," a man painting a wall said. And so I went through the house, walking across painter's tarps and around ladders straight along a hall and out into a little back yard by a brook, where I found her sitting on a low stone wall overlooking the water. She had not heard me approach, and so I rather surprised her. But she was expecting me.

"Come, have a seat," she said. She had set up a pot of coffee and some sandwiches and cakes on the wall. It was a breathtakingly beautiful place to have lunch.

"Sorry about the workmen," she said, "but I'm building an addition onto my house. All my kids and my grandkids come to visit. And they take up all the bedrooms. So I decided to build another bedroom. For me."

I asked her about her family.

"I have my daughter, the doctor, and her two kids, *and* my son the engineer and his wife the rabbi."

We both giggled. This from the founder of the women's movement.

"And my other daughter-in-law, who is the only engineer in Iceland but who now lives in Princeton. All together three children, eight grandchildren, age two to fourteen. They're here a lot and I love it."

"You're quite the softie," I said.

"Yup."

She asked me if I was from the East End, and I told her I was not, but had moved here with my parents when I was sixteen. She asked how I had started my newspaper and I told her I had originally started it in Montauk, because one was needed since there was none. And she wanted to know more about my family, and so I told her I had four kids. She already knew about my divorce.

Soon, lunch was done, and amidst the sounds of the babbling brook, the birds and the banging and hammering, we were talking again about the women's movement.

"The women's movement was a throwing out of the baby with the bath water," she said. "I never said, 'down with motherhood, marriage, and men.' I just said a woman can't be defined in those terms alone. It's liberating to have a choice and its just as valuable to choose to have children as not. I've repeatedly told people in the movement: stop wallowing in victimhood. There are other issues."

At that moment, out of the corner of her eye, she saw two workmen struggling to bring in a new four-poster bed.

"Excuse me," she said, and she got up and walked over. I followed.

"Put this in the living room for now," she told them.

Without asking, I grabbed one corner of the bed and helped them with it. It was difficult to maneuver. She stood to one side and directed the operation.

We talked more about the women's movement. Now she was writing a book about aging.

"It's what you have to look forward to," she said. She was seventy, I was forty-eight.

Soon afterwards, I left. I felt we had shared something quite lovely. I was almost ready to forgive her for the women's movement.

A few years later, Ethel and Robert Scull went through a bitter divorce of their own. And soon after that, they went broke. It was a very big deal to see their vast art collection up on the auctioneer's block at Sotheby's, their antique car collection sold off, and their house sold on the courthouse steps.

I thought—ha! see what happens when you don't let me put my newspapers in your front hall?

Norman Mailer

~~~~~~

Early on a sunny morning in April of 1968, I drove up a hill in Sag Harbor along a narrow, winding road to arrive at the aptly named Hilltop House. It consisted of a white clapboard home with a screened porch, a swimming pool with lounge chairs all around, an outdoor bar, and some gardens. A gardener, on his hands and knees, was clipping some roses in a flower bed. He was the only person around.

"Are the movie people here yet?" I asked. I had been told that Norman Mailer, the great novelist, was producing and directing a film there.

"No. I think they're coming in two weeks," he said.

"Thanks."

Two weeks later, I drove back up there again, expecting to see a movie being made. However, I never did get to the top of the hill. Halfway up, there was the unmistakeable smell of burnt wood. Three-quarters of the way up, a chain across the road blocked the way. I stopped, got out, and walked around the chain and up the rest of the way to see

NORMAN MAILER

just two stone chimneys standing amidst the smoking ruins of the place. Hilltop House was no more.

No movie, is what I thought. And dammit, I didn't even know about the fire. What kind of newspaperman was I?

The following year, however, I learned that Mailer *had* made an art movie at Hilltop House that spring, a whirlwind affair filmed in just one weekend. It was called *Maidstone,* and it had been made the week after I had been there and one week before the big fire. The film was shown for just one night at a movie theatre in Manhattan. The *New York Times* theatre critic Pauline Kael had gone to see it, and she called it "the worst movie I ever saw all the way through to the end." I had even missed the review at the time.

Goddamn it again, I thought.

As the years went by, I hoped the film would return to a theatre for a showing somewhere, but it never did. I wanted to see it. Realize that it never entered anybody's mind in those days to buy a copy of an art movie. And that was because you couldn't. Films were made on big reels and shown at movie theatres. Unless you had copyright permission and knew someone who could get the reels, you were never going to see it unless it came around again at some art house somewhere. *Maidstone* never did. Or at least I never noticed that it did. So I sort of gave up.

In the early 1980s, however, videotapes came on the scene. You could buy a VCR and play tapes over your TV set. People were making collections of videotapes. I certainly was. Could *Maidstone* be on tape? It was not.

I still wanted to see it. Then, in 1993, I started a sort of fun promotion for the newspaper called "The Dan's Papers They Made the Movie Here Film Festival" (TDPTMTMHFF).

There had, by that time, been a big important movie festival started in the Hamptons called "The Hamptons International Film Festival," which attracted such celebrities as Steven Spielberg, Mercedes Ruehl, and Kathleen Turner.

It was held for the first time in October 1993, and it consisted of four days of nonstop showings of about a hundred new films. The festival was a big success and it has continued annually to this day.

I thought—why don't I have a mini-film festival the week after the festival? We'd show films made in the Hamptons. I'd get a small lecture hall in a school somewhere in town, rent some VCRs of movies made here such as *Son of the Sheik,* starring Rudolph Valentino; *Death Trap,* starring Michael Caine; and *Sweet Liberty,* starring Alan Alda—all of which were made in the Hamptons—and invite people in for free. Maybe I'd even be able to find that monster movie they'd made in Montauk years before. And maybe, finally, I'd see *Maidstone.* But *Maidstone* never got to be part of it. I never could find it. Indeed, I was warned off it.

"This is not a decent movie for a regular audience to see," someone said.

Our film critic, Guy de Fromenai, who was a judge at the Sundance Film Festival, and who introduces the films at TDPTMTMHFF, agreed with that assessment. He had actually seen it and reviewed it for a magazine in New York when it came out.

"This was made a month after Robert Kennedy was assassinated. *Cinéma vérité* was being born. Mailer made a plotless, filthy, drug-addled sex movie that is essentially a poorly made home-movie. It's disgusting and it's boring. Don't show it. At least not with kids around."

At that point, I wondered if, years earlier, the fire at the Hilltop had been set by some crazed right-wing zealot in reaction to the making of a godless movie up there. Who knew?

Oh, how the world had turned since 1968, when the anti-establishment was winding up the fight to be able to say dirty words and do X-rated acts on film for the sake of "art"; and you could go to the Hampton Arts Movie Theatre, which I did, and watch the rawest of X-rated films right in a theatre in our community.

Of course, I had to see it. And finally, in 2006, I got a bootleg DVD of it. I got it by attending a lecture given by

Norman Mailer at Southampton College. After he finished, I spoke to him about *Maidstone.* And a few days later, an unmarked manila envelope arrived in my mailbox. I went home, pulled the shades down, and I watched.

Well, it was everything they said it was. And it was filmed not just at the Hilltop House—which was the headquarters for the great assemblage of attractive young people Mailer brought out—but at a great many other locations, some of them so exclusive that it seemed amazing to me that they had ever gotten permission to film at them. Well, it was another time. Sex, drugs, mayhem, and all manner of other bizarre behavior was going on all over the place.

Norman Mailer, in addition to directing it, starred in it as the lead, playing a famous filmmaker named Norman T. Kingsley, who has decided to run for president. As a filmmaker, he is a wild man, and he has a large and merry entourage of groupies who follow him around.

Then there's a smaller group of people who dress up as FBI agents, in suits, ties, and dark glasses, and lurk in the background to watch the proceedings. They keep talking to one another about whether Kingsley's run for the presidency is illegal, perhaps seditious, and whether he ought to be killed. But when—now, or later? Permission has not yet been granted. Occasionally, they grab one of the merrymakers and interrogate them, or do whatever to them.

Mailer did not have any written script for the movie. There wasn't even a plot. Apparently, at the start of every scene, Mailer would assemble this group, which included the Andy Warhol star Ultra Violet, various models and photographers and friends of his, Mailer's third wife Beverly Bentley, his two ex-wives (there would be six wives in his lifetime), the actors Herve Villechaize, the *Fantasy Island* star, and Rip Torn, and several hangers on. He would tell them he was going to shoot footage for a while, so get ready and just say whatever you want to, but stay in character. Among the filmmakers, and there were several, was D. A. Pennebaker, the well-known documentary filmmaker who now lives in Sag Harbor. It was quite a crowd.

As I watched the movie, I recognized many of the locations where the FBI observed, grabbed, interrogated, and plotted, and the entourage cavorted, ran around naked or topless, and had regular or oral sex as Kingsley/Mailer strutted around importantly nearby.

I was ready with the remote in case something involving underage teenagers showed up on the screen—it's illegal now to even *watch* children in sexual contexts, as you know—but none did. It's all grown-ups.

The scenes took place—I recognized them all—at the Gardiner mansion on Main Street in East Hampton (which had once been the summer White House for President Tyler), at the home of Grove Press publisher Barney Rosset on Georgica Road, at the home of a disco nightspot owner Peter Rangell, and at the sixty-eight-acre Georgica Pond–front home owned by artist Alfonso Ossorio, which today is owned by Ron Perelman of Revlon. There were also scenes shot at the exclusive and private Gardiner's Island, access to which could only have been obtained by permission of Robert David Lion Gardiner, the sixteenth lord of the manor. Otherwise, caretakers would have scared them off with guns.

There is one particular scene which takes place in a small boat in a harbor not far from my house. The girls undress, then the guys undress. Everybody gets drunk and runs around as best they can on this small boat.

What is surely the penultimate scene in this scatological disaster takes place on Gardiner's Island. Norman Mailer could have died from it.

Mailer is in an open field talking to the crew about the philosophy of his filmmaking, about the film as an allegory and a separate reality from the regular reality—the cameras are rolling, of course—when actor Rip Torn bursts out of a nearby shed brandishing a hammer.

"I'm going to kill you, Norman T. Kingsley," he shouts, and he runs over and leaps on Mailer, bashing him in the head with his hammer. Mailer and Torn now wrestle around in the grass—people are screaming—and blood is dripping down the side of Mailer's head. People run over to try to pry these two apart, but by this time Mailer has gotten his teeth locked around Rip Torn's right ear and won't let go. Torn is shouting and screaming in pain, until finally the two of them are pulled apart.

In spite of being hit in the head with the hammer three times—I rewound it and saw it in slow motion—Mailer seemed uninjured. He apparently had a very hard head. Soon, they are standing up, facing one another, breathless.

Torn's ear is also bloody. "I wasn't trying to kill *you*, I was trying to kill Kingsley," Torn says.

Mailer does not appreciate the distinction. He doesn't speak to Torn again. Then the film ends.

And that's it.

I give it half a star. But four stars for effort, when you consider everybody is pretty much wasted the whole time.

Just to round things out, I should note that I had years earlier met Mailer without even realizing it. It was the second year I was publishing *Dan's Papers,* I was twenty-one years old, and I was at the print shop where it was being run off in Freeport, Long Island. Several newspapers were being printed there that Wednesday night, because Thursday was the day all the weeklies came out. One particular Thursday at the shop, I met three guys who had just started a new newspaper in New York called the *Village Voice.* I'd heard about the paper but had not seen it. The men were in their late thirties, but at age twenty-two I was the old-timer, having started my newspaper the year before.

We talked for a while. There are long waits while newspapers are produced, and you sit in a front room away from the presses and wait for galleys to be brought out to proofread. I told them my newspaper was free. They told me it would never fly. Theirs was a paid paper and it was the only way to go. Free was just for fliers. The three men introduced themselves to me by their first names, and they were Dan, Ed, and Norman. A free paper may be a new thing, I told them, but it would surely work where you had a captive tourist audience staying in motels, and you could leave the paper in the lobby in stacks.

Norman, or one of the others, told me I should be looking for other work.

A few years later, I learned that Norman Mailer and the two others had been the founders of the *Village Voice.* Thirty-five years later, the *Village Voice* became a free paper. It is free to this day.

William Power Maloney Sr.

〰〰〰〰〰〰〰〰〰〰〰〰〰〰〰〰〰〰〰〰〰〰〰〰

In 1969, I moved my newspaper office to a two-story, hundred-year-old former private home on Main Street in the quiet little town of Bridgehampton. Completely surrounded by potato farms at the time, it consisted of one main street three blocks long with a feed store, a meat market, a print shop, a grocery store, and six grimy gas stations where grease-covered mechanics worked on cars, tractors, and potato trucks to keep the potato crop going. At the westerly end of Main Street, two potato-packing barns operated seven months a year. The trucks would back in and dump their loads onto tables where the black migrant workers, laboring in these hot, dusty, windowless buildings, would sort them out, discard the bad ones, and pack the good ones into burlap sacks. Later, the sacks would be sent off to the market, which was at the railroad depot in Riverhead twenty miles away. Here, the sacks would be loaded into railroad cars along with lots of other eastern Long Island farm produce—cauliflower, corn, beans, strawberries in season—to be sent off to New York City.

MAIDSTONE GOLF CLUB

BRIDGEHAMPTON GOLF CLUB

(Courtesy of the author)

It was hard work. Sometimes you'd see the migrants during their day off congregating in small groups on Main Street, talking and occasionally taking swigs of the Thunderbird wine they kept inside paper bags. As night fell, they would shuffle off to the makeshift barracks that the farmers provided for them on the farms themselves; and in the fall, when it was all over, the migrants would be shipped off in big yellow school buses back to Georgia or Alabama.

My dad, at his drugstore in Montauk, approved my move to Bridgehampton.

"I think it's good," he said. "You can mingle with the chic bull crap in East Hampton or Southampton. Then you can go home to a working-class town."

By that time, my newspaper was being distributed over the full sixty miles of the South Fork peninsula and was a clear success.

Of course, there were wonderful things about Bridgehampton. There were beautiful Victorian homes on residential streets just off Main Street. There was a classic old drive-in movie just west of the potato-packing barns where, if you wanted to take a dare, you could try to sneak somebody in in the trunk of your car. Directly across the street was the Carvel, open until midnight for a drive-in ice cream. Also, amid the dirt and grease of downtown, there were four sparkling white churches, a four-square bank, a soda fountain, and a drugstore with a pharmacist who knew my father. At the most easterly end of town, there was the town's single traffic light, and directly below it, a memorial monument to those from Bridgehampton that gave their lives in all the wars. A bronze eagle stood atop it, defiantly, spreading its wings. At the time it was built, in 1899, there were plaques on the monument to four different wars. Today there are ten plaques on it.

It did occur to me, because of my college studies in architecture and city planning, that unlike East Hampton and Southampton, downtown Bridgehampton had gone very wrong. The four corners defining this monument had, years earlier, been a splendid space. One corner had been an open field, the mustering grounds for the Bridgehampton Militia during the Revolutionary War. Another corner had had an old colonial inn called Wick's Tavern on it. And the two remaining corners had grand, three-story-high Georgian mansions facing the monument.

When I moved there though, one of the mansions was falling to ruin and another was in poor condition, and to pay for the upkeep the owner had leased his front lawn to a gas station. Where Wick's Tavern had been was now a gas station—with a metal sign on the street noting that once Wicks Tavern had been there. And the fourth corner, where the militia had been, was now a white-stucco commercial building with stores in it.

Three miles south from the center of town, beyond the last potato field, was the Atlantic Ocean. Here, hard up against the dunes, were big summer homes, with beautifully groomed lawns and gardens. These were owned by the same wealthy old WASP families from New York City who had established summer colonies in East and Southampton. There were only a few of these summer homes here in Bridgehampton. I thought they had come here for the same reason I had—to get away from the chic, although a different chic, since they were all WASPS.

Of course, they did have an exclusive beach club. And they all belonged to a private nine-hole golf course just a short walk from Main Street. The Bridgehampton Golf Club wasn't as exclusive as the Maidstone in East Hampton or the Shinnecock in Southampton, and indeed I knew several local merchants who belonged to it. I thought that since I was a new young businessman in town, I might become a member, too. I enjoyed playing that game.

I not only moved the office to Bridgehampton, but a year later, I bought a home in town, a big six-bedroom Victorian mansion on Lumber Lane, off Main Street. I had paid fifty thousand dollars for it, and realtors told me it was the most money paid for a home in downtown Bridgehampton at the time. A new benchmark, is how they put it. It would be a good place for my growing family.

After I moved in, I noticed changes in the community. A few shaggy hippies had set up art studios on side streets. Bobby Van's, the soon-to-be-famous literary bar, had opened on Main Street. Right next door to where I rented my first big newspaper office on Main Street was the newly opened Benson Art Gallery, a series of buildings and barns which would soon become the center of the art and literary community in the Hamptons.

Perhaps most interesting of all were two new offices that appeared the same year I got there. They were right across from one another on Main Street. The first was an environmental action office called The Group for America's South

Fork. People with headbands and bellbottoms worked there. The issues they were concerned with were pollution—air and water. There was nothing about saving the farmland—the farmland was fine—and global warming had not yet been detected.

The other office was a small storefront that had now become the headquarters for a young hippie lawyer named William Power Maloney Jr. I'd met him covering an earlier environmental battle for an article for the paper. He viewed the world with wry humor, something I enjoyed too. And so I'd often go over there and chat with him when things were slow. I soon learned he was a member of the wealthy WASP summer community. He had married a Wellesley girl. And he lived in a Victorian house that was even bigger than the one that I had just bought.

"Who is William Power Maloney Sr.?" I once asked him. "It's such an amazing name."

"Oh, you'll meet him someday," Bill said. "He's everything I'm not. He works on Wall Street."

Bill did wear a suit and tie to work every day, however, because he was always in court. Everyone knew where he stood, though. He defended the migrants. He battled those polluting the water.

I did walk down one day to have a look at the golf course. I stood on the sidewalk. The clubhouse wasn't much—it was just a low, one-story extended bungalow—but the course looked good, although it was just nine holes. The president of it, I was told, was William Power Maloney Sr. So I asked Bill about it.

"Not my department," Bill said. "You're on your own."

One day I came to meet William Power Maloney Sr. in Bill's office. He burst in. I immediately thought about the golf course. But this was not the time to ask him about it, of course.

"Where's your mother?" the old man asked Bill. He had not even acknowledged me.

"I don't know," Bill said.

"She said she was coming in here."

"Well, she's not here yet," Bill said. The senior Mr. Maloney turned and walked out. And that was that.

"I guess that was your father?" I asked.

"That's him."

After that, I saw Mr. Maloney Sr. around town on numerous occasions. He was a stern, humorless man and he always wore the same neatly pressed three-piece suit. He must have had a closet full of them. He wore shiny black shoes.

Physically, he looked awful. He was stiff and bent. He might have been a handsome fellow at one time—Bill was—but that was gone. He had liver splotches on his face. What little hair he had was white and in a comb-over. He was altogether an unpleasant little man, not somebody I would ever want to introduce myself to. Certainly there would be no direct way to talk to him about playing golf.

So I wrote a letter. "Dear Sirs," I wrote. "I'm inquiring about becoming a member of the Bridgehampton Club. When I was a teenager I belonged to a private club in Livingston, New Jersey, called Cedar Hill and became pretty good at the game. I was on my golf team in high school. I played in the New Jersey Amateur in 1957 at Baltusrol which, I am sure you know, Jack Nicklaus won. I would be pleased and honored to be accepted into the club."

The response was swift. It came in a phone call, not from the golf club, but from Bill Jr.

"I hear you applied to join Bridgehampton," he said. "I think you ought to come over so we can talk about this in person."

"Is there a problem?"

"Just come over," he said. And so I did. I sat in the chair on the other side of his desk.

"They don't want you," he said.

"Why?"

"Because you're Jewish. They don't accept Jews."

"Bill. You've got to talk to your father. This is not right."

"My dad is who decided there would be no Jews," he said.

"I want to file a lawsuit."

"Dan, it won't do any good. It's a private club. They can do what they want."

I felt awful. "One of the reasons I moved here is that the golf course is right down the street," I said.

"When I fight my dad on his turf, he wins," Bill said. "He'll die someday. After that, maybe things will be different. But for now, you're blocked."

This business about Bill Sr. dying in the next year or two actually seemed to be coming about. It's a small town. As the years passed, Mr. Maloney's gait got slower. His clothing became more slovenly. He became nastier. And sometimes, he got lost.

I actually saw this once. He was right on Main Street and it appeared he had forgotten where he was. But then a man appeared.

"I'll take you home," the man said, guiding him to a car.

"I'm fine," Maloney said. He wasn't.

In those days, in a small town, when somebody got old and their mind began to fail, what you did was simply help them out. There were old-age homes, but they were not for the wealthy. There were no "assisted living" places in the 1970s. Your assistance was around you.

One night, I was at the Village Tavern, a local hangout, having a beer at the bar. We had worked late at the newspaper. I wasn't up to going to Bobby Van's to get into conversation with all the intelligentsia.

In came William Power Maloney Sr. in all his babbling glory. I was the only person at the bar. In fact, I was the only person in the whole place other than the bartender, but Mr. Maloney would have none of me. He sat down at the far end, where the bar meets the wall, where he could prop himself up.

He ordered a scotch. The bartender hesitated, Maloney bellowed something and banged his fist on the bar, and so off the bartender went and got it for him. Maloney belted it down.

In just a few minutes, however, it was apparent that William Power Maloney Sr. was completely in another world. It was midnight. The bartender looked at me.

"I can't leave this place for another hour," he said.

"I'll do it," I said.

I came over to him gently and tried to help him off his stool, but he waved me away. So then the bartender joined me, and between us we got him out the front door and into the passenger seat of my car parked out front. I locked the door so he wouldn't get out.

"Only one problem," I said to the bartender.

"What?"

"I don't know where he lives."

The bartender told me. It was the big mansion down by the school where Bill and his wife lived, and it was not at their end of the mansion but at the other end. There was a cottage. Knock on the cottage door. Someone will help you. Just wake them up.

We drove along. The car began to smell. Maloney made some point or other, jabbing a finger in the air. Satisfied at whatever it was, he settled back down.

Why don't I just dump him in the woods? I thought. What a horrible thought. I banished it from my mind. What kind of person was I? My face flushed.

I got to the house, knocked on the cottage door, and, despite the late hour, a man soon appeared, a servant by the looks of him, full of apologies for my inconvenience. He helped me get Mr. Maloney out of the car and into his house where, he indicated, there were others who would take over from here.

And so I left.

Soon thereafter, William Power Maloney Sr. passed from the scene. I did see Bill at the time and offered him my condolences.

But I made no more overtures about golf to Bill ever again. Indeed, that they had rejected me put the idea of playing on that golf course completely out of my mind forever.

Some years later, I attended a party there, and I got to see the shabbiest of interiors. It was WASP country living—clanking radiators, sturdy but wobbly wooden chairs and tables. I wasn't even sure if they had hot running water. And there were no women in there either. This was *golf*. But not for me.

Snow

~~~~~~

On warm summer days in the early 1970s, young black men wearing ragged clothing could sometimes be seen lolling about in front of stores on Main Street in Bridgehampton, enjoying the day. One of them might have a brown paper bag wrapped around a pint bottle of Thunderbird, their drink of choice back then; and if that were the case, you could watch him hand it around to the others, one at a time, and they would each take a swig, exhale with satisfaction, and then wipe their mouth with their sleeve before passing it on. The men were disheveled and often caked with dirt.

Under other circumstances, I might cross the street and walk on the other side of Main Street to avoid men such as these. But these men seemed so peaceful and relaxed, so friendly, talking to one another with big smiles on their faces, that I quickly saw these were not like other circumstances.

"Good day," I might say, walking by and smiling.

They'd stop whatever conversation they were in the midst of. They'd nod. "Yazzuh," one of them would say, tipping an invisible cap. They spoke in that deep Negro dialect that was

LARGEST POTATO COMPETITION, AGWAY,
BRIDGEHAMPTON, 1983
(Courtesy of the author)

so prevalent back then in the Deep South. I couldn't really understand much of what they said. Certainly, they weren't from the Hamptons.

Soon, however, I found out who they were. They were migrants, the men who worked on the potato farms that surrounded Bridgehampton. They'd arrive in early July, brought up on old buses from places like Arkansas and Alabama. They'd be promised good wages for picking the crops, driving the trucks, working in the potato-packing barns, and they'd have been cajoled onto the buses by straw bosses. Work hard. Make a good wage. The bus will take you back down south in September.

Here in the Hamptons, the migrants would be assigned to different farms and shown to makeshift wooden barracks where they'd live. I had never been in one, but I'd heard about them. There'd be a bathroom down at the end, a potbellied stove for heat on cold summer nights in the middle. Some of the barracks had electricity, others did not. Some had running water, some did not.

Every once in a while, you'd read in the local weekly paper about a knife fight that took place in one of these barracks. It's what happens, I thought, when you put a lot of people up in a building like that.

Oddly, there didn't seem to be much objection by the white community about this situation at the time. It was one of those things that had been taking place for almost forever. How else were the farmers supposed to get the potatoes out of the ground before they rotted? The workers were paid well for their hard labor—but then they had to pay rent for their bed in the barracks, and also for the food they ate at the daily meals the farm owners provided. There really wasn't much left over at the end. But they seemed to enjoy it. If they didn't, people figured, why had they been making this trip, year after year? Many, I was told, would come back again and again.

Also, when summer ended, many of them simply went on to other farms in other communities where the harvest started later in the autumn than it did here. They were migrant workers, and that is how they lived.

In many ways, they seemed to me to be just part of the street furniture in the summertime there in Bridgehampton, lollygagging around on their one day off each week, enjoying themselves. Didn't have much to do, so they'd come into town and hang around and talk and get a buzz on. Tourists and regular locals just passed them by.

If the young men would congregate on Main Street down near the monument, where most of the stores were, there was an older black man who did not. His name was Snow. And on certain days—sometimes three days a week—you could find him, a small, slender, slightly bent black man walking somewhere on Main Street all by himself, very slowly, heading toward one end of town or the other. Sometimes he walked silently. Sometimes he could be heard talking to himself.

His route never varied. He was always on Main Street, never on any of the side streets. As most of the potato farms were based to the west of town, I imagined he would start there and commence walking east at some point in the early morning. He'd pass the drive-in movie theatre, the Carvel, the One Stop Market, our *Dan's Papers* newspaper office (where we could sometimes look out the window to see him slowly walk by), then down the street past the Benson Art Gallery, the Pulver Gas Dealership, the Community House, the Candy Kitchen, and then that entire row of stores that went down to the monument and the single traffic light there at the east end of town. Then he'd walk back.

You'd see him on either the north or south side of the road—there were no sidewalks back then except where the stores were down by the monument, so he'd either walk on the grass or, if there were bushes or a big tree in his way, in the street itself. He never said a word to anybody, not to the white world or to the black world, as far as I could see. He just walked.

One day, I got it in my head to interview him for the paper. I'd walk along with him. What a story he would tell. I'd ask him questions about himself. He'd talk slowly, I was sure, and he'd tell me about who he was and where he was from. He was probably too old to work anymore. So he walked.

One morning, I asked George Stavropoulos about Snow. George ran the Candy Kitchen Luncheonette, and with the morning rush over I found him at the cash register by the front door of the place. He was free to talk for awhile.

"Oh, I don't know any more about him than you," he told me, "but he's certainly been on that walk for at least ten years."

It occurred to me that I'd never seen a black man in the Candy Kitchen. Ever. Early in the morning, it was a gathering place for the farm owners themselves, big white men usually, with florid complexions, big hands, overalls, and boots. They were mostly Polish-American, and they'd occupy the place for breakfast from six to seven-thirty every morning before heading out. They'd gossip or talk about the price of feed or the fluctuating market price of potatoes.

"You know," George said, "there was a terrible tragedy involving the migrant workers here fifteen years ago. A fire. It swept through one of those barrack buildings in the middle of the day while the men were out working. The women were out working in the fields too that day, and the children had been left alone in the building unattended. Five of them burned to death."

I told George I had not heard about that.

"The farmers felt terrible about this, and they did something about it. They raised some money and purchased a small twelve-acre dirt farm on the Sag Harbor Bridgehampton Turnpike—that's where the black section in town is today, you know—and they made it into a daycare center for the black children. It's a daycare center to this day. The Bridgehampton Child Care Center. It's where the black grammar-school kids go after school is out. And during the day, it's for the preschoolers for when the moms work in the fields. All paid for by the farmers."

"Maybe Snow knows something about that fire," I said.

"Maybe. Come to think of it, that's when he started taking his daily walks."

A customer came to the cash register to pay. There were no written checks accepted at the Candy Kitchen back then. You just went to George and told him what you'd eaten, and he'd add it up in his head and tell you what you owed. So I said thanks and went out into the street.

I didn't lay in wait for Snow or anything. There was no sense to that, because you never knew when he would come by. However, what I did do was just keep the project in the back of my mind. In the course of things, I always had a pen and paper in my pocket and in the car I always had a camera.

And of course, one day, there he was. I was driving along heading east and there was Snow, just passing the Elaine Benson Gallery and coming up on Pulver Gas. I pulled over to the side of the road behind him, parked, grabbed my camera, and started to walk toward him.

It wasn't necessary to break out into a brisk trot to catch this man because he was always just toddling along really slowly. I just walked regular. I caught up to him past Pulver Gas, alongside the front lawn of the Bridgehampton Community Center with the tall white pillars out front.

"Hi," I said, as I came alongside. "Mr. Snow, could I talk to you for a minute?"

He turned, saw me, and then stopped. He looked me right in the eye and raised his arms.

"RRRRAAAAHHHH!" he shouted. He bared his teeth. He flapped his arms over his head.

I turned and ran. And that was the last time I ever tried that.

I never did learn the story of Snow.

The Free Life

~~~~~~

To this day, almost forty years later, a thrill goes through me as I recall the absolutely magnificent morning of August 23, 1970, on George Miller's Farm in East Hampton. Books have been written about it. There are people in town who share a bond about that day. We all know who we are. And we are bound together for life.

First of all, there was the farm itself. I'd been up there many times. And I always thought, leaning on the split-rail fence on the southern border of this pasture, what an unbelievably magical place this was. The land, all grassland, stretched out low and flat and green to the edge of Gardiner's Bay several miles away to the north. In this whole stretch there was but one tree, a single giant weeping willow, way off in the distance. Horses often grazed there.

To the east of the pasture, the land melted into miles of swamps to become Accabonac Harbor, a body of water extending for nearly three miles along that side of the pasture. You could see the horizon in that direction, too. Since what was behind you from that railing was the small village of

(Courtesy of Bill Henderson)

Springs settled deep into a woods, it was a great flat expanse to the horizon. What a stage it was for what was to happen on that day.

By noon, more than two thousand people were standing on the lawn, talking excitedly, next to Springs-Fireplace Road where the split rail was. With them were TV crews, photographers, television commentators, and newspapermen.

In the center was Rodney Anderson, a young Wall Street stockbroker, now in hippie garb, who had tuned in, turned on, and dropped out, and would now make this astonishing attempt to fly across the Atlantic Ocean in a balloon.

Others had attempted to do this, but none had succeeded. This would be a first.

With Anderson was his no-nonsense British pilot, Malcolm Brighton. And most important of all, there was Pamela Brown, the daughter of millionaire John Brown Sr. of Lexington, Kentucky, and Rodney Anderson's twenty-eight-year-old wife. It was her money that supported this venture.

Pamela was already in tears. She would not be going. Her father had forbidden it. Much of the time, she held hands with her husband, as if to hang onto him so that perhaps he would not go either. She was a beautiful young woman with thick black hair that fell over her shoulders and glistened in the sunshine.

"I work as a commodities broker in the city," Anderson said into the microphone that was thrust out to him. "And I've decided there is more to life than just Wall Street. I need a Free Life. I can't give you any other explanation. You have to do what you have to do."

Brighton, the Englishman, stalked around the great deflated balloon lying flat on the ground next to Anderson, periodically examining it, shooing people away from it. He was of stocky build and wore black rubber boots, rough trousers tucked into the boots and held up by green suspenders over a blue denim shirt.

The balloon had three words in large orange letters on it, and you could read them there flat on the ground. *The Free Life.* Adjacent to the balloon and attached to it with ropes was the large wicker gondola with sandbags hooked to the railings. Nearby was a flatbed truck, a Styrofoam cooler, and metal bottles of propane. Off in the distance, by the single weeping willow, the horses, eight of them, frolicked and kicked and nipped at one another.

You could walk right up to the wicker gondola if you wanted to. And I did. I was astonished to see that glued to the inside of the wicker were ping pong balls for flotation. It seemed to me to be a sort of amateurish thing. But everyone was caught up in the excitement of the day. They were going to go no matter what. And we were all going to cheer them on. There was little doubt they would succeed. In three days, they would drop down in Ireland. And there would be another celebration.

A test inflation was ordered. Brighton wanted to check for leaks. Shortly, after whooshing blasts of propane flames were applied, the balloon became a mound, then a mountain, then, with a popping-canvas sort of sound, a sixty-foot-high, brightly colored psychedelic globe, wavering in the breeze, pulling at the ropes and the basket, which creaked and thumped a foot or two along the ground. Brighton ordered it taken back down. It was fine, he said.

I had been standing there, taking notes. Now I looked up to see John Strong, the realtor whose office was downtown next to the post office in East Hampton. He was in a sport shirt and slacks. I was halfway between sport shirt and slacks and hippie garb. *Everybody,* practically the whole town, was there.

"Hey," he said.

He was eating a sandwich.

"Where'd you get that?" I asked. It suddenly occurred to me I hadn't eaten lunch and I was hungry. It was 2:15.

He motioned to a workmen's coffee and food truck that I had not seen arrive.

"Looks like they're finally going to do it," John said. "Crazy, no?"

"It's a celebration," I said.

"A celebration of craziness," John said. "I hope they don't go. They're going to kill themselves."

I walked over to where the balloon was now slowly coming down. Brighton was talking to somebody about safety equipment. Something wasn't right about the radio. I went over to the coffee truck and bought myself a ham sandwich.

The preparations for the *Free Life* in East Hampton had taken two months, although, according to what I was told, the attempt had really been in the planning stages for years. Rodney and Pamela had been staying at the home of an older Bonac woman named Mary Damark, who, it seemed, had met them when they came into Damark's Deli on Three Mile Harbor Road. Mary had fallen in love with them and had sort of adopted them. She said they'd have to stay at her house. And so they did. The crew stayed elsewhere.

I first learned about this project by reading an article about it in another local newspaper in July. After that, I followed events with considerable interest, writing occasional articles in the paper about it myself. The date for the launch was postponed. Then it was postponed again. I had been unable

(Courtesy of Bill Henderson)

to get through to Rodney or Pamela, but through Mary Damark had met some of the crew. They had been expecting a pilot by the name of Crown to join them. He should be coming in from St. Paul, Minnesota they said, but in the end, he never did come. Now they had a line on somebody from England. A professional balloonist there named Malcolm. Soon thereafter, he arrived. And now, today was the day.

At ten minutes to three, with the *Free Life* once again inflated, Rodney Anderson and Malcolm Brighton climbed into the gondola of the balloon. The wind had picked up. Brighton said they should be off before it died down again.

The crowd, all colorful in their headbands and beads—this was just one year after Woodstock—was cheering loudly. Suddenly, without ceremony or fanfare, the ropes were dropped and the gondola started to move bumpily along the ground.

"Goodbye."

"We love you."

"Have a nice trip."

And then, from out of the crowd, weeping and emitting terrible cries, came Pamela Brown, running along with the gondola, holding out her arms, tears streaming down her cheeks.

"I'm going, I'm going," she cried.

At the very last minute, as the gondola began to lift off, Rodney Anderson, with the help of Malcolm Brighton, lifted her in. And they were gone.

Watching that balloon, sweeping away from the crowd across the pasture to pass just over the weeping willow and out over the bay, was a true fairy tale. There was the prince and princess, leaving from Oz, waving and waving, then turning to embrace one another.

They got smaller and smaller. Soon they were a speck. Can you still see them? Can you? People were pointing and squinting into the sunshine. What a foolish thing she did. Oh God, oh God.

And now the speck was gone.

Around us, among the thousands and thousands of spectators, there were people crying. Other people were embracing one another. This was *perfect*. Off in the distance, the horses continued to frolick in the green clover under the weeping willow tree.

The *Free Life* was never heard from again. A storm came up off Newfoundland that night and they radioed that they were going down. They said they would call to announce their position when they set down in the sea. Then, 'please rescue us.' And that was the last message those on shore ever received.

Pam's millionaire father, John Brown Jr. was frantic. Later that day, he flew up to East Hampton to participate in the Coast Guard search himself. He flew out with them. After two days of nothing, after the Coast Guard called it off as a dark summer storm moved in, John Brown hired his own planes to crisscross the sea. But in the end, even he had to give up.

Something other than just the physical fact of the deaths of three young people settled over the people of eastern Long Island after that. As people, particularly young people, remembered that day, with the glittering sunshine and the horses and the magical balloon, they spoke in low tones.

How could it have happened the way it did? All people wanted to do was forget. And they couldn't.

Don Clause

~~~~~~

I would do anything for my customers. If there was some-body I knew they wanted to meet I would set it up. If they wanted my advice about something I would do my best. If they wanted a story in the paper about some new widget their wife had invented, they'd get it.

"You're good with words," Don Clause told me in the summer of 1972. "I've bought a billboard. You know the one on the north side of the highway in Sagaponack by the Blue Door antique shop?"

I knew it well. It was a billboard for Agway Farm Supplies the last time I looked at it. It stood fifteen feet high and thirty feet long in the middle of a potato field adjacent to the highway. It had a bright green Caterpillar tractor from Agway advertised on it, with a happy farmer fifteen feet tall waving to the passing motorists from the seat of it. At night, it was lit up.

"So I've bought it for a year," Clause said. "Help me design it. Maybe this is an opportunity for you. Go into the advertising designing business."

1.67 ACRE GIFT
FROM
DONALD J. CLAUSE
TO
THE INCORPORATED VILLAGE
OF
EAST HAMPTON

(Courtesy of the author)

"If I can help you," I said. "I will."

Don Clause and his wife, teenage daughter, and son lived in one of the old WASP mansions on Woods Lane in town. They were rich, they were Italian American, and Don, anyway, had a certain mafia inflection in the way he spoke. I thought maybe it was an act. Who could know for sure?

Don Clause was the new owner of the beautiful old Victorian seaside inn at Main Beach in East Hampton called the Sea Spray. Don had also opened new real estate offices in Amagansett and Sag Harbor. And at the time Don offered me the task of making his sign, we were standing in the main room of the two-hundred-year-old saltbox that Don had bought for his new office in East Hampton. It was where Skimhampton Road met the highway. He had just given me the tour of his renovations. Everything was now covered in baby blue shag, even the ceilings.

"Nice, huh?" he said, indicating a post wrapped in the shag.

"Yup," I said, unenthusiastically.

Don Clause was about forty-five, slender, movie-star handsome, with big dark eyes and a great shock of black hair. No way this guy was mafia, I thought. Just a good Italian businessman.

"So what do you think?" he asked, now referring back to the billboard he had bought. Clause advertised big in the paper. Real estate. Sea Spray. Several pages a week. A tough pay though, though eventually he would always pay me.

"I could do it."

"How about this time next week. Write up what you think that billboard should say. I'll pay you a hundred dollars to design it. I've got to give the design to a sign painter by a week from Tuesday."

Wow, I thought. A hundred dollars, for something not involving publishing the newspaper.

I gave it some thought. What I came up with, working in pencil on paper at home on my dining room table, was, I thought, brilliant. The background of the billboard would be white. But there would be a thin pinstripe of brown inside the border of it. Inside that, in the center, would be the silhouettes of two geese flying side by side. Above the geese would be the words SHARE OUR TRADITIONS. Below it would say, DON CLAUSE REAL ESTATE, 324-5355.

It's hard to imagine, all these years later, just how important and how excellent this billboard really was. First of all, billboards were getting fewer and fewer as the years went by. There were laws being passed against them. When we had first moved to the area in the 1950s, there were hundreds of them. They were everywhere as you went down the street. I recall one that the Southampton Police had put up by the side of the road as you came into Water Mill from the west.

ENTERING WATER MILL

SLOW DOWN AND ENJOY IT

SPEED CONTROLLED BY RADAR

How excellent that was, and how excellent all billboards were, can be demonstrated by the fact that I can still, in my mind, see that sign in Water Mill. Motorists would hit the brakes. No sense roaring through Water Mill at high speed with that warning and with cops about. I was, however, personally against billboarding up the Hamptons. But if there were still a few left, I at least ought to make a handsome design for one.

In any case, Don Clause, too, loved what I did as a design for his billboard. He not only put my SHARE OUR TRADITIONS design on the billboard, he also made it the logo for his stationery and put it on the side of his real estate agents' cars. But I never got the hundred dollars. When I mentioned it to him, he said, well, I had been giving him a discount for his advertising. Next time, let's make it *less* of a discount by a hundred dollars. How was that?

Five years later, the billboard was still up with SHARE OUR TRADITIONS on it, and every day I'd go by it on my way home from work. Yes, indeed. We locals had a beautiful life here. It goes back three hundred fifty years. Buy some real estate and we'll share our traditions. There were not many summer people back then, and we wanted to encourage them to come out.

As for the Clause family, it seemed to be thriving. I was invited over to their mansion a few times. It was really quite beautiful inside, all Turkish rugs and wicker, flocked wallpaper and fake gas lamps on the walls.

Don was very strict with the kids. Tough with his wife too. But maybe that was a good thing. By that time I had one daughter age two, who I was spoiling terribly. It was just another way.

One evening at the Clause home that spring, Don suggested that perhaps he would buy six full-page ads every week for his expanding real estate business. I was ecstatic. We were sitting in his study, and he had a copy of my paper on his coffee table.

"Ever have anybody buy six full pages?" he asked.

"Never did," I said.

"So this would be a first. Well. I'd need a good price for the six."

I gave him a good price. But it wasn't good enough.

"Tell you what," he said. "I'm going to fill each of these pages with classified real estate ads. I'll pay you (he named a ridiculously low sum). But I'll give you a commission on anything we sell. We'll advertise only in your paper. If we sell something, you know, we get a six percent commission. I'll give you a third of that. What do you say?"

In my head, quickly, I did the math. If we sold just one house, it would pay for everything five times over.

"Done," I said.

Late that autumn, as the activity in the Hamptons slowed down to a crawl—I'd be shutting down my newspaper business for three months in the wintertime—I had dinner at my parents' house in Montauk where I met a lovely middle-aged couple by the name of Rothholtz. Barbara was a beautiful woman of French extraction. Peter was British, with this clipped British accent. He also had a wonderful sense of humor and an occasional twinkle in his eye. I learned that he and Barbara had just bought a house in East Hampton, that they also had an apartment in Manhattan, and that Peter was in the public relations business. His firm had the contract to do the marketing and public relations worldwide for the island of Barbados in the Caribbean.

"You should come down sometime," he said. "I could arrange it for you. Write about it in the paper—a great place for a getaway in the wintertime—and the hotel will be on me."

What a wonderful offer. I was living with a woman named Ann Nowak at the time. And so we took Peter up on it. We stayed a week at a wonderful beachfront resort called Cobbler's Cove, located between Sandy Lane and Speightstown. When we first got there, on a Friday, all the islanders were caught up in a very important cricket final. Everywhere you went, you'd see people with portable radios to their ears. People would ask each other the score. I had no idea what any of it was all about. It lasted two days. Then everything returned to normal. On the third day, Peter Rothholtz showed up at the hotel. We didn't know he was even on the island. But he came by and said if there was anything we needed just let him know. He'd be there for a few days.

Of course, I wrote about this trip in the paper, and it seemed to spark a friendship between Barbara and Peter and myself and my girlfriend. One day, two months later, they invited us over for dinner. They wanted to show off their new house.

We walked through the dining room and the den, and then upstairs to the three bedrooms; and it was there, in the master bedroom, that Peter Rothholtz had this to say.

"You know, we bought this house because of your paper."

It was an odd thing to say.

"You did?"

"We did. We're big fans of your paper. We read it every week. There was a classified ad from one of your advertisers. Don Clause. He had pages and pages of classifieds. And so we saw this house there. And we bought it."

"You did?"

One week later, back home, I marched into Don Clause's shag-covered office in East Hampton, situated in a kind of low-ceilinged upstairs room. You climbed a shag-covered spiral staircase to reach it.

"You owe me a commission," I said. It was, indeed, a lot of money. I explained it all to him. He looked puzzled.

"I must have missed that," he said. "Let me look into it."

"You might look to see if there were any other houses sold. We had a deal."

"Yeah," he said. "Unless we advertised it in one of the other papers too."

"You said you were going to advertise exclusively in my paper."

"Like I said, I'll look into it."

Needless to say, after Don Clause conducted his investigation, he reported back to me that indeed that ad had been one of those that had been in another paper. So, too bad.

I've never been a particularly combative person. Don Clause was a big advertiser. And that was fine. But I did ask Peter Rothholtz a second time where he saw that classified ad. And I also told him about my deal with Clause.

"Well, I hope you got your money," Peter said.

"Working on it," I said. But, of course, I wasn't.

About three years after that, this would have been around 1979, the real estate market began to tank as it periodically does. Clause had been paying for his ads fairly well, for Clause anyway, but now the money seemed to dry up. And then the Sea Spray Inn burned down.

This was a real catastrophe for the town, the loss of a great jewel of a property right on the ocean across from the wood-shingled beach pavilion at Main Beach. It was a magnificent three-story Victorian inn with a wraparound porch. There was a big lawn with a flagpole. And there were five bungalows around the lawn, all of which survived the fire. But the inn was gone.

Don Clause, I was told, was distraught from the loss of the inn, but I don't know. I didn't have much I was doing with him at the time. He owed me too much money.

It was said that the inn had been in the process of being sold. In fact, I had met the people who were supposed to become the new owners, three guys who were big football and baseball jocks. They had rented the property from Clause for a year, and were now coming up with the cash to buy the place.

I never did see them again after the fire.

Then things went rapidly downhill for the Clause family. The mansion was sold, and it seemed it was some sort of mortgage forclosure action, although I could not be sure. Then the new Southampton real estate office closed up. Later I heard that the Clause family had picked up stakes and moved to Fort Myers, Florida and had gone into the real estate business there.

As for the big SHARE OUR TRADITIONS billboard, it remained up for another year as the Clause businesses were falling apart, and I now had a very different view of it. It was not just that things had failed to go the way they should have between me and Don Clause; it was that by this time it was 1985, and this was one of the very last billboards left standing, and so it looked very out of place in the community. Also, what was a very good thought in 1975, that people should come out here and buy a lot and build a house to share our traditions, had now become a very alarming reality.

There were just too many summer people in 1985. There were traffic jams, loud obnoxious people with poor manners, expensive European cars, and an entitled attitude. Whoever had thought up this SHARE OUR TRADITIONS slogan should be shot. Who the hell was the idiot who thought that up?

And I'd still go driving by it every day going home from work.

Today, there is another monument in town to Don Clause. It's been down Ocean Road in the town parking lot just before Main Beach since the late 1970s, and it's a big boulder with a plaque on it attesting to the good works of this man:

> 1.67-ACRE GIFT
>
> FROM
>
> DONALD J. CLAUSE
>
> TO THE INCORPORATED
>
> VILLAGE OF EAST HAMPTON
>
> MARCH 1979

That parking lot, paved and striped today, had once been the gravel parking lot for the Sea Spray Inn. I don't know the details about how it came into the Village's hands, but what I remember at the time was that Clause offered it—he didn't need it because there was no inn there to park for anymore—and that the gift was offered with the contingency that a big boulder with a plaque on it attesting to his generosity be placed in the parking lot.

And so it has. You can go down there today, anytime, to be reminded of it.

Steven Spielberg

~~~~~~

In 1971, a member of the Southampton social set named Peter Benchley wrote a book called *Jaws,* in which the people of the Hamptons, fearful that the culinary habits of an angry killer shark might scare away tourists, try desperately to keep the whole thing hush-hush.

Things were tough in the Hamptons at that time. The farming and fishing economies were faltering. Many locals were on welfare in the wintertime. And even in the summertime, the small wealthy WASP enclave that came out from the city, living behind hedgerows, simply did not provide enough jobs—landscapers, cooks, chauffeurs, etc.—to make up for it. If the visitors could be prevented from knowing about the killer shark until they could kill him, why tell them?

Benchley's book was a bestseller. As a result, the book was picked up by a movie studio, Universal, so a film could be made of it. They selected a young filmmaker, Steven Spielberg, to direct it and announced they would produce it in the summer of 1974.

Everyone in the Hamptons thought—what a boost this will be for us. But it was not to be. The filmmakers decided

STEVEN SPIELBERG (RIGHT) SPEAKING AT
HAMPTON SYNAGOGUE, 1990.

(Courtesy of Hampton Synagogue)

to make the film in Martha's Vineyard. The Hamptons, they said, was now "too busy" to capture the sense of isolation and dread needed for the movie. It would be the Hamptons. But it would not be the Hamptons.

I spoke to Marty Lang, the town supervisor of Southampton about this at the time.

"What the hell did they mean by 'too busy'?" he asked me, waving an arm at the empty street outside. We were sitting in Sip 'n' Soda on Hampton Road in Southampton. He'd have done just about anything to get that film production. "The book was set in the Hamptons. It says so. I don't get it."

The following year, with the filming done, a man from Universal Pictures, Ben Salweather, came out to see me about the premiere of this upcoming movie, which was now just a month away.

"It's going to be a very big deal," he said. "And it's going to be *here,* at the East Hampton Theatre."

He handed me some glossy photos. The size and ferociousness of the shark was quite frightening.

"There will be celebrities and limos and red carpets just like you see in Hollywood. The movie is going to scare the daylights out of everybody. I wanted you to have a heads-up. I want to give you literature about it. Maybe you'll write about it in your paper."

"Have you seen it?"

"I have. It scared the bejesus out of me."

People were certainly talking about it. Some said they would see it. Some said they would never see it. I planned *never* to see it. I loved to swim in the ocean and I didn't want to give that up.

It had been a busy spring. Edward Albee, the playwright who had a summer home tucked away in Montauk, had written a play called *Seascape,* about four people lying on the beach, and it had won the Pulitzer Prize for drama.

I wrote about that, and also noted that the Rolling Stones were still rehearsing in Montauk at the Manor Stable owned by Edward Albee for their upcoming world tour to begin in June in Baton Rouge; but now, with the word out, security guards were stopping crowds of uninvited people at the gates to the stable.

I concluded by saying that we were all so pleased to have these celebrities living quietly at the beach to enjoy the

JUNE 25, 1975

solitude and the ocean, far from the glare of publicity, and what was now going on was just too bad.

Another big story was about a single-engine plane that had gotten into trouble and landed in a potato field near Mitchell Lane, in Bridgehampton. The next morning, I was out there as the locals helped haul it out onto this long, straight road that separated two potato fields, and cheered as it roared off, with Mitchell Lane as its runway.

And I wrote stories trying to fool the tourists. On May 29, as the tourists arrived for Memorial Day, I had published a "Hooter's Guide," which explained the meaning of the hoots given off by the Montauk Lighthouse. It had to do with the Coast Guard staff there ordering pizza. One hoot was plain, two hoots were pepperoni, and so forth.

The main theme of the paper that spring, however, was an ongoing feature where I asked readers to write in and give examples of the "Hampton Spirit," which I defined as kindness, friendliness, and helpfulness.

People wrote in to praise the owners of the Carvel in Hampton Bays, the owners of a taxi service in Amagansett, the owner of a motel in Shinnecock.

Looming over everything, however, was the upcoming premiere of *Jaws*. It was now clear that it was going to be a major national event. I went to see a new nightspot opening in Southampton called "Jaws." I got the tour.

"You just walk in the front door and, here you are, right inside the shark's mouth. The teeth hang down. So you sort of *escape* into the disco."

What if the movie simply scared everybody out of ever coming to the Hamptons? Two weeks before the premiere, I made another call to Mr. Salweather. I told him I thought the Hamptons might have grounds for a lawsuit against Universal when this film came out if, as a result, people stayed away. Had he thought about that? He referred me to the lawyer for that company, a man named Shel Middleman. So I called him.

"Does Universal Pictures still have those studio tours for the general public?" I asked.

"Yes, we do."

"Well, suppose I wrote in a newspaper that you had a real live sniper along that tour. And as a result of this, business dropped off. Couldn't the studio sue my paper?"

"Probably."

"Well, then the reverse is also true. A movie studio cannot cause economic hardship to a resort town without bearing the responsibility."

There was silence on the other end.

"If a town could sue for loss of business," Middleman said, "then W. C. Fields would have been sued long ago. Remember his famous line? 'I went to Philadelphia last week. But it was closed.' "

"Still, if this movie is *so* vivid as to scare the wits out of everybody, it should have a disclaimer on it. No man-eating shark has ever been seen around here in the history of the Hamptons. Have you seen the film?"

"No. Let me get on this, and I'll call you back."

Three hours later, Middleman called to report that a "reader" in the studio, a young woman named Camille Smith, had read the script to consider exactly what I had called about.

"The name of the place the film takes place in is a town called Amity," he said.

"Amity?"

"There are references to resorts up and down the northeast coast from Maine to the Jersey shore. Even the Hamptons. But it's Amity. At the beginning of the movie, there's a big billboard at the entrance to town that reads WELCOME TO AMITY. It's Amity."

Now I was just completely frustrated.

"It was supposed to be the Hamptons. So first you film it somewhere else and then you name it somewhere else?"

"Yes."

"You get us coming and going, huh?"

He had no answer for that.

And so it was that on the sunny day of July 1, 1975, the movie made its east coast premiere at the East Hampton Cinema on Main Street with the full celebrity experience—red carpet, spotlights, photographers—I had never before seen anything like this in this town. Attending were actors Richard Dreyfus, Roy Scheider, and Robert Shaw, along with director Steven Spielberg, all of whom smiled and waved to the crowds before going in.

I, however, after wavering this way and that, finally decided to remain steadfast to my earlier decision about not going in. So I hovered silently in front of the James Marley Stationery Store across the street from all the hoopla, and watched the amazing scene of this full-blown movie premiere from across the way. There were movie trucks, TV vans, limousines, herds of photographers that some people called "paparazzi"—it was the first time I had heard that term. So I waited there and when all that came to an end, and everybody went inside, I waited around for a little more, hoping to hear screams or something from those within, and when that didn't occur, I finally decided I ought to go down to the beach for a while to go for a swim—definitely a defiant act—and then return in time to be there when everybody got out.

The first people to come out were a couple, who were laughing and singing to one another. "It wasn't so bad," they said when I asked.

A mother came out with a ten-year-old boy who was whimpering and crying.

Two teenage boys came out totally spooked—eyes wide, hands in their pockets.

At that point, almost right on schedule, a delivery boy driving one of *Dan's Papers* red-and-white delivery vans appeared coming down the street. He pulled over, jumped down, grabbed several bundles of papers under his arm, ran into a store, came out with fewer bundles, went into the next store, came out with no bundles, then went back to the truck for more. Pretty soon, he got to across from where I was standing, came out of the truck with two bundles, and left both of them just inside the front glass doors of the movie theatre. He smiled at me and waved. Then he was gone.

Other drivers in other *Dan's Papers* trucks were doing the same thing in other towns. By the end of that day, all the towns of eastern Long Island were saturated with the delivery of fifty-nine thousand copies of *Dan's Papers* featuring a front-page story consisting of my own personal take on what was happening. People wandered over to pick up their copy—this was the only free paper in town—and here is what they read.

An Important Letter from the Chief of Police

From: The Office of the Chief of Police
To: The Editor of *Dan's Papers*

With the movie *Jaws* now playing at the East Hampton Cinema, I think it would be a good idea, at this time, to allay the fears of some of your readers that a big, man-eating shark might eat them up during this summer.

As you know, the movie is about just such a man-eating shark, and it describes how half a dozen people lost their lives as they swam around in the ocean just off our shores. The movie further describes how we government officials are unable to cope with this shark, and it alleges that we cover up every incident in which a tourist is eaten up by a fish.

All of these allegations are false in every respect. For one thing, the number of people eaten by the man-eating shark is nowhere near a half dozen a day, as shown in the movie. Through careful feeding of the man-eater, we have now reduced the number of people lost to the shark in any given day to just one, or at the most, two. And for this, I might add, we owe a vote of thanks to every member of this police force, including both the present membership and those deceased members of the force, may they rest in peace, who gave their lives so that others may swim. Our force, during the last month or two, has worked night and day continuously feeding the shark raw meat so that he is constantly well-fed and not in a serious mood to eat swimmers. This feeding, conducted by helicopter, has been made possible by the generosity of virtually all of our local meat markets, who have sacrificed thousands and thousands of pounds of raw meat that they might otherwise have sold at a profit to the general public. It is this sort of unselfish generosity which makes America the great nation that it is today.

With the arrival of the summer tourists, we are hopeful that the amount of meat donated for the feeding of the shark might double or even triple, so that even less than one tourist a day might be eaten by the man-eating shark.

To this end, I would ask your readers to please join in this raw meat drive, just as your readership responded so generously during World War II with contributions of tin, rubber, and bacon fat. Anyone with leftover meat at the dinner table, or with uncooked meat (preferably), is asked to pack it up and bring it down to the police station in Bridgehampton between the hours of nine and five for collection. The man-eating shark has shown a distinct preference for lamb chops and spare ribs, if that should make any difference.

One final note. Due to the great help of marine biologist Alfred Silverton, we have been able to train the man-eating shark to eat his meals in different places at different times. On Mondays, Wednesdays, and Fridays, he is fed in the ocean, off Main Beach, in the center of town. But on Tuesdays, Thursdays, and Saturdays, the shark has been trained to take his meals over in the shallow waters off Peconic Bay. On these days of Tuesdays, Thursdays, and Saturdays, it is absolutely safe to swim in the ocean, since we can positively assure you that the shark is in the bay. On Sundays, incidentally, the shark naps.

We would like your readership to take note of the following silhouette of the shark. (Silhouette shown.) There are many large sharks swimming around in the ocean, and although other sharks might come up and gnaw playfully on your arm or something, this particular shark is the only one which will actually eat you up.

As time goes by, Dr. Silverton assures me that he is more and more able to teach the man-eating shark tricks, thus heading him down the path toward domestication. Already Dr. Silverton reports, the man-eater will come when he is called, sit, stay, and clap his fins playfully after each meal.

Tourists in the Hamptons should be assured that with the increased meat drive, we can cause the shark to give up eating swimmers altogether. And in the event that the meat drive does not live up to standards, and there simply is not enough meat available, your readership should know this police department, every one of us, has taken a vow of personal sacrifice.

We here at the police department are determined to make every tourist's summer vacation a happy and enjoyable one, no matter who has to get eaten in the process.

Sincerely,

Martin Brody

Chief of Police

Bridgehampton

Call it the revenge of *Dan's Papers*. The Hamptons needed the publicity. This was going to get it for them. Before the day was done, the phone was ringing off the hook at our office, and within the week, articles appeared about this caper in *Sports Illustrated*, the *Wall Street Journal*, *Town and Country*, a journalism trade publication called *[MORE]*, and the *Christian Science Monitor*. Two weeks later, *Time* magazine ran a whole spread in their "Press" section headlined "Hoaxer of the Hamptons," and wrote about not only the *Jaws* letter, but the pizza-ordering Montauk Lighthouse and several other good times had by all.

After *Jaws,* the Hamptons were on the map big-time. And *Dan's Papers* took off like a shot.

In 1990, my son David, then eight years old, was introduced to Roy Scheider in our living room when Roy and his wife Brenda were over for dinner. By that time, the Scheiders had moved to Bridgehampton. Steven Spielberg was now living in East Hampton. Richard Dreyfuss had been out here visiting many times.

"This is the man who was the police chief of Amity in the movie *Jaws*," I told David, indicating Mr. Scheider.

David wasn't even born when *Jaws* premiered. But he had seen it later and he knew all about it.

"How big was that shark?" David asked.

"Twenty-five feet," Roy said.

"And how did they get it to wiggle around like that? Was it made of metal?"

"Some parts of it were," Roy said. "But it kept breaking down."

ON THE SET OF JAWS

"Were you really on that boat when the shark killed Quint and it was sinking?"

"Yes."

"Did you fire the gun?"

"Leave Roy alone," I said to David. "He came here for dinner."

"Oh, I don't mind," Roy said, grinning.

In 2006, both Roy and Steven Spielberg hosted a screening of the movie at the John Drew Theatre in East Hampton.

It hadn't been screened in thirty years. They were there to raise money for a private school called the Hayground School and for the theatre, which was to be renovated.

"Remember all the trouble they were having with the shark?" Steven said to Roy on stage after the movie was shown. "It kept breaking down."

"There were days and days we did absolutely nothing while they worked on it," Roy said. "We just stayed in our rooms. You have no idea how boring Martha's Vineyard was out of season at that time."

"Do you remember the food fight?"

"How could I forget the food fight."

"We were staying in this old wooden hotel that had maybe eighty rooms," Spielberg said. "There were very few people there. We'd come down and have our meals in this vast empty dining room. One evening for dinner, with the shark still broken, we came down and, in the next room over, which was their big catering hall, they were just beginning to have this big coming-out party or cotillion or something. There were a hundred people or more there, including all these sixteen-year-old girls in white formal dresses with crinolines and high-heeled shoes. And there was a dance band and balloons and these very serious people with slicked back hair and tuxedoes and the women in low-cut gowns and everybody all holding drinks yakking away. And we all just sat there, glumly, another day with a broken shark, and I forget who it was, maybe it was you . . ."

"It was me," Roy said.

"We had been served this steak and Roy had cut a single piece of it and he picked it up in his hand and, like this, he just flicked it at me, and it hit me in the forehead."

"That's what started it. He flicked it back."

"And I added, as I recall, a second item, which was a French fried potato, which missed."

"Next, somebody else, maybe the cinematographer, flicked something. I don't know. And then it kind of just grew."

"It was one of the biggest and best food fights in the history of the world," Steven said. "Mashed potatoes sliding down the wall. Peas bouncing around in the chandeliers. Splashes of wine. Rolls and butter flying. And these women in the catering hall, you should have just seen them, standing there, their mouths open . . ."

The Hamptons became a glittering first class resort after *Jaws*. Celebrities moved here. Movie stars moved here. Billionaires moved here. We were awash in money. And so began some very wealthy, very interesting, and very fascinating good times.

Clifford Irving
(and Howard Hughes)

~~~~~~

When I was a small boy in the late 1940s, seeing an airplane make its way across the sky was a big deal. It might happen twice a day. You'd stop and look up at a slow, propeller-driven affair with its engines rumbling away and propelling—that really was the right word for it—a beautiful streamlined silver aircraft along.

I was not living in the Hamptons then, but much later on, when I was a man, I heard about this slow-moving yellow seaplane that would come to the Hamptons during the summer of 1948 and begin to circle down for a landing on Georgica Pond.

It was Howard Hughes, dashing pilot, movie producer, and millionaire, at the controls up there. The kids in the community would see it in the sky, and they'd run or bike over to the dock at the pond where they knew he would end up. When he did, he'd get out and stand by his plane there on the dock, with his hands in his pockets, and look down at these farmboys and pick one or two. Just you two,

CLIFFORD AND HIS WIFE, EDITH, JANUARY 1975
(Photo © Bettman/CORBIS)

he'd say. And he'd help them up into the cockpit and roar off, climb back up into the sky, and give them the thrill of a lifetime for about fifteen minutes, circling over the town before coming back down to the pond again.

When he got out this time, he'd take from the luggage compartment a small suitcase and a bouquet of roses, and he'd wave goodbye to the boys and walk up the path to the Herrick's house at the back of that lawn.

He was courting the Herricks' beautiful daughter Adrianna, and he had come, as everyone in town knew, to spend the night with her at her family's home. In separate bedrooms, some people said. Maybe not, said others.

You couldn't miss seeing that yellow seaplane take off the next morning.

O n a Friday evening in the summer of 1973, my wife and I got dressed up and headed out to tour the art galleries of the Hamptons. Gallery-going on a Friday evening, from five to seven, was a very big deal in those years. You'd go and stroll around looking at the paintings while drinking wine and eating crackers and cheese. You'd see the latest work of Willem de Kooning or Herman Cherry or Fairfield Porter or Saul Steinberg, the very low-key New Yorker cartoonist who lived quietly up in Springs.

We went to the Pantigo Gallery in East Hampton first, stayed a few minutes wandering through, then headed over to Bridgehampton and the grandest of all the art galleries, the Benson Gallery. Here, the paintings were on display in a series of barns and courtyards, and there was not only food and wine but, on that particular evening, a classical guitarist sitting on a high stool in the central outdoor courtyard.

Our last stop on that particular Friday was the Tower Gallery in Southampton, a three-story fairy-tale turret at the corner of Main Street and Jobs Lane in the center of downtown Southampton. The art was not only inside the tower on the second floor, but often outside, on the roof of the adjacent one-story building. Larry Rivers had shows here, as did Andy Warhol and Fairfield Porter.

We went in and climbed up the spiral stairs to the tower. Edith Irving, the Swiss wife of Clifford Irving, the writer who had been accused of taking a half-million-dollar advance from a book publisher to write what turned out to be a bogus autobiography of Howard Hughes, was having a showing of her work. The money raised from the pieces sold would go to their defense lawyers. People I spoke to at the Benson earlier in the evening said they were going to make a special effort to buy something at the Tower. Edith Irving had only been involved in this in a peripheral way, they said. It was her husband who had done the dirty deed.

Edith was a beautiful blond woman with a soft voice and a graceful walk who did these small watercolor abstracts wherever she and Clifford were living. When we arrived, there were about fifty people noisily milling around in the tower among the paintings. And Edith, who I had met once before, seemed very happy.

"Thanks for coming," she said in her adorable Swiss accent, extending a hand.

There were many, many paintings, including some on clotheslines out on the rooftop of the adjacent building, which you accessed by simply stepping through a large open window of the tower.

As it happened, we were out on the roof when all the commotion began. There was the sound of crashing footsteps on the spiral staircase, a lot of shouting, and then screaming. We didn't know whether to stay out there or come back in. So we just stayed where we were.

Then we heard a man inside the tower, near the food table, shouting.

"Everybody out. IRS. The show is over. Paintings seized for unpaid taxes."

Through the open window, I could see him, a plain man in a dark suit. He was holding out a badge. Two other men in suits were in there too.

From the roof, we could see lights flashing down below. Southampton Town police cars were parked on the street at odd angles. We could also hear the gallery owner, a Mrs. Beckett, trying to tell the men to please leave, that they could do this after the show was over—but it was not doing any good.

"The show's over now," the agent said.

There was no other way down from that rooftop, other than stepping back through the window. And so we did. We joined a thundering herd of people going down the spiral stairs. Edith was there, weeping, standing by a painting with a red dot on it, which meant that it had been sold. There were lots of paintings with red dots. Checks had been written. You might as well tear them all up now.

But then, there were some people *not* going down the stairs. They just stood there, drinks in one hand, hors d'oeuvre in the other, too stunned to move.

I didn't know what to say as we walked past Edith in her time of crisis. We just headed down the stairs, at which time, to our amazement, we passed people coming up, chatting to one another amiably.

"You're late," I said.

I first met Clifford Irving at Bobby Van's restaurant three years earlier. He was sitting at the bar with a stunning redhead. She was on a stool to his left, and there was an empty seat, the only empty stool at the bar, to his right. So I sat, ordered a drink and talked to the bartender for awhile and, as these things sometimes happen, was soon joined in conversation with Clifford.

"So you publish *Dan's Papers*," he said. He had picked up on a comment the bartender had made about an article in the paper. "I thought you'd be older."

"I am," I said.

Clifford was charming and engaging.

"I'm a novelist," he said, pressing on. "Not a big deal novelist"—he motioned to Truman Capote, who was telling some sort of story in a booth behind us. He gave me a sly smile. "Not yet, anyway.

"I have a new book just coming out," he continued. "It's *Tom Mix and Pancho Villa.* And I'm in the middle of writing another one. Perhaps you'd like to come by. I'm living at the Warren House on Lily Pond Lane in East Hampton. You know the place?"

I said I didn't. He proceeded to describe how to get to it in great detail. "Stop by and I'll give you a pre-pub galley of the Pancho Villa book. Maybe you could write about it. How about tomorrow at two? I'm there writing all day."

"Okay."

Now it was back to the redhead.

The strange thing about all this, considering what happened later with both Clifford and Edith sentenced to prison terms for what they did involving Howard Hughes, was that just three weeks before my meeting with Clifford, I had published a big fat hoax of my own in *Dan's Papers* about Howard Hughes.

Howard Hughes, the richest man in the world, had, since the late 1950s, been living in seclusion in penthouse apartments around the world, protected by his beefy Mormon bodyguards.

Just eight weeks before my first conversation with Clifford, Hughes secretly checked out of his hotel in Las Vegas—he'd been up there seven years—and nobody but his Mormon legion, sword to secrecy, had any idea where he'd gone.

One day during this time, which was in the summer of 1969, I was standing in the plaza in the center of downtown Montauk, looking at the abandoned seven-story building with the penthouse up at the top that was the centerpiece of that town, and a thought came to me. Why not write that Hughes was up there? What a very merry idea it would be to put him up there, and publish it as an exclusive in *Dan's Papers*. No other newspaper had *that* story.

HUGHES IN MONTAUK was the headline. I published a photo I had taken of this very raggedy and forlorn building. And below the building, in the body copy, I published a head shot of the great man. Look closely at the penthouse. Here's who to look for.

This article did create a great local sensation. Everybody was talking about it. Tourists stood across the street from the building taking pictures of it. Was that him? Some people had binoculars. Meanwhile, the locals looked at all this and thought boy, some people are just jackasses.

To this day—and this is now forty years later—I still come across people who remember that little prank fondly and tell me so. Best thing you ever did, they say. It was wonderful, and I enjoyed it very much too.

In any case, the day after I met Clifford Irving at the bar, I drove down to Lily Pond Lane and followed the directions to the Warren place.

It was a grand, three-story mansion on vast landscaped grounds that had a gravel driveway leading up to a circle at the front door. Indeed, as I drove up, there he was, right out front, this tall man, a bit hunched over to make him look less tall, I suppose, with his hands in his pockets, smiling and rocking back and forth, waiting for me. He was surely the gracious host.

Clifford ushered me into the living room, which featured, along with sofas and chairs, a large table that appeared to have been pushed into the center of the room. On it, all spread out, was the new book he was working on, he said, a mystery novel.

At that moment, the phone rang in a library just off the living room.

"Here's the galley of *Tom Mix and Pancho Villa*," he said, handing me a book as he got up to answer it. "Have a look."

He strode off and picked up the phone.

"Hello? No, he's not here. None of them are here. Do you want me to take a message? This is Clifford Irving, a friend of his. No, I'm sorry, I don't know when they are coming out. Okay. I have a pencil."

The cover of the book featured a sombrero, two crossed ammunition belts, and two six-shooters. I turned it over. "Galley Proof. Not for Sale" it said in small letters on the back. Pretty special.

Clifford returned shortly, and for the rest of my time there, he told me the virtues of the story he had written and how true it really was even if it wasn't true. We had a rum and coke together, and shortly after that, I left.

As I opened the door to my car, I saw a white Mercedes convertible pull up and a beautiful dark-haired woman get out carrying several bags of groceries. Hi, I said. She smiled and nodded back.

I never did read, and therefore never did review, *Tom Mix and Pancho Villa.* But a month later, Irving called me as if we were old friends to ask if I knew another place he might stay in East Hampton for awhile.

"You know, I stay here and there. I move around. It's good that way."

I got the distinct impression he had been staying at the Warrens' without their knowledge. I told him I really didn't know anybody.

Two years later, in 1973, McGraw-Hill announced that they would shortly be publishing a sensational, fully authorized autobiography of Howard Hughes, written in collaboration with the writer Clifford Irving.

Irving had been given a then unheard-of advance of nearly half a million dollars. And the book would be out within a year. *Time* and *Life* would publish excerpts from it.

"Irving has shown us long handwritten diary notes, written to him, by Hughes," an executive from McGraw-Hill said at a press conference. "Handwriting experts have confirmed their authenticity."

The excerpts appeared. Clifford Irving's picture appeared on the front covers of magazines, along with accounts of how Hughes had met Clifford at midnight at strange places such as the Great Pyramid of Cheops in Egypt to give Irving intimate details of his life. Irving embarked on a series of television interviews and special appearances.

McGraw-Hill said that they would shortly be announcing a worldwide tour for Irving. And they had now completed a press run of four hundred thousand copies as a first printing. This was the largest first printing of a hardcover autobiography ever. The books were being kept, on skids and under guard, at several warehouses that McGraw-Hill owned. The combined weight of all these books exceeded one thousand tons. The whole world was waiting breathlessly for this complete account of the life of Howard Hughes.

On May 23, 1973, Hughes sent a message out via Mormon courier to say he would hold a press conference. At first, executives at McGraw-Hill—hoping it was really him—were thrilled. The fact that people would not get to see him and that he would be conducting the press conference by speakerphone from a secret location just added to the mystery. What better publicity could there be for the book? We knew we could count on Howard.

Further rules were revealed. There were to be just nine reporters in attendance, personally selected in advance by Howard Hughes because he knew them. They could verify his authenticity from his voice and what he said about meetings he had had with some of them long ago.

And so, the press conference was held. The reporters were in a studio in New York. As for Hughes, it was now impossible to keep his location secret because of the cables and equipment needed for him to hold this press conference. He was up in the penthouse of the Paradise Island Hotel in Nassau, Bahamas.

Hughes got right to the point. "I only wish I were still in the movie business," he said, "because I don't remember any script I ever saw in Hollywood as wild or imagination-stretching as this autobiography yarn has turned out to be."

He said he had never met Clifford Irving. He had never been to any pyramid in Egypt. His handwritten notes were a forgery. McGraw-Hill had fallen for the whole thing hook, line and sinker, and he felt it was just too bad for them they had done that.

The roof had just fallen in on Clifford Irving.

Irving was arrested and charged with fraud for fleecing a half million dollars out of McGraw-Hill—a $150,000 check made out to Clifford Irving and $350,000 made out to H. R. Hughes, which McGraw-Hill had given to Clifford to give to Hughes, but which instead, it was soon learned, was put into a Swiss bank account that Edith Irving had opened in the name of Helga R. Hughes.

As for those handwritten letters from Hughes, Clifford Irving now freely admitted he had written them, having learned how to write like Hughes by carefully copying a handwritten letter that the great man had penned that appeared in *Newsweek*.

Irving was convicted and spent a year and a half in jail. Edith returned to Switzerland because that was where her crime was committed. She was sentenced to six months in jail, but that was reduced to parole by an understanding Swiss court.

McGraw Hill was ordered to burn or otherwise destroy the one thousand tons of books they had printed. And Edith and Clifford Irving were ordered to somehow return the half million dollars they had fleeced from McGraw-Hill.

I never saw Clifford Irving after that. However, twenty years later, in 1992, I got a phone call from a mutual friend of ours named Marty Shepherd, who owned a small publishing house in Sag Harbor and had published some of my work.

"Clifford wrote a book while he was in jail," he told me, "which tells the whole true account of what happened when he did this swindle. He tried to pitch it to all the big publishers, but surprise, surprise, they wouldn't give him the time of day. So I'm publishing it. Can I send you a copy?"

I told him I'd love to see it. And so he dropped a copy of it off for me at the office.

The book came, a big, five-hundred-page hardcover tome with a white cover and *The Hoax* in big red letters. I'm a slow reader. I was looking at maybe a month's worth of reading. So I gave up and never did anything about it. The book is still in my library at home in East Hampton.

But that was not the last of it. Two weeks later, I got another call from Marty Shepherd.

"McGraw-Hill says they will sue us if we publish *The Hoax*," he said. "So forget it."

So here was a book publishing company, which had a few years earlier destroyed four hundred thousand copies of an earlier Clifford Irving book, now insisting that a second book by this same author never sees the light of day.

And it didn't end there.

Six months later, Marty called to tell me that *The Hoax* was now available on the internet. These were the early days of internet publishing and there were few rules about how to conduct yourself on it.

"You can go online, and with a credit card 'purchase' the book, and then you can print it out," he said.

Needless to say, that didn't work either.

Finally, however, something worked big-time. In 2004, Marty called to tell me that Universal Studios wanted to purchase the movie rights to *The Hoax*. They offered two hundred thousand dollars to Marty, who had the rights, and three hundred thousand dollars to Clifford Irving for having written it. And so, the half million dollars filched from McGraw-Hill had, in a way, returned.

"This you can write about," Marty said.

And I did.

The movie came out in 2007 and starred Richard Gere as Clifford Irving—it's amazing how much he looked like Clifford—and Marcia Gay Harden as his wife Edith, and it had a pretty good run.

I interviewed Clifford by phone in Aspen. I knew from having read about it that he had been divorced and remarried and then divorced again. But I was more interested in how he felt about this large sum of money coming back to him.

"For a year and a half, I was paid twenty-three cents an hour working in jail," he said. "I figure, this kind of balances things out."

Florence Palmer

~~~~~~

In the spring of 1976, I gathered up my sales pack and went around the Hamptons and Montauk selling my advertising as I always did. But all I could talk about was the pain I was in. It truly was terrible. Never in my wildest dreams did I expect I would be going through a divorce. We owned a six-bedroom house on Lumber Lane in Bridgehampton. We had two children, ages five and three. We had dogs and cats. A sports car. Everything had seemed so peaceful and wonderful, and then all hell broke loose.

"Where are you living now?" Rudi DeSanti, the owner of Dreesen's Market on Newtown Lane in East Hampton asked.

"In the attic at my office," I said.

The ads got sold. But sometimes, in my saner moments, I wondered how. Where was my enthusiasm to sell bigger and better and more and more? Nowhere. I would explain about the price of the advertising and the big circulation and the stories I would write and somehow, by the end of the second paragraph, I would be talking about my divorce.

THE "PHOENIX"
(Courtesy of the author)

One day, after about a month up in the attic, help came from an unexpected source. I was up on Three Mile Harbor Road in East Hampton, a long, winding lane that went through the deep woods along the eastern shore of Three Mile Harbor, and I was trying to sell an ad to the owner of one of the four marina resorts along the shore.

Florence Palmer, in 1975, was an older woman, what you might call a fading beauty. She was probably seventy-five then. Her heyday would have been during the roaring twenties, but in her adult life she had apparently settled down with a husband, now deceased, on about ten acres of waterfront property, and in 1950, they had built a little resort. It was called the Silver Sea Horse and it was completely out of character with everything else in East Hampton.

The Silver Sea Horse consisted of an enclosed, protected, boat basin with fifty boat slips. Walk up the docks from the boat slips and you crossed a lawn to a concrete patio with lawn chairs surrounding a small, kidney-shaped swimming pool. An undulating concrete wall six-feet high separated the pool from the road; and on this wall, which was painted white, were bolted a series of three giant pink concrete seahorse sculptures. There was a restaurant and café adjacent to the pool, a gravel parking area next to a wooden sign with a mermaid on it, and four small cottages set in the woods alongside. All together, it looked like something that belonged in Miami. It was probably modeled after something in Miami.

I found Mrs. Palmer standing out on the lawn of the restaurant looking out at the boats and asked her to renew her ad for the restaurant. Again, sure enough, my sales pitch veered off into the sadness about my divorce. Soon I was talking about the little makeshift apartment I had made at my office. It included a closet I had converted into a tiny kitchen area—hotplate, toaster, and cube refrigerator—and a steep stairs to a bed in an unfinished attic.

"It's going to be getting hot in the attic," Mrs. Palmer said, referring to the imminent arrival of summer.

"I haven't thought about that yet," I said.

Florence looked down the hill and out to the marina. Some boats, mostly sailboats, were already tied up in some of the slips.

"I have a boat you could stay on for the summer," she said.

"You do?"

"Yes. See that sort of beat-up wooden touring yacht way down almost to the end on the left?"

"That's the biggest boat in the marina."

"It's fifty-four feet. It's been abandoned here for a couple of years. I had my staff living on it last summer. But I don't have to give it to them again. If you want to live on it, it's yours. Go down there and have a look. Meanwhile, I have to go into the kitchen. And yes, I'll repeat the ad."

On my way down the wooden dock, I passed a number of serious yachtsmen doing yachterly things on big ketches and yawls and sloops. They waved to me and I waved back. People do that when they are on or near boats. Halfway down but off in the reeds at the northern fringe of the marina, I passed another bit of abandoned wreckage. It was a classic wooden houseboat, square, with wooden railings bordering a deck all around, and a main cabin with broken windows. It lay in the mud at about a ten-degree angle. Mrs. Palmer took in all kinds at the Silver Sea Horse.

I arrived at what Mrs. Palmer referred to as the touring yacht and I was overwhelmed. It had been the yacht of some long-ago millionaire. And it was magnificent. I climbed aboard and inspected it.

Below-decks, in the bow, there was a V-shaped bunk bedroom for a crew of two. One mattress was okay, the other torn. There were empty beer cans all around, probably left over from the prior summer or something unmentionable over the past winter. There were two round holes in the hull where portholes had once been. Makeshift screening to keep out bugs was tacked over the holes.

A Dutch door separated the V-bunk from a small galley. Inside were counters and cabinets and a large empty space where there had been a stove and an icebox.

The galley opened through a beautiful mahogany door to what had been a splendid little dining room. There were no chairs, but there was a mahogany table still firmly attached to the floor in the center. Along the walls were four magnificent stained-glass cupboards for dishes and silver, although, of course, there weren't any in them.

At the end of the dining room, two steps led up to the captain's bridge. There was a dashboard filled with gauges and dials, levers and gears, and two high captain's chairs made of old leather, now ripped, one of which faced a big ship's wheel and a great domed glass compass, still intact.

Behind the captain's chairs, four steps down, was a smelly engine room. In the dim light down there, I could see two giant inboard gasoline engines, all rusted and peeling paint, obviously seized shut. Water sloshed on the floor and a pump was going. There was a long extension cord that ran from the engine room, up the steps, and out into a socket on a post on the shore.

I was so excited. "I can't believe this," I said to nobody in particular. "God bless you, Mrs. Palmer."

At this point, of course, I was not even halfway through the ship. I continued on. Walking from the bridge and down a smaller set of stairs, I went down a hallway that led all the way back to what I could see was a master bedroom. On the left, were two smaller bedrooms, and on the right, one bedroom, with the other space a simple but serviceable bathroom. Well, I thought, all the fixtures were here. I stepped on the lever that flushed the toilet. Nothing happened.

And so I entered the grand master bedroom at the end of the hall. There was a foam mattress behind which was a beautifully carved wooden headboard. It was a scene from a Grimm fairy-tale with foxes and cottages. Wow. *My* bedroom. This sure beat hell out of sleeping at the office.

But there was still more. Above decks, a two-foot walkway extended around the ship, opening up in the rear to a grand outdoor dining deck, about fourteen feet wide. It had been meant to be covered with a flat canvas roof—there was the metal frame for it—but that was long gone.

Breathless with excitement, and with the tour complete, I climbed off the boat and headed back toward the marina. The hotplate, toaster, and box refrigerator at the office I would have here within the hour. And I'd have to visit a hardware store. I'd need a big painter's tarpaulin for the canvas roof, and maybe half a dozen kerosene lanterns.

"I cannot thank you enough," I said, when I got back to Florence Palmer. She was arranging some flowers on a table in the dining room. "Thank you, thank you, thank you."

Florence waved a hand. "And feel free to use our swimming pool. Also, we have bathrooms and showers that are for the people in the marina over here, open from the outside." She pointed to the far side of the restaurant. "And we have a washer and dryer in there. Feel free to use them too."

Off in the distance, beyond my yacht, the sun was beginning to slide low across the sky on the far side of the harbor. I had a sunset!

"Your ad is free this summer," I said.

"Don't be silly," she said.

I got towels and sheets at the five-and-dime, knives and forks and glasses and plates at the hardware store, at which time a helpful clerk sold me clothesline and a strange-looking device that could create grommets, so I could lash the canvas painter's tarp to the metal frame. Also at the hardware store I bought a set of large metal letters. *Phoenix*. Rising from the ashes. As the ship faced bow-in in its berth, I attached these letters to the wooden frame just below the captain's cockpit windshield. And then I moved in.

At midnight that first night, I was lying alone up against the Grimm fairy-tale headboard staring at the ceiling, too excited to sleep, when I began to think about the sound of the baling pump in the engine room, alternately going off and on. The water, I knew, was seeping through the seams of the ship. When it got to a certain level in the hold, the pump would rumble to life, suck out some water, and, when the level was low enough, click off.

It was a nice sound. Sort of. But I began to wonder what might happen if there was an electrical outage at the outlet on the shore late at night. Nothing would be pumping the water out then. And the hold would fill. But sleeping so soundly, how would I know? I wouldn't know.

I sat up in bed. Just how deep was the water in this marina anyway? I got up, found a long stick lying on the floor of the

FAMILY DAY ON THE PHOENIX
(Courtesy of the author)

galley, and there in my pajamas climbed out onto the deck and lowered the stick into the water. Nothing. I wriggled it around. Still nothing. I rolled up my pajama sleeve, held the stick at the very end, and leaned way over with it into the water. Once again nothing. It was way down there.

My first inkling of trouble would be the cold water sloshing over the foam mattress against my sleeping body. It would happen quickly. Confused and struggling, I would suffer a horrible death, drowned while pinned to the underside of the ceiling in my opulent master bedroom with the Grimm fairy-tale characters dancing around.

Gaaah.

The next day I asked Florence what the depth was in the slips. She told me. From the lawn, I eyeballed the height of the side of the *Phoenix*. I did the math. Maybe it was okay.

I hosted many wonderful dinners and parties on the *Phoenix* that summer. How could I not? The place was amazing. One evening, the second week I was aboard her, I invited a five-piece band, part of a summer-stock troupe in town for a two-week run at the John Drew Theatre, performing the Broadway play *Oklahoma*. They played on the deck as the sun went down. A dozen friends, bearing food and drink, came to hear them, and we all sat around eating and drinking and, with the other yachting people, enjoying the entertainment until the sun finally set and the chirping of the crickets accompanied a last song.

"You should do this every Saturday night," somebody said. And so we did, all summer, with the music now provided by local talent, banjo, harmonica, guitar and slide guitar players. By mutual agreement with the neighboring yacht owners, the music stopped at ten. But the party went on till twelve, with everybody welcome.

And then came the girl. She was, it seemed to me, very much in keeping with the whole atmosphere of that summer at that marina. Her name was Johanna Vanderbeek, she was stunningly beautiful, blond, a former Miss Florida, and she and a girlfriend had leased the restaurant in the next marina up the road, which they called Georgette's. Georgette cooked. Johanna hosted. And after the dinner crowds dispersed around nine or nine thirty, the two of them would wander over. They had heard about the jam sessions and when the wind was right, they could even hear the music—and they'd come and bring leftover desserts, which Johanna had baked.

The first night they came, Johanna later told me, they were so dazzled by this remarkable scene on this old boat that at the end of the night, as they walked down the dock walking and talking, they failed to see a right angle turn, and talked their way right off the dock and into the water.

Johanna and I hit it off right away. She was, I learned, a young widow. Her husband had been the famous experimental filmmaker Stan Vanderbeek. They had two kids. She was living in their small summer home on Fort Pond Boulevard not far away. And she was older than me. I was in my thirties. She was in her forties. How could this be? I didn't care.

Sometimes when the jam session ended, if Johanna hadn't come, I'd go over and get her. Johanna's two teenage children, August and Max, both worked at the restaurant waiting tables. They, like all the other waiters, wore T-shirts that had been painted to look like tuxedoes, complete with bow ties. Sort of a tromp l'oeil thing. It was that kind of place.

One night, long after everybody left, Johanna gazed out into the harbor and she said this:

"Why is it," she said, "that every time I come on your boat I have this immediate urge to take off all my clothes? And then I have to wait until everybody's left."

As the summer went on, I learned a lot more about the yacht. I actually found, in a metal case in a drawer, the ship's ancient instruction manual. This ship had been built in 1932 by the American Car and Foundry Yacht Building Company. It was indeed a touring yacht, designed so that a rich man and his family could go from one yacht club to another. The twin engines, frozen below, each had eight cylinders, developed between them 600 horsepower, and at full throttle could push the ship at eighteen knots. Proper top speed would be achieved at 800 rpm. Do not exceed this if at all possible.

I was astonished at this rpm number. I looked on the dashboard gauges. Each engine went up to 1000 rpm and that was it. My car, as any car would, topped out at 4000 rpm. Vroom. These engines, topping out at 800, must have made a sort of budda budda budda sound as they burbled along.

I imagined myself captaining this ship as it made its way between yacht clubs, perhaps from Newport or Martha's Vineyard to Hyannis or Block Island, with my wife and her friends, drinks in hand, sitting in floppy hats, out back on the deck under the roof canvas, enjoying cocktails.

Excuse me, we'd *all* be out on that back deck under the awning. My *hired* captain would be piloting my ship.

I also learned the ship's recent history from Mrs. Palmer.

"It's been here for three summers," she said. "Ever hear of George Gallup?"

"Yes. He runs that polling service."

"Yes. He has a brother named Fred. Apparently he isn't as good with business as his brother, but George gave him a job and he's a vice president. The home office is in Princeton.

"One day, Fred was up in Groton, Connecticut, and came across this boat in drydock in a boatyard there and fell in love with it. He had it put in the water and towed here. I met him and he paid for that summer and said he intended to restore it. But apparently, when his wife got wind of it, she said no way are you bringing this wreck of a yacht to New Jersey. I will leave you if you do that. And so he didn't. He left it here the next year and never paid the fee for the slip. Last year when he never showed up, I had my workers stay on it. You know the rest. I don't think he's coming back."

Another time, she told me about the wreckage of the houseboat.

"That's a famous houseboat," she said. "It was the house-boat used in the movie by that name starring Gary Cooper and Sophia Loren. They filmed it in Westhampton Beach. I had it towed here. Somebody will find a use for it."

One day, about two weeks after I had moved aboard the *Phoenix,* a brand new Chris-Craft called *Wonderful Time* pulled into the empty slip just adjacent to the *Phoenix,* and between the *Phoenix* and the sunset. By a matter of about twelve feet, the *Phoenix* stuck out further than the Chris-Craft so the view of the sunset from our deck was not blocked.

The morning after this ship arrived, I woke up to see a man in a captain's hat puttering around aboard it. I hailed him.

"Jed Carlson," he said as we stood across the railings. He held out his hand and I shook it.

I thought at first that Jed owned this big Chris-Craft, but he explained he didn't, he was just the captain of it.

"A really rich guy owns it," he said. "I brought it up the inland waterway from Fort Lauderdale for him, and I'll be on board here for when he uses it. You'll meet him."

The weeks went by, however, and I didn't meet him. Jed was the only person on board. Of course, I invited him to the Saturday night jam.

One day, I saw Jed walking down the dock carrying two big bags of groceries. There was a big smile on his face.

"He's coming," he shouted across to me. "I've got filet mignon, champagne, caviar."

But that night, which was a Friday night, the owner did not come. Nor did he come on Saturday. Jed brought a bottle of Piper-Heidsieck to the jam. And on Sunday evening he invited me on board to help him devour the filet mignon. He changed his mind, Jed told me.

The owner never came all summer. And the day after Labor Day, Jed pulled *Wonderful Time* out of the slip and out to sea.

As for the newspaper, an odd thing happened. I wrote articles about being on this boat. And the word got out. What a crazy and romantic thing this was. Dan's this crazy editor living on a boat running a newspaper. I was now some sort of character, and the advertising, which had dipped during the months of my sorrow, now returned stronger than ever. I bought a captain's hat, which I now wore everywhere.

In the second week of August, Johanna came by, but seemed agitated.

"I got a call from a friend of mine in the city," she said. "He's going through a crisis. I have to go be with Sholom a few days. But I'll be back."

The wounds from my divorce were still fresh. "Is he your boyfriend?"

"He was. But he's twenty-six. So we're just friends now."

Twenty-six? I was thirty-six and she was forty-two. "Don't go," I said. But what could I do? She left. I consoled myself with friends. One of them bought me a T-shirt that had an inscription on it.

IF YOU LOVE SOMEBODY, LET THEM GO,
FOR IF THEY RETURN THEY WERE ALWAYS YOURS,
AND IF THEY DON'T THEY NEVER WERE

I wore it for the next few days. I also stopped shaving. As the days stretched into weeks, my stubble became a beard. I have the beard to this day. I don't know why. Johanna never did come back that summer. However, every year in the years that followed, on my birthday in August, she would bring me, either because I asked her or because she just showed up with it, a version of the special Georgette's chocolate cake that she'd made while hosting the restaurant that long ago summer. We're still friends.

I wanted to live aboard that yacht for as long as I could into the fall, I was having so much fun. People said I'd find it impossible, it would be too chilly after Labor Day, but I didn't believe them.

The day after Labor Day, however, a damp fog moved in, slid through the screened open portholes, left all the tabletops and counters wet, and chilled me to the bone. And so that was that. I was gone within two days, back to the attic.

As for Florence Palmer, the following spring she began going through her own terrible time. It was about her son, a grown man with a terrible temper, who had now returned to the property to stake his claim to what his late father had left them.

I still stopped by once in awhile. And Mrs. Palmer did continue to advertise. Indeed, apparently having been inspired by my long-ago Saturday night jam sessions, she had launched, on Memorial Day weekend, a Sunday morning brunch on the front lawn that featured a steel-band concert hosted by a well-known local group known as Vivian and the Merry Makers. But she wasn't enjoying it.

That June, there appeared a long line of impenetrable cedar trees dividing the property all the way from the road to the harbor, a distance of more than a quarter mile. On one side was Mrs. Palmer's marina and restaurant. On the other were the cottages, and now, a new restaurant building going up and a competing marina. I went down there one day and found her son, Rick Hamilton, laying cinderblocks in a rectangular wall, one layer on top of another layer, surrounding a seventeen foot racing yacht.

"Yeah, the racing yacht will be inside the dining room," he told me. "It's racing days are over. And no, I don't want an ad."

The next year, with my life in many ways back in order, I was visited in my office by a man who wanted to see me about the touring yacht at the marina. A secretary ushered him into my office. He was a little man in a three-piece suit with a bow tie and slicked back hair. He sat down in a chair opposite me.

"I understand you lived on the touring yacht at Florence Palmer's place last summer?"

"Two summers ago."

"My name is George Prescott, and I am from Tom's River, New Jersey." He reached into a breast pocket and pulled out a card, which he handed to me. "I have bought that yacht. And I have had it towed to a marina near my home. I intend to restore it."

"That's wonderful."

He leaned forward. "Did you know," he whispered, "that that touring yacht was the featured centerfold of *Motorboating* magazine in August of 1932? It was the foldout!"

"No, I didn't."

"Well, it was. It's a very famous and very valuable touring yacht. And it is missing all its portholes and other brassware. Someone apparently took them out. Did you take them out? I bet they fetched a pretty penny."

"It was like that when I lived on it," I said. "It sure is a beautiful boat."

"In particular, I am looking for the tender for this boat. Surely, the tender for this boat was on it when you lived on it."

"No, it wasn't."

"This tender is mahogany. It's worth a considerable sum. I must know where that tender is."

"I can't help you with that. I never saw it."

"Are you *certain* you never saw it?"

"Look," I said. "The ship was a wreck. No tender. No portholes. Perhaps one of the local baymen has it and takes it clamming. It wouldn't surprise me if there was a ten-foot-long mahogany tender, painted white and with an outboard on the back, chugging around in Three Mile Harbor somewhere. But I haven't got it."

He sighed.

"That ship is going to be a thing of beauty when I get done with it."

"I'm sure it will. And I would love to see it when you've got it all fixed up. Here's my card." I handed my card to him.

He left, and that was the first and last time I ever saw him.

A few years after that, Florence Palmer sold the Silver Sea Horse to a German man who turned it into a steak house he called Sea Wolf. He removed the seahorses from the curving white wall, he removed the mermaid from the sign, but kept the Sunday morning steel-band brunches as a tradition.

Years later, I saw Florence Palmer one last time. She was elderly and frail at almost ninety, but she was back in town and wanted to see me. She came by my office in the back seat of a long black limousine driven by a uniformed chauffeur who seemed to dote on her. She had a little white dog on a pink leash, and she was too frail to come upstairs, so I came down and met with her in the conference room.

"I see everything is all right with you again," she said. "Those sure were wonderful times, weren't they?"

In 1991, the newspaper, as a promotion, began running the *Dan's Papers'* They Made the Movies Here Film Festival. Every spring on Saturday afternoons, we would show six films in six weeks, all made in the Hamptons. Every fall we would do it again with six different films.

In searching for films, I had, of course, come up with *Houseboat,* starring Cary Grant and Sophia Loren. And we would show it. But although I sometimes came to the festival to introduce one film or another, I never attended the showing of *Houseboat.*

In 1999, the Town of East Hampton tried to get the owner of the former Silver Sea Horse property to remove the wrecked houseboat because it was an eyesore. I rallied the town against this idea with an article in the paper, declaring that the houseboat was an historical treasure and should be restored and sold to a museum, and the town backed off.

Finally, in 2004, I got a chance to see *Houseboat* at our festival. It was showing fourth in the series, right after *Deathtrap, Grey Gardens,* and *Rocket Gibraltar.*

I sat in the audience after introducing it and watched. It was so embarrassing. In the background where the houseboat was docked, were palm trees and Spanish moss. And the houseboat in the film was a much different shape than the one at the Silver Sea Horse. After the film ended, I quietly ordered that it was not to be shown again at the *Dan's Papers'* They Made the Movie Here Film Festival.

"I think we might have copyright trouble," was how I explained it to those running the show, who had apparently never noticed, as everybody else had never noticed, that there was no way this film was made in the Hamptons.

Evan Frankel

~~~~~~

In 2006, I went to a fundraiser on a vast estate near the ocean in East Hampton owned by the Wall Street millionaire Jeff Tarr and his wife Patsy.

From the entry gates of the estate, we were taken in a parade of golf carts a quarter mile down a long driveway through beautiful landscaped grounds to a big tent set up on the front lawn of this vast modern mansion. The tent had looked small as we drove up, but in fact, it was quite large, just dwarfed by the huge lawn and the grand stone-and-glass confection that overlooked it. It began to rain, and shortly, the few hundred people that had spilled out of the tent to chatter with one another on the grounds scurried back under the tent with the rest of us. There must have been more than five hundred people squeezed in there at one point, all dressed up in their summer finery, and swarmed over by waiters and waitresses in white shirts and black bow ties, along with a wide assortment of photographers. I talked with Christie Brinkley, who I hadn't seen since a celebrity benefit the week before, and I talked with Barry Sonnenfeld, the producer-director, who I hadn't seen in several years. He was

EVAN FRANKEL, THE SQUIRE OF EAST HAMPTON
(Courtesy of the Evan Frankel Foundation)

wearing a cowboy hat and I was wearing a safari hat, and I noted that we were probably the only two men in the place wearing such accessories. The photographers took pictures of us, holding drinks and smiling at the camera.

Amidst the din of the conversation and the rumble of the rain and the flash of the cameras, I found myself wondering where it was on this property that an *X* would mark the spot where I had years earlier had a wild and torrid dalliance with a young woman named Zoe Mathias.

The house, where all this took place, is not there anymore. When the Tarrs bought the property in the 1990s, they tore down the century-old twenty-room mansion that I remembered, and they had built their even bigger house of steel, glass, concrete, and waterfalls to replace it. It had been in that earlier, older mansion, specifically on the floor in the living room, that I had my romantic encounter.

Maybe it was over there by that stand of big tall trees. They looked like newly planted trees, and they probably were new trees, hauled in full-grown on flatbed trucks to be planted in exactly those spots. Where was the old house in relation to the new, anyway? I couldn't tell, and it annoyed me. Frankly, I treasure my memories. Particularly memories of love. Or lust. Sometimes you never know which.

In June of 1976, I had met Zoe Mathias at an artist's dinner party in East Hampton where they served vegetarian food. She was slender and small, had big black eyes, a perfect figure, a turned-up nose, and with her short dark hair, Indian headband, and hippie dress, she dazzled me. She was twenty-four.

"Are you living out here?" I asked.

"Just for the summer. I've rented a place with my girlfriend Lynn," she said, motioning her pretty head to a blond girl across the way. "You?"

"I live here. I run a newspaper."

She asked me about it and I told her. She'd never heard of it.

There was no mistaking my intentions. I sat with her all evening and talked to her. And at midnight, I took a chance.

"Ever been to the Walking Dunes?" I asked her.

"No."

I took her out at midnight that night to visit the most romantic and isolated spot I knew. This was an enormous group of sand dunes, isolated along the northern shore of Napeague, miles from anywhere. Few people knew about them. Years before, Richard Gilmartin had introduced me to them. They are called the Walking Dunes because the winds are strong there, coming in from the north, and this wind slowly drives them southward. From the top of the tallest one, you could see forever, and you could also see where along its southern slope that a dune was smothering a forest. The tops of trees were all that were visible, and under the top they disappeared entirely, apparently inside the dune.

We sat on a blanket, and we drank wine and kissed and hugged and, under the great dome of stars late that night fell in love. And she said this: "I am going to be the worst thing that ever happened to you."

Two months later, we were still going at it. I would come see her and my knees would buckle and my stomach would churn at the very sight of her.

One night, I was sitting with her and her girlfriend Lynn, having dinner at Bobby Van's restaurant in Bridgehampton, when out of the corner of my eye, I saw through the front window the figure of one of the richest men in town, Evan Frankel. Frankel, in his mid-seventies, was wearing what he always wore every day in his later years—a hunting cap, a half-belted tweed sports jacket, and a half cape around his shoulders. He was also carrying a walking stick, and he was looking in at me. What was this all about? Now he was coming in and he was heading over to our table. I don't think I had ever exchanged more than ten words with him in all the years that I knew him. Honestly, I thought he didn't like me. And now this?

I introduced him to Lynn. And pointedly noted that Zoe was my girl friend. He took it all in. Then he smiled.

"May I join you?" he asked.

"Sure," I said.

And so he sat. Next to Lynn, also age twenty-four. And he smiled at her.

At that time, Evan owned much of the commercial district of East Hampton, and as I walked around town, I sometimes heard him referred to in uncomplimentary terms by his tenants. He'd raised the rent. He didn't fix this or that. At the same time, he was spoken of in glowing terms by the Jewish community in that town. Evan had, three years before, contributed about a quarter of a million dollars to become the major benefactor of what would soon thereafter become the first synagogue in town, the Jewish Center of the Hamptons on Woods Lane in East Hampton. It had been a very dramatic thing to do.

My parents were Jewish. I was raised Jewish. And in fact, in 1956 when we moved to Montauk, we were the first Jewish residents. Others followed. By 1965, when Evan Frankel of East Hampton proposed that a synagogue be built in East Hampton, we were one of maybe five families in Montauk who were Jewish. If you added to that the families in Amagansett and East Hampton, there were perhaps thirty families. Hardly enough for a synagogue.

But Frankel, this wealthy gentleman from Brooklyn, was determined. I do recall my father, one evening at dinner at our home in Montauk, saying that he told Evan that we could not afford a temple. We were too few. Evan replied, Dad said, that he would buy them a temple and pay for it himself. Dad said he thought this was pie in the sky.

Two years later, the deed was done. Evan had bought an old mansion on Woods Lane in East Hampton, right at the entrance to the town. He had found a three-story home for sale that was owned by one of the wealthy WASP families and which, by a clause in its deed, could not be sold to Jews or Negroes. Evan had a Christian friend who did not approve of this nonsense. And so the friend had bought it, removed the restriction, and immediately turned around and sold it to Evan. Evan offered to give it to the families. But the families said who would maintain it? Evan found another Jewish millionaire in town, Jacob Kaplan, the wealthy owner of Welch's Grape Juice. He persuaded him to put up enough money to endow the maintenance of the place forever and ever. A Jewish Center would appear right at the entrance to a very Christian town.

As for me, years before we moved to Montauk, I had separated myself from organized religion. I had been bar mitzvahed, but that was it.

"In Hebrew School they said the Jews are the Chosen People," I told my parents. "I don't believe that. I believe Jews are no better or worse than any other people. Where do we get off saying that?"

"Will you come to temple with us?" my mother asked.

I was fourteen. I said I would not.

"What about on the High Holy Days?"

So it was a negotiation.

"I'll do that," I said.

When we moved to Montauk there was no temple within twenty miles and I thought I was done with organized religion. My parents would drive to New York City with my sister and I to go to temple on the High Holy Days. They could have gone to Sag Harbor to a temple there. It was the only temple in the Hamptons. But my parents were liberal and that synagogue was run by an old Orthodox sect. There were customs in the Orthodox sect, such as men and women worshipping separately, that my parents could not abide.

And then came Evan Frankel. In short order, there was a big sign put up just as you drove down Woods Lane to enter downtown East Hampton. It is there today.

THE JEWISH CENTER OF THE HAMPTONS

So that is where I met Evan Frankel. At the High Holy Days. The services would end and we'd sit there and listen while the rabbi gave his sermon, and then Evan would get up—he was the president of the congregation—and deliver a second sermon about the necessity of the membership to contribute funds to the institution. I thought this was pretty ridiculous, everything considered. He was determined to continuously remind everyone of how it had begun and how much he had done for everyone.

EVAN AT HIS 80TH BIRTHDAY WITH
GIRL FRIENDS FROM YEARS GONE BY
(Courtesy of the Evan Frankel Foundation)

"I hope to live to see the day," he would say, "when we can afford to build a true sanctuary, a true chapel for our synagogue. That is my dream."

The services were being held, at that time, in the living room of the former mansion. The thirty or forty of us would sit on folding chairs and when Frankel finished his sermon, the service would be over and we would get up and wish everyone Good Yontif.

Then in an adjacent room we would have food, Jewish food, wine, little sandwiches and cakes, and we would stand around and talk. Frankel, a handsome man, would talk animatedly with my parents, but seemed to have for me what appeared to be to be a mild dislike. I attributed this to the fact that I was the next generation and, unfortunately for him, not particularly enthusiastic about the place.

"Have you ever been to my home, 'Brigadoon?' " Evan asked, looking around at the three of us in Bobby Van's restaurant years later. "No? Well, why don't we all go there for a nightcap?"

I paid the bill—I had wondered if he would pick up the check, but he didn't—and then we all walked out the front door to the bright lights of downtown Main Street to his automobile.

"Just leave everything here," he said, apparently referring to my car. "We'll go to Brigadoon, and then I'll bring you back here."

So Evan drove, and talked animatedly with Lynn in the front. In the back, Zoe and I took advantage of the darkness to grab a few kisses and hugs. I looked out the window at one point. We were on Middle Lane in East Hampton six miles away from Bridgehampton. Then we were curving up this long winding gravel driveway to the front entrance of the Frankel mansion, "Brigadoon." It was a three-story brick affair, built in a sort of High Renaissance style. There were columns out front. Statuary. There were shutters on the windows. It would have looked perfectly at home in a shire in England.

On the way over, I had considered from my lofty moral perch what was going on in the front seat of that car. Frankel was forty-five years older than this young woman. And then I remembered. Frankel was a ladies man. I had never thought anything about him before in that regard. But in the dining room after services, I would hear people ask him why he had never married. Here he was. Handsome. Rich. Getting a bit on. Wouldn't you think there was a woman out there for you? Wouldn't you want a son?

I just haven't found the right woman, he would say, looking forlornly at his feet. One will come along. I keep looking. Well, and so he now was looking again. At the restaurant, I was just someone in the way of his sitting down next to Lynn.

We walked between the columns of Brigadoon to the front door, then went into a foyer, and then into a huge living room filled with statues, nineteenth-century paintings, and overstuffed furniture.

"Can I get you something to drink?" he asked.

We said we would like that and he went to a bar and rattled around with some glasses, ice, and liquor for awhile. He put some classical music on a record player.

For a considerable time, we sat there in the living room sipping drinks. Zoe and I sat on a sofa. He sat in one club chair, Lynn sat in another. After two drinks, he suggested to Lynn that he show her the rest of the house. It was what it was.

"You people just enjoy the living room," he said. "We'll be back."

Zoe and I liked this idea. We drank and snuggled and finished our drinks. Then, after a moment's hesitation, I got up and went to Evan's bar and made us more drinks. We continued with this. And one thing now led to another.

But we held back. We were in Evan's living room after all. He and Lynn might come back at any moment. But you know what? They didn't. Twenty minutes passed. Then thirty. The music on the record player came to an end, and the record player automatically shut itself off. And still we drank and kissed and hugged. And things now had gone further and further. So, sort of natural like, I kind of shifted Zoe a bit, and then pulled her toward me onto the floor between the sofa and the coffee table, and then to behind the sofa. We were, I thought, safe there. And this wouldn't take too long.

And then, at the worst possible moment, we heard footsteps. A single set of them.

"Oh my God," I whispered. Zoe giggled. "Shhhh."

As quickly as we could, we began to find our clothes and put them on behind the sofa. And then Evan spoke.

"Dan?" he said. Clothes askew, we stood up to face the music.

He was wearing the same thing he had been wearing when we had last seen him. Double belted sport jacket. White shirt. Pressed blue pants.

"And just what do you think this is?" he said, raising his voice. "I invite you to my home. And *this* is what you do?" There was a sweep of his hand.

We said nothing. But I thought, isn't this what this was supposed to be all about? Wasn't this the planned major activity of the evening? I tried to say it. Nothing came out.

Soon thereafter, Evan drove us all back to Bobby Van's in silence. In the back seat, Zoe and I sat as far from one another as possible. And then Evan began to talk to Lynn. I tried to pick up some inflection, some phrase, that would suggest they had done the same as we had. But there was nothing. Sinners were sinners, and he would have nothing to do with us.

And yet, weeks later, there was no doubt that Lynn and Evan had become a couple. Zoe and I lasted for another month. Lynn and Evan Frankel lasted for about a year.

Even after Zoe and I broke up, we remained friends. As for Lynn, she would give us reports from the front.

"I think he's falling in love with me," she said at one point. "How do I feel? I don't know. He's a real gentleman. And I really like him."

At another time she said, "I have to tell you he's pretty good in the sack for a man his age."

In the end, a year later, Lynn dumped Evan for a much younger man, a fiery writer of scatological essays that were published in such magazines as *Playboy* and *Hustler.* This was Marco Vassi—funny, unpredictable, outrageous, ridiculous. He wrote a book, an alarmingly bad one in my opinion, filled with four-letter words. He was the Howard Stern of that age, now that I look back at him from this vantage point. But she and Marco didn't last either. And five years after that Marco died of AIDS.

"Are you going back to Evan?" I asked her one day.

"I think about him," she said. "But I don't think he's ever forgiven me Marco." And they never did get together.

Evan continued to treat me with distain on the few occasions I went to temple in the years that followed. I considered that he had every right to. In his late eighties, giving his sermon at the temple, he began referring to himself as the "nanogenarian," a sort of premature honor for himself that he hoped soon to enjoy as he waited for his beloved sanctuary to be built. He was eighty-eight.

Architect Norman Jaffe was designing it. It would be the crowning work of this great architect's career when it was completed. But Evan never lived to see it.

In his eighty-ninth year, before the ground was even broken, he took a severe turn for the worse, as my parents put it. He was in the hospital. He might not have long to go now, my dad said sadly.

But then Evan rallied.

"I heard this story," dad said, shortly after that. "It happened yesterday. Evan was almost gone, semiconscious and delirious. They thought this was the end and now it was his death bed. A nurse leaned over, and even though Evan was completely out of it, his hand went up her skirt to, uh," he couldn't complete the sentence but there was a big smile on his face.

"That's Evan," he concluded. Partying to the end.

And though he rallied from that deathbed, six months later he died. And the whole congregation mourned.

In 2008, on a rainy night, I was taking a taxicab from Kennedy Airport to Manhattan when the cabbie noted that traffic was pretty impossible on the major routes, and he said it might be better for him to take a shortcut through some of the lesser roads if that was alright with me. I approved. And thus, in the dark, winding through the back roads of Queens, we began to talk about religion. He was, as I learned, an orthodox Jew who observed the kosher laws and the sabbath. I told him my views. And he suggested this might not be in my best interest in the end, when I would face my maker.

"I really think it's not just about the Jews," I said. "I think we're all equal under God. I believe in God. But when I was a teenager, in schul I was told the Jews are the Chosen People. I just couldn't believe it. What does that make everybody else? And how do we expect to all get along with one another with this attitude."

The cabbie was quiet for a long time. Then he said, "I think you misunderstood what this says in the Bible. The Jews are chosen, but not because they are better, but because the Lord God has honored them by choosing them to deliver his message to everybody."

I thought—have I misunderstood this all this time? And I said this: "Oh."

And so we drove along in silence after that, for thirty more minutes, until we came to the Queensboro Bridge and into Manhattan toward my apartment there.

Ralph George

~~~~~~

In 1977, I bought a small house on a hillside overlooking Three Mile Harbor in East Hampton. The house itself was tiny, a former fishing camp built at the turn of the century. And the property itself was just a patch. But what sold me on this place was the amazing view you had when you were up there in it. The house opened out to several marinas filled with boats, and a spectacular sunset over the far shore of the harbor. At night the lines clanked on the aluminum masts of the sailboats. And almost exactly across the street from me, in a no-man's-land between two marinas, there were four or five wooden rowboats bobbing in the water, available to the local baymen for free. The rowboats were on pulleys, one end attached to a stake on the beach, the other end to a stake in the water. The baymen, or "bonackers" as they were known, would pull them in, then row out and go clamming.

As I signed the papers for the house, I thought I'd buy a boat slip. The marina on the right had no slips available. So then I tried the town marina on the left, which had slips available at half price if you were a homeowner, which

RALPH GEORGE ON ONE OF HIS POLICE BOATS
(Courtesy of Ralph George)

I certainly now was. But when I called, I found out such possession would be many years into the future.

"There's a long waiting list of people who want those slips," the town clerk told me.

"How long?" I asked.

"Well, people renew them every year. They can keep them as long as they want. So it depends on when they decide not to renew."

"How long?"

"At the rate it's going, maybe four years. Longer if people don't drop out as much."

"Well, put me on the list," I said.

I was disappointed that I'd have to wait four years, but I still wanted a boat out there. I know, I thought. I'll be a pretend clammer. Who could say I was not? So that's what I did. I bought a rowboat, carried it down to the no-man's- land, and installed it in the water next to one of the others. I even put a metal pail in it and a clam rake. Even the bonackers wouldn't know it was just me, the newspaper publisher. I hated the idea of actually clamming.

What I really had in mind to do with this boat, however, was take my two little kids out in it on weekends. I had the oars, and also, I had a three-horsepower engine I'd carry down there and clamp on the back when I wanted to use it. If we rowed out too far, I could chug back.

Those were wonderful times. Sometimes we'd motor up the harbor to one of the three waterfront restaurants that were up there, and have dinner watching the sunset over the far shore. It was quite an excursion in this little boat, about forty minutes each way.

Unlike today, when everything waterfront is so chic and expensive, back then the waterfront restaurants were clam bars and fish-and-chips and fries and hamburger joints. The kids were six and four years old. One time, on the way back from lunch at one of these places, then called the Upper Deck, we stopped and I dropped anchor, and without taking off our life jackets we all jumped into the water for a swim. Turned out, we'd jumped into a herd of jellyfish. We all got stung and got back into the boat as fast as we could. That was the last time we did that. There sure was a lot of crap in Three Mile Harbor. Waterbugs, clams, fish, horseshoe crabs, water beetles, eels, and an occasional nurse shark—these are the little sharks that chase off the bigger sharks, I told the kids, so they can nurse you back to health if a big shark bites you.

On one of these trips I met Ralph George. It was around six in the evening on a July day and the engine was bashing our little rowboat through some heavy seas (eighteen-inch waves in the harbor, anyway). We were on our way up to have some dinner (and then bash back) and there he was, just alongside in his little police boat that wasn't much bigger than our boat.

The kids looked at him wide-eyed. He wore a white uniform with a shoulder patch, had a badge on his chest, and, at about thirty-five, looked much older and weatherbeaten than his years. He was the only person on the police boat.

"Just thought I'd say hello," he said. "Want to keep an eye on you. See you coming up and back every once in a while."

I was comforted that he was looking out for us. "We don't go out of the harbor," I said. I introduced the kids to him and he offered up his name, Ralph George.

"Don't see any registration numbers on that boat," he said, motioning to the side of the rowboat.

"Just a clammer's boat," I said. "The others don't have numbers."

He raised an eyebrow as in, you, a clammer? Then he looked at the pathetic little engine on the back that could take the boat up to a screeching four miles an hour.

"Well, I won't be giving you any speeding tickets," he said, referring to the five-mile-an-hour limit. "And keep wearing those life jackets."

"We will."

And so he left, and as he did, he turned on the flashing police lights above the roof of the cabin, and he made the horn sound like a siren briefly. He tipped his cap. The kids cheered and waved.

There were about a hundred and fifty slips for boats in the four marinas near our house at the most southerly end of the harbor. If today many of the slips, owned by second homeowners, just have the boats rocking in the slips from week to week, back then the place was a beehive of activity. The clamming boats would go out every day. There were fishing boats and sailboats and catamarans and speedboats. People were out there in the boats, moving along amidst seagulls, mallard ducks, and other wildlife all the time. It was a busy time being a marine patrol policeman. I soon learned the Ralph George was the chief of them.

I also soon saw that he kept the police boat at the floating dock, which was right outside our living room window. It was a comforting thing to know he was there. It was like living right next door to a police station.

Late one Sunday afternoon, three men knocked at my door to ask if I knew any place they might buy gas for their boat. They had dropped anchor in the little inlet right out my window, had paddled in in a rubber inflatable, and said all the marina owners had locked up and were gone for the day. They'd walked right up my driveway. I told them, because I knew this from Ralph, that there was always one place open on Sundays and you'd just have to find it. So they came inside, and we called the marinas one by one until we found one open. After that, they left, took the inflatable back out to their sailboat and went there.

After this experience, I decided I ought to get a two-way police radio and watch over things. I already had a marine scanner, which I had chattering away on many afternoons in the living room of the house so I could listen in on what was going on. So I bought a two-way, and with a ladder and great effort put an antenna up on the peak of the roof of the house. On channel nine, the emergency channel, I announced myself as "Dan Ashore."

This didn't last long. I was soon visited by one of this community's real characters, a woman named Fannie Gardiner. Born and raised amidst great wealth in the town, she decided on her own to renounce her heritage and become a "bonacker." She was unmarried. She wore jeans every day and a cowboy hat. She drove around in a fifteen-year-old sedan filled with junk. I have no idea where she slept at night, maybe in the car. And she came right up my driveway. At this time, she had three antennas right on the roof of her car, held on up there with magnets. They signified that she had three police radios inside. She didn't knock at my front door. She simply honked her horn, so I came out and walked over to the driver's door. She never turned off her engine.

"Who you think you are, buddy boy, tryin' to be a bonacker. I heard you. You can't have a two-way in a private home. Not allowed. Only on the water. You keep that on, I'm going to report you. It's a federal crime. You could get five years in jail. Just turn that off, Mr. Dan Ashore."

And she drove away. I wanted to ask her before she left about having two-ways in her car, but I didn't. I talked to Ralph about it and he said it was true and there was a law. So I reluctantly took out the two-way. Even took out the scanner. Dan Ashore was now out of business. I felt terrible about it, but it was either that or five years in the slammer. Today, thirty years later, I still have the antenna on the roof of the house. But inside it goes nowhere. It was too much trouble to try and get it down.

One Friday late in the day around 1985, I had a truly terrifying experience. I was chugging up the harbor toward the entrance when a big seaplane came in overhead, circled around, and then slowed itself down as it prepared to come in for a landing on the water. I'd seen seaplanes land on Three Mile Harbor from time to time, but always in a distant part of it, where there was no boat traffic. Not this time. This seaplane came down just above the water at eighty miles an hour, and set up to land directly in front of me heading right toward me. There was no way it would be slowing down enough to avoid me, and I sure didn't have enough time or power to get out of the way. The pontoons hit the water with a splash and all the pilot could do, after he saw me, was swerve around me and continue on until he came to a stop.

The kids, who were with me, loved it. "That was *fun*," one of them said. I thought we had come pretty close to being made into mincemeat.

I spoke to Ralph George about it the next day.

"I've seen him before," Ralph said. "He's been bringing in some big shot here every Friday. Right into the marina directly across from you. I'll see what I can do about it."

"Is it legal, what he's doing?" I asked.

"No."

I'd forgotten all about it when the next Friday came, but as it happened I was home about six o'clock in the evening when, out the window, I saw the little police boat chug away from the floating dock, and, with the red police lights on top flashing, head slowly up to the end of a marina where a dock stuck out.

Now, Ralph was behind the dock. He turned around, turned his lights off, and just sat there, waiting. Sure enough, after awhile, there was the sound of an airplane.

I grabbed a camera. This, I thought, needed to have its picture taken. A few minutes later, out in the bay somewhere beyond our little inlet, I heard the seaplane's engine slow as it began to set up to come in for a landing. I went out on the deck. It was a cool evening, with the sun beginning to set low across the water.

Sure enough, at well over the speed limit, this big white seaplane, the same one, touched down and roared along the harbor at a skittery forty miles an hour, to finally arrive and come to a halt at the marina in the harbor on my right. It rocked silently there, the front of the plane facing me. And then, off from the side of a big seventy-foot yacht parked in a slip at that marina, there came a little rubber boat with the word *Serenity* on the side chugging out toward the seaplane.

Why hadn't I seen this on previous Friday evenings? Hadn't I been home? I guess not. I had been at work.

A side door behind the pilot opened, and a man in a dark-blue suit and yellow tie got out, reached in for a black briefcase, and climbed down the little metal ladder to the

RALPH GEORGE
(Courtesy of Ralph George)

pontoon of the seaplane just at the moment the little rubber
boat pulled up. He stepped in and sat down. And then they
were chugging back into the marina. With that, the white
seaplane turned around and began to head back out of the
inlet, first at two miles an hour, then at five, then at ten.

At twenty miles an hour, it passed the spot where Ralph
George was. As it did, George turned the flashing lights of
his police boat on and began to pull out from behind the
dock. Ralph was too late. And he was too slow. Suddenly,
the seaplane let out a roar, lurched forward, and with exhaust
coming out the back directly into Ralph George's face, went
plowing through the water until it rose up on its pontoons,
lifted off at what must have been a hundred and twenty miles
an hour, and flew away.

Ralph just stood there with his hands on his hips, staring. He turned his flashing lights off. He coughed. He hadn't gotten him.

The following Friday was a whole different story. The seaplane appeared, and just moments after it came to a stop, Ralph George was racing over across the inlet, his lights flashing and his horn whooping.

Once he got alongside, Ralph took his good sweet time. I know, because I was up on the deck watching and taking pictures. He said something over his loudspeaker, and in a minute the pilot opened his door and climbed down to the pontoon, leaned forward, and handed some paperwork to Ralph. His registration and license, I supposed. Ralph took out a pad and started writing something down.

At that moment, the fellow in the little inflatable appeared from the side of the same huge yacht parked there from the week before. It still said *Serenity.* But I can tell you, this was not serenity—but, on the other hand, it was. While Ralph stood there with the pilot, this man with the black suit and the briefcase crept quietly down the metal ladder on the far side, got into the inflatable along with the mate, and motored stealthily over to and behind the big yacht which I now noticed also said *Serenity.* This was not his problem.

Now came the coup de grace. With the ticket written and the pilot back up in his cockpit in a great funk, Ralph George backed up his police boat in reverse—still with the flashing light—waited until the pilot maneuvered his seaplane around, and then got directly in front of it to lead it back up the harbor to the jetties. This was only three miles, of course—that's why they call it Three Mile Harbor—but with Ralph keeping under the five-knot speed limit, it would take almost as long for the seaplane to chug out into Gardiner's Bay to take off as it would to fly back to New York.

It was nearly an hour later that I heard the roar of the engine way up there in the bay. I imagined Ralph standing on his police boat, the lights still flashing, watching him go, watching that he did this right. It was legal to fly into and out of the bay, but you never know what sailboats or buoys might be out there that the seaplane would have to look out for.

Of course, that was the last time we saw this seaplane in the harbor.

The following spring, it suddenly occurred to me that it was now four years since I had made the application for the boat slip. I felt a bit conflicted about this fact. I really liked my life as a fake bonacker, carrying my engine across the street every time I wanted it on my rowboat. That it was free down there was a plus. Even at half price, a town marina boat slip would still cost about four hundred dollars, which was a hefty bit of money at that time, but it would be mine then, and, I thought, my house would be complete. Nice Jewish man from New Jersey, has a house in the Hamptons, water view, yacht parked in his slip right outside. You could even see it out the window. There it is. Now let's get something to eat.

So I called the town clerk and I asked her about it. There was a long pause and a rustling of some papers.

"Your name?"

I gave it to her.

"Mr. Rattiner, I don't see your name on the list. Are you sure you put your name on this list? Maybe you just think you did?"

I rarely lose my temper. But this was one of those times. Boy, did I let her have it. I described how I had come to buy this house right across the street from the slip, how this was one of the first things I did after I bought the house, how since I had bought the house exactly four years earlier—which she was welcome to look up wherever she had to look that sort of information up—and that for all these years I had been completely patient, not bothering her, not trying to sneak my name up anywhere or anything and not pestering her, and so now, here it is four years later and . . .

"Okay, okay," she said. Pause. "You're next."

And I was. The kids were now twelve and ten. And I bought an old, used thirty-four-foot cabin cruiser with a shag rug and an eight-track down in the cabin. But that's a whole other story.

Albert Einstein

~~~~~~

Every Saturday night, for three years after I lived on Florence Palmer's boat in 1976, I continued to hold covered-dish jam sessions at my home. People would bring salads and spaghetti along with banjos, guitars, and auto-harps, and we'd sit in the living room and watch the sun set over the water. Usually six or seven musicians would attend, and they would bring their wives or husbands or boyfriends or girlfriends, and sometimes even their dogs and children, who would run around in the living room with us. Often it was fifteen or twenty people. We'd eat whatever people had brought—spaghetti or couscous or salads—and we'd harmonize, singing "The Erie Canal" or "The Wabash Cannonball" or even something as hokey as "You Are My Sunshine." I recorded all these sessions. I still have the tapes.

One of the regulars in 1979 was a twenty-five-year-old man from the North Fork named Ron Rothman. He played guitar well, he had a strong voice, and he often brought new songs with him. He had a girl friend, Madeline, a girl he met a few years earlier in college, and she would sit next to him, watching him adoringly, the whole time.

DAVID ROTHMAN AND ALBERT EINSTEIN
(Courtesy of Ron Rothman)

I don't recall the exact way this came about, but one evening, after we'd played for awhile, Ron mentioned that his grandfather had quite a story to tell. He'd been a friend of Albert Einstein in 1939 when that scientist came to live on the North Fork for the summer. I didn't know that Einstein had been here. I took down Ron Rothman's phone number and told him I'd sure like to meet his grandfather. Coincidentally, I was born in 1939.

"Just come up to Rothman's Department Store in Southold," Ron said. "He runs the place and he's there almost every day."

And so I went. Rothman's was not nearly as big as I thought it would be with the name, "Department Store." It was about the size of a small drugstore, although to be fair, it was the biggest store in the row of little stores on the block. Over the front door was the grand sign, ROTHMAN'S DEPARTMENT STORE. Sleigh bells jangled when you pushed open the front door.

Inside, there was just about everything. Beach umbrellas, toasters, bathing suits, suntan lotion, candy, kitchen utensils. Though smaller, it reminded me of my dad's store in Montauk. A real country store.

At the counter, I asked an older man if David Rothman was there.

"Dad? He's waiting for you. You must be Dan Rattiner."

I was really confused by this at first. Off to one side, at a cosmetics counter, Ron Rothman, our guitarist, was waiting on a customer. The older man, apparently, was Ron's father. And I was looking for *his* father.

"Follow me. I'm Bob Rothman," he said.

In the back room, I came to meet David Rothman. He had white curly hair, a lined face, and wire-rimmed glasses. He was a man approaching eighty, and it was clear he was not running the place. He was just there to hang out.

David Rothman shook my hand, his son quickly went back to work, and there we were, just the two of us, separated from the busy front of the store by a curtain. David motioned for me to sit down on one of two high stools, and I did. He sat on the other. And after just a few pleasantries, he told me the story of his time with Einstein. Sometimes, he'd stop and open a picture album he had made of just the two of them at Nassau Point in Southold. There was David, as young as his grandson out front was. And there was Albert Einstein—no mistaking him—with the spindly legs and the big shock of white hair.

It was quite a story. I took notes. And two weeks later, I published David Rothman's account of his summer with Albert Einstein in *Dan's Papers*. It appeared on August 12, 1979, as told by him to me. Here it is.

In June of 1939, a woman walked into my store and began looking at things on the shelves. At the time, I was at the back, listening to a record player that was playing Handel's Water Music. I turned the volume down. It seemed to me I had seen her before.

"May I help you?"

"Yes. I don't suppose you would have such a thing, but I'm looking for a tool that is used to sharpen a sculptor's chisel."

I thought for a moment. "I have such a thing. I'll be right back."

I took one out of a glass showcase nearby and came back with it.

"Here it is," I said. "We don't sell many of them. But do you mind if I ask? You look awfully familiar to me. Have you been in my store before?"

"No, I haven't. As a matter of fact, we're new in town. My father and I have rented a place for the summer on Nassau Point."

"You're Margot."

"Yes."

"I recognize you from your picture. You're Margot, and your father is Albert Einstein. I've read everything he's ever written. Everything about him. I've seen your pictures in magazines."

"My goodness."

"Please take this sharpener with my compliments. And give my regards to your illustrious father."

"Oh, I couldn't."

"Yes, you could. It is a privilege to have Albert Einstein in our town."

The next day, at eleven in the morning, Einstein himself walked in. You couldn't mistake him. There was the hair, the broad midriff, and white boxer shorts and sandals. I think he was sixty at that time. I must treat him like any other customer, I thought.

"May I help you?"

"Yes. My daughter told me I could find anything I wanted in your store. I am looking for sundials."

"Sundials? Sundials?" I said.

I didn't want to disappoint him. But I didn't think we had sundials. I looked everywhere. In some drawers in the back. Under some counters. No sundials. But then I got an idea.

"You know, I do have one of my own in the yard out back. Come with me. If you like it you can have it. If not, I can always order one for you."

I took him past the record player, which was playing Mozart's G Minor Symphony, and out to the backyard where I showed him the beautiful cement sundial in the middle of the lawn.

"No, no."

"Mr. Einstein, it would be my pleasure to let you have this."

Einstein lifted a leg and touched his foot with his hand. "Sundials, sundials."

Oh my God, I thought. He's wearing sandals. "Them I got!" I shouted. And so we went back inside.

I charged him the regular price for the new sandals, which was one dollar and fifty cents, and as I was putting them into a bag, I noticed that with one finger he was absentmindedly conducting the Mozart.

"I see you like music."

"Oh, yes, I am an amateur violinist."

"Well, that's a coincidence, so am I. Mr. Rothman, we must play together some evening."

"Oh, I don't want to interfere with your vacation."

Einstein took the package and tucked it under his arm.

"Monday night will be a good night," he said. "Bring some sheet music. Do you know where I live?"

As you can imagine, I was very excited. A concert with Albert Einstein! What does he play? Easy pieces? Hard pieces? I'll take a little of each. And so, with about two dozen sets of sheet music, my violin and case, and my music stand, I drove my 1937 Durant Sedan to Nassau Point, where I knew that Einstein lived on Old Cove Road. When I got there, I was greeted at the door by Einstein's personal secretary,

Miss Ducas, who led me across a porch and into the living room where the scientist was waiting.

"Let me take your things," Einstein said. "Sit down, make yourself comfortable. Did you bring some music? Something easy? Something more difficult?"

We talked. Then Einstein went through the sheet music and chose Bach's Double Concerto. This was one of the most difficult pieces. We set it out on the stand and began to play. In just a few bars, I knew I was out of my league. Einstein played his half of the pieces with ease. I struggled with mine. After a brief time, Einstein stopped the concert in the middle.

"Let's put the music down for now," Einstein said. "Let's go out on the porch and talk awhile."

And so we did. We settled in two wicker chairs.

"Where did you learn to play?" he asked.

"I'm self-taught," I told him. "But we have a quartet at my house every week, so I try to keep up."

"I'm largely self-taught, too," Einstein said. "I learned in Germany."

"When did you leave Germany?"

"I fled the Nazis two years ago. I've just recently come to America. So you'll have to pardon my English."

"I have read almost everything you have ever written," I said. "And I have so many questions. For instance, what are you working on now?"

"A unified field theory. I am working out a relationship between the macrocosm and the microcosm."

"It would seem easy, on the surface anyway," I said. "The planets revolve around the sun. The electrons revolve around the nucleus. Clearly there is a relationship."

"It's actually rather difficult," he said. "I'm not interested so much in the particles as I am in the spaces between them."

"Oh."

"And when I get it down, I'm not sure I'll be able to prove the theory. Tell me. You seem so curious about everything, Mr. Rothman, and here you are a dry goods merchant. Are you an educated man?"

"I am self-educated," I said. "I was never very interested in school and the current events they teach. So I studied myself. Plato. Newton. Bacon."

"I wasn't much interested in school either," Einstein said.

We sat on that porch for the next three hours, talking about every subject, about every great book. And we became friends.

At midnight, Miss Ducas appeared in the doorway in her nightgown.

"You are keeping the doctor up so late," she said to me.

"But I am keeping Mr. Rothman up late," Einstein said.

As he got up, Einstein asked me if he could join the quartet that I had mentioned earlier in the evening, and I told him that surely he could.

"We'll be having a musicale at my house this Wednesday."

Miss Ducas gathered up my things and ushered us to the door. As we were saying our goodbyes, she leaned forward and whispered, "This quartet, Mr. Rothman, it must not be jazz players."

And so I left.

In the days that followed, Einstein and I took hikes and went on other outings together. Einstein had a tiny sailboat, not much larger than a rowboat—he called it "Tinif," which is Yiddish for "Junk"—and he sailed this little boat on Peconic Bay wearing an undershirt, baggy shorts, and a folded-up newspaper hat on his head to keep his white hair from blowing.

Einstein told me he had asked his neighbor for permission to use a path alongside the neighbor's yard as a shortcut to the beach. But the neighbor refused.

"We're here for our privacy, just as you are, Mr. Einstein," the neighbor told him. He smiled when he said that.

Twice a week, Einstein would come to our house to play in the evening quartets there. Attending these quartets were my brother-in-law, Milton Samuel, a viola player; Howard Cook, a cellist; and Robert Lyon, also a cellist.

Also at this time we had taken in for the summer a troubled, twenty-six-year-old composer named Benjamin Britten. Occasionally, Britten would play in the quartets, but for the most part he spent his time upstairs building model airplanes with my son. Britten made almost no contact with Einstein, though he was to go on to be the most famous contemporary composer of the age. At that time he was simply a confused young man, a British subject who refused to join the war, then fled London to eastern Long Island. In fact, one day Britten asked if he couldn't take a job as a clerk in our store. Perhaps this was his calling. I told him to stick to composing.

Once, Einstein and I were walking on the beach together at night by flashlight.

"If I take this flashlight beam and shine it up," I asked him, "then it would travel forever? Is that true?"

"If it gets through the atmosphere."

"Do you believe in God?" I asked.

"I do not believe in an atmospheric God," Einstein said. "You know this word 'anthropomorphic'?"

"Yes."

"For me, religion takes the form of a rapturous amazement at the harmony and beauty and mathematical preciseness that obtains in the universe. It reveals an intelligence of such superiority that human intelligence is totally insignificant before it."

I memorized that and later wrote it down. Several hours later, I was talking to Einstein's secretary. Miss Ducas.

"Miss Ducas, you should be taking notes," I said. "If we only had notes about Newton, about Galileo, it would be so wonderful to read them now."

"Don't worry," Miss Ducas said. "I'm taking them."

A week later, I was taking Einstein on an outing to the Riverhead Telegraph Receiving Station. This was a major station that could receive messages from all over Europe, and I had a lot of friends at the station. I thought Einstein would enjoy meeting them and seeing the place.

So we started out, driving slowly in my sedan, and we'd gotten as far as Peconic when another car cut us off and pulled us over. I recognized the driver as he was getting out of his car as a salesman from the Allen Card Company.

"Hi, Mr. Rothman. Gee, is that Ein*steen?*"

"Yes, it is, Andy."

"Sorry to pull you over like this. But I stopped in your store and they told me you had just left and if I hurried I could catch you. I won't be back out this way for another two weeks. You need anything?"

"Andy, I don't need a thing. Stop and see me next time."

"Okay, Mr. Rothman. And sorry again."

And he drove off.

I turned to Einstein, "I hope this didn't frighten you, his pulling us off the road like that."

"No," he said. "In Germany maybe this would have frightened me, but not here."

"What was Germany like?"

"Well, the Storm Troopers came to my house one night and they took my wife and I outside into the yard. They had to search my house for weapons, they said, and so they went inside and out they came with my carving knives. 'See, we have found weapons,' they said. And they smashed my sailboat. After they left, I said to my wife, 'Look good on this place, for you shall not see it again.' And that night my friends took us to Holland and then to England." Einstein turned to me. "And you know, if they had catched me, they would have killed me. Of that, I am sure."

At this time, the Riverside Church in Manhattan had sent out letters to fifty scientists across the country. Their plan, they said, was to erect statues at the church to the eight most famous scientists that ever lived. Could the fifty scientists send in their lists of eight? They would like to know of whom these statues should be made.

The lists came in and on every list there was only one name of a scientist still alive at the time: Albert Einstein. The statues were erected. I read about it.

"How does it feel to have your statue there among Moses, Newton, and Christ?" I asked him.

"From now on," he said, "and for the rest of my life, I must be very careful not to commit a scandal."

Einstein would often show up at my house unannounced. He would come in the back door, play with my children, lie down on the couch, and take a snooze.

"Where is Ruth?" Einstein asked one day.

"My wife is in the hospital. She is quite sick and I've just come back."

"She'll be alright?"

"I think so. She is such a wonderful woman. I am so in love with her. I don't know what I would do without her."

"You know, I've had two wives," Einstein said, "but I have never experienced the love that you have. My wives have been good women who've looked after me."

In a few weeks, my wife recovered.

"Rothman. You want me to teach you the theory of relativity?"

"What? Are you kidding? With my eighth-grade education?"

"If you had a college education. I'd be suspicious. With an eighth-grade education, I think I can do it."

"How do we do this?"

"I need you to do a few things. Promise me you'll give me three full hours of your time. And promise me, if you get lost with what I say, you'll tell me. That way I could clarify things and we won't get all tangled up. Okay?"

"I need a promise from you."

"What's that?"

"That you won't use any mathematics."

"Agreed."

Einstein took out a pad and a pencil.

"I said no mathematics," I said.

"I'm just going to take notes while I talk. You don't mind if I do that."

"No, of course not."

Einstein began his discourse, talking about how a spinning metal rod contracts in the direction of its spin. As he talked, Einstein wrote numbers and formulas on the paper he had in front of him. And then, forgetting himself, he lapsed into a complicated mathematical formula.

"We said no mathematics," I said.

"But this is so *trivial!*" Einstein said.

And so, he gave up the effort. I did, however, ask if I could keep the piece of paper on which he was scribbling, and he gave it to me.

On one occasion, Einstein, wearing his newspaper hat, undershirt, and baggy shorts, was hauling his anchor in the middle of Peconic Bay when his boat capsized. Einstein was thrown into the water, and, since he could not swim, began thrashing around yelling for help. A fifteen-year-old boy who was swimming nearby and who never identified himself, saved Einstein.

"I made a triple error," Einstein later said.

On another occasion, I got a phone call from Miss Ducas to inform me that Albert Einstein had decided to sail his little boat from Nassau Point to my house in Southold.

"He left at six this morning," Miss Ducas said, "so he should be there soon."

But Einstein did not arrive. After the sun set, I became hysterical. But then the phone rang. On the other end was a friend of mine, a vacationing New York City cop who lived at the Southold beach.

"Rothman," he said. "There's a weird-looking guy who needs a haircut—some helluva looking looney—down here on the beach wanting to know where you live."

And so, of course, I went and got him.

Another time I got a call from the minister of the Southold church who said the reason he was calling was that he wanted me to get a message to Einstein because he knew I knew him.

"Next week, I'm moderating a meeting at the firehouse about getting refugees out of Nazi Germany. I know Mr. Einstein has been active in getting Jewish refugees out. We're going to try to get some of the Christian refugees out. What I wondered was, could you ask Mr. Einstein to attend? Just his presence there would be a big boost to us. You come too."

I told him he would probably come if I asked him, but in return I wanted to ask if he could be treated like an ordinary person, because that is what he was. Don't ask him to speak or anything. But you could mention that he's in the audience.

"Of course."

The following week, I put on a suit and a tie and drove over to pick up Einstein on Nassau Point. Einstein came down to meet me wearing an undershirt and baggy pants tied up with a rope and sandals.

"My. You are looking elegant," I said, and he disappeared back upstairs. Ten minutes later he was back, dressed in more proper attire.

The meeting was attended by perhaps two hundred people who all sat on folding chairs facing a dais. Einstein and I were about halfway back.

"And we have with us," the minister said, "the famous scientist, Albert Einstein. Mr. Einstein, come up to the dais and join us and give a little speech."

Einstein gave me a funny look, then went up and sat. One speech followed another, and finally Einstein was asked to say something.

"You must organize just as we Jews have organized," he said. "Otherwise you will have a big problem."

Then he sat down. That was it. So everyone applauded.

After the meeting broke up, literally dozens of people crowded around trying to say a few words to Einstein.

"Mr. Einstein," one woman said. "I'm from Europe. I understand you've come from Europe, too?"

"Yes, Europe, a fine place," he said. Then he turned to me and cupped a hand over his mouth.

"Get me out of here," he whispered.

I led him through the crowd and out into the street to get to our car. From behind a tree there jumped an older man who identified himself as a physicist from Johns Hopkins University. He just wanted to meet Albert Einstein he said, and so they shook hands and exchanged a few pleasantries. A week later, this Johns Hopkins' physicist was at the counter of my store.

"Mr. Rothman, you've got to lend me a hundred dollars. I'll win it back."

I never heard of anything like that. So I refused. Later, I told this story to Einstein, reminding him that he'd met this professor outside the firehouse.

"We scientists are not good businessmen," Einstein said. "If we are good businessmen, we are not good scientists."

On the morning of July 30, 1939, an old Plymouth arrived at Einstein's home on Nassau Point bearing two scientists from Princeton University. I was there at the time, and Einstein met them in his traditional undershirt, rolled-up pants, and sandals, and then introduced them to me. They were Leo Szilard and Eugene P. Wigner. It seemed they were there on serious business, and so I excused myself and went back to Southold.

It was only four years later, after World War II ended, that I learned that Szilard and Wigner, together with Einstein, had drafted one of the most famous letters in history. It was addressed to Franklin D.

Roosevelt, and it outlined the discoveries made by the Germans in developing an atomic bomb, and it asked him, to save America, to create an American program to build our own atomic weapons.

"A single bomb of this type," the letter said, "might very well destroy a whole port together with some of the surrounding territory."

Though Szilard and Wigner worked with Einstein in drafting this letter, only Einstein signed it. Szilard and Wigner believed, correctly, that only a scientist of Einstein's stature could carry the weight necessary to see to it that the letter arrived on the president's desk.

The letter was mailed from Nassau Point on August 2, 1939, and reached the president on October 11. President Roosevelt ordered the creation of an atomic bomb study group as a result.

Einstein left Nassau Point in the autumn of 1939 and returned to Princeton. He never returned. But the following spring, he wrote and asked if his sailboat could be trucked to Saranac Lake in the Adirondacks. For family health reasons, he said, he would not be able to return to the beach, for which he was deeply grieved.

We exchanged letters for the next five years. One day I read where the government had asked Einstein to write down, in his own hand, the theory of relativity so they could raffle it off. He did that, and in the raffle, a total of six million dollars was raised.

I wrote Einstein and reminded him of the piece of paper that I still had. And I asked him what had become of his original manuscript on relativity? Did the Nazis get it?

"My first manuscript was not burned by the Nazis," Einstein wrote back. "I myself threw it into the wastebasket after it was printed, judging it good for nothing."

A year later, Einstein published his unified field theory. It appeared as a front-page story in the *New York Times,* and the *Times* quoted scientists who said that it was unlikely that this theory could either be proven or disproven in this generation. As for me, every year I sent Einstein a new pair of sandals.

"I miss the nights with your quartet group," Einstein wrote me back. And then, in a later letter, he wrote, "I am thinking often of the beautiful hours we spent together in the last years . . ."

So that is what appeared in *Dan's Papers* in 1980. A few final words should be said about Einstein's visit to the North Fork in 1939. At that time, it had already been about twenty-five years since Einstein had advanced the theory of relativity in Austria at the age of thirty-six. It was also twenty years since that theory had been proven by scientific demonstration.

In 1939, Einstein was preoccupied with his unified field theory, because he felt that since he had been able to develop a theory of relativity, he should be able to develop a corresponding unified field theory.

Unfortunately, during the decades that Einstein was working on his unified field theory, other scientists advanced quantum theory, which explained the field situation in a way quite different from what Einstein proposed. Thus, for the entire last half of his life Einstein worked as a maverick, totally out of the mainstream of scientists who embraced quantum theory. By 1939, Einstein, though respected for his earlier work, was largely isolated from the scientific community

"It is a shame that such a brilliant man could waste the last half of his life in such a way," one of his students said.

But was it wasted? We must wait and see.

I drive down the Main Road in Southold every once in a while. Rothman's Department Store is still there. And the generations are still there. But now they are Bob, who is eighty-one, his son Ron, and, well, they're hoping Ron's son Gregory will come into the business. But so far, he's not biting. Or so says his mother Madeline.

Barry Trupin

~~~~~~

In the late 1970s, a man named Barry Trupin bought the big abandoned Henry Francis du Pont estate known as "Chesterton House" on the beach in Southampton at auction. He did so through a dummy corporation so nobody could know who he was. His intention was to follow up the half-million dollars he had spent to buy the place with the expenditure of about thirty million dollars to fix it up, and then, one day, move into the largest mansion in the estate section of Southampton. It would be an enormous French castle complete with towers, turrets, gargoyles, and spires. It would take two years to complete. Everybody would want to come visit him there.

But first a chain-link fence with barbed wire went up around the property. And after that came a small guardhouse, manned by security people with guns. With that, things changed.

"Who *are* these people?" I overheard somebody say in Shep Miller's clothing store at the head of Job's Lane. Another patron in the store commented, "They have to be mafia. I've heard they'll be helicptering in drugs. Frankly, I'm afraid. Everyone else is afraid too."

BARRY TRUPIN AND HIS DAD
(Courtesy of the author)

Shep Miller catered to the rich. He sold scarves and sport jackets and golf shoes. There were certain colors, sort of the official colors of the wealthy in Southampton, that he traded in. The colors were pink and lime green. He'd sell a pair of green socks with pink elephants on them. Or he'd sell a pair of pink men's pants with green bullfrogs on them. I had no idea what anybody was thinking about with this, but it seemed to amuse these people. Maybe, I once thought, it meant you were in the club if you bought clothes in pink and green colors. Maybe these colors were the vacation version of all the black suits these people wore every day in the city. Or maybe they had something to do with the clans of Scotland. It was all very ridiculous after all. Any one of these theories seemed to fit the bill.

I might note that the "Estate Section" of Southampton, down at the beach, was very clearly defined. For about eight blocks back from the beach, along a three-mile stretch, the homes were all mansions, with manicured lawns and tall hedgerows along the narrow lanes; there were gardeners out by the swimming pool and tennis courts, and there were cooks and maids inside, and chauffeurs out by the carriage houses. This was a safe and peaceful place. And now this terrible thing had come into their lives.

Three weeks later, the *Southampton Press* had a name—Barry Trupin. He was behind the dummy corporation that had been set up to buy the property. Nobody had heard of him. Who was he? Nothing came up about him on Wall Street except that he had arranged his life so that nothing could be figured out about him. There were those who said he was connected with a shadow investment corporation called Rothschild's Investments, which bore no relationship whatsoever to the wealthy Rothschilds banking family of Germany.

The next week there was a full-page ad in the *Southampton Press* about the formerly abandoned du Pont mansion. I had picked up a copy of the paper at Silver's Cigar Store on Main Street, another favorite haunt of the old guard. Construction was now under way at the du Ponts, the ad said. And it had to be stopped. Those placing the ad, which was signed by the Southampton Corporation, a non-profit group that the old guard had set up around 1910 to protect their interests, had had a look at the plans at the Building Department. The building was hideous. Furthermore, its turrets and chimneys were going too far up. They were exceeding the legal limit. STOP THE CONSTRUCTION.

There was also an article.

"How would you like your teenage daughter and her friends to come walking down the beach late at night from a party and have to cross in front of *this?*" a resident of the Estate Section said to a reporter from the *Press*. And then, reading further on, I learned that that had actually happened. A guard with a gun had stopped just such a group of people on the beach late at night and questioned them about where they were going. After a bit, he let them through.

The mayor of Southampton, Roy Wines, a man who owned a local plumbing company, was asked about all this by the newspaper reporter. What could he do? His hands were tied, he said. Construction had now begun.

And still nobody knew who this man was.

A few days later, I walked into Bob Keene's Bookstore on Hampton Road in Southampton.

"The whole town is talking about this guy Barry Trupin," I said to him as I came in. "What do you think?"

Keene had a big smile on his face.

"You're smiling?" I asked.

"You really ought to see this new book I got in last week."

"What book?"

Keene reached over to a little display on a counter, and picked up a thin volume entitled *Elias Pelettreau, 1726–1810: Goldsmith of Southampton, Long Island, New York*. He handed it to me.

I flipped through it and read a sentence or two. The Pelletreaus were one of the famous artisan families in South-ampton. Although they were long gone, their workshop on

Main Street had survived the centuries. And it was open as a little museum. As for the book, it was pretty technical. And rather badly written.

"What's so special about this?" I asked.

"It was written by an elderly retired man who lives in Hallandale, Florida. He was here about two weeks ago and he dropped off some of these books for me to sell. I figured I could sell them. You can see his name right on the front cover."

I looked. It was written by Bennett W. Trupin.

"He's a very nice guy," Keene continued. "Maybe you ought to meet him and write a story about his book. He told me his son has just bought a house here that he is now in the process of fixing up. He's very proud of his son. He's coming back again in another week. He's going to stop in to see how the book is doing."

"Have you sold any?"

"Three, so far."

"Have you told anybody else about this Mr. Trupin?"

"No. And nobody seems to have made the connection."

"This is what I truly hate about being a newspaperman," I said. "Newspaper people sometimes have to lie."

"You don't have to take me up on my suggestion to write about him."

"No, I'll do it."

I left. Then I went back in, and for twelve dollars bought a copy of the book. Then I left again, all in a funk.

I was flushed and excited when I came back two weeks later to meet Bennett Trupin. Maybe he'd figured me out.

Keene introduced us and we shook hands. He was a Jewish man with a Yiddish accent. And he was very sprightly and he had a sparkle in his eye.

"Well, you *should* write an article about the book," Bennett Trupin said, when I told him that was why I wanted to meet him. "It's all about your famous fella. He was very important in the world of goldsmithing. I've written a very good book about him."

Keene had customers, and so Bennett and I went for a stroll down Main Street, which wound us up in the Driver's Seat Restaurant on Job's Lane, where we had lunch.

At that lunch, I learned more about the classic ways Elias Pelletreau and his son went about silversmithing, and about Bennett's silverware factory in New Jersey, from which Bennett had recently retired. I also learned everything I needed to know about Bennett's son, Barry.

Barry Trupin was born and raised in Astoria, Queens. He went to public high school and then to Adelphi University on Long Island. On graduation, he had, along with a friend, opened a bar in Manhattan, but when that didn't work out, he got a job that entailed security clearance, working on something top secret for Republic Aircraft in Farmingdale.

"He wouldn't even tell me or his mother about it," Bennett marveled proudly between bites of pastrami.

Soon after that, Barry Trupin opened Rothschild's Securities and made hundreds of millions of dollars.

"He found this big corporate-tax loophole that nobody had ever seen before," Bennett said. "If Ford Motors had a fleet of trucks and was losing money, and if FedEx had a fleet of trucks and was making money, the trucks at Ford could be sold to FedEx and then leased back to Ford. They would still be at Ford. But FedEx, which could use the tax write-off, would get to do so, while Ford, which could not use it because they were losing money, didn't need it. And this was my son Barry's brilliant idea. Now he is building his dream house for his wife, Renee, who he dearly loves and who wants to be part of Southampton society. Maybe I can introduce them to you?"

The thought terrified me.

The next week, all of this information was on the front page of *Dan's Papers*. In addition, was my opinion, that if a man were doing anything wrong, that was for the courts to decide. People were allowed to live wherever they wanted in America. In the back, there was a review of *Elias Pelettreau, 1726–1810: Goldsmith of Southampton, Long Island, New York*.

Less than twenty-four hours after the paper came out, the phone rang in my office.

"Hi, Dan?"

"Yes."

"This is Barry Trupin. My wife and I would like to invite you and your wife over for lunch next Sunday. Are you free?"

"Yes, as it happens, I am."

"I thought you might like to see what we're doing down here at the beach."

"I would."

"I don't understand why this is such a big deal. Anyway, we're on Meadow Lane, I think you know the house, and how would noon be?"

"Sounds good."

The following Sunday, my wife and I drove to Meadow Lane where, as we rounded the bend to where I knew the old du Pont house to be, I realized I had made a tremendous mistake. Nobody could possibly be living in this mess. Scaffolding was all around the house, there were trucks filled with building materials skidding around in the mud, and there were workmen hammering and sawing away.

"Uh, oh," I said.

"Ask that man," my wife said, pointing to the guard-house.

I pulled up and came to a stop, and the man inside swaggered out to the car. He wore rubber boots and a windbreaker. You could see his shoulder holster. And he peered into my car suspiciously. What were we doing here?

"Uh, we've been invited to have lunch with Barry Trupin?"

"Name?"

We told him.

He nodded and disappeared into the booth. Two workmen walked by, little men in hard hats, gesturing with their hands, talking in a foreign language.

"Italian," my wife said.

The man reappeared.

"Go five houses down. You'll see two white pillars with stone lions on them. They're expecting you."

"Thanks," I said.

We followed his instructions, and soon drove up a long driveway past perfectly mown lawns and landscaping to this *other* beautiful oceanfront house, which was about half the size of the du Pont mansion. But everything is relative. The du Pont mansion, as I knew, had sixty-four rooms.

Barry Trupin, a heavyset but otherwise pleasant-looking fellow of about thirty-five, met us at the front door with a smile, and led us in to meet his wife Renee. She was strikingly beautiful, and, as we soon learned, the daughter of an army officer. She had grown up moving about from place to place.

"Renee wants us to have a home in Southampton," Barry told me, as we sat down on some giant sofas in front of a grand fireplace in the living room. "She wants to be a member of society. We intend to have great and very fashionable parties here. You'll see."

"I had no idea you owned a second house," I said.

"We don't. We've rented this one while we finish the other one. It's only a short stroll down there. This house used to be Roy Radin's house."

A shock of surprise went through me.

"You know about Roy Radin?" Barry asked, leaning forward.

"I sure do. But I didn't know this was his house. Sad what happened to him."

"Yes, it was."

Roy Radin had been killed five years earlier, his body found in a canyon in California with a bullet in the back of his head. He was just twenty-nine years old. Prior to that, he had lived in this house in Southampton with his mother. He was a familiar character on the streets downtown. He was extremely heavyset, wore a black cape and cap, and carried with him a silver-handled cane. He also had very wild parties at his house. The police had raided one and found drugs, whips, chains, video equipment, and sado-masochistic costumes. Also, all sorts of guns and pistols and ammunition. Radin was arrested and had to be bailed out of jail at four in the morning. His mother, who lived in the house and who accompanied him to the police station, said she had no idea all this was going on.

Lunch was served under a white silk tent set up by the staff on the lawn between the Radin house and the sea. The side panels of the tent were all drawn back and tied to the poles with thick, gold-threaded sashes, so the grand table, which could have seated twelve, was open on all sides.

I still remember this meal fondly. It consisted of seven courses, served by cooks and servants, with the wind ruffling the tent roof and the sea sending billows of mist up from the beach to mix with the smells of the steamed salmon and boiled potatoes, or with the filet mignon and rice, and everything else we ate. It was a remarkable lunch that day, just the four of us.

Barry Trupin sat at the head of the table, of course, with his wife on his left hand and his guests on the right. After the dessert came and after he tasted it, he called the waiter over to heartily praise the chocolate mousse, and then ask him to relay that information to the pastry chef. The waiter walked off mightily pleased.

After lunch, we took a tour of the Radin house. It was filled with all sorts of European exotica from the old castles of that continent. There were oil paintings of kings and queens on the walls, crossed swords and shields on the mantlepieces, suits of free-standing armor by the doorways, and huge religious weavings a thousand years old or more leading you down the hallways. I briefly wondered if all this dusty old stuff had been left there by the Radins. But I knew that could not be. All the Radin possessions had been auctioned off by his estate at Sotheby's after he died. This stuff was getting ready for the French castle.

Renee led us excitedly down to the basement of the Radin house. This was her pet project, she said. Barry trailed behind, smiling.

"It was just a regular old basement when we got here," Renee said, "but I wanted to make it into something. I chose the beach at Coney Island."

The walls featured continuous trompe l'oeil paintings of ferris wheels and roller coasters and merry-go-rounds. The paintings wound their way through the many corridors of this vast basement, now all brightly lit, and as we walked along on a wooden boardwalk built a few feet above the concrete floor, occasionally Renee would stop and show us a turn-of-the-century game you could play—they actually worked—pinball, hit the clown with the ball, knock over the pins with a beanbag, and so forth and so on. The four of us played a game where we bet on tiny mechanical metal horses which chittered and chattered around a little iron track after you wound up a key. Neither my wife nor I had ever seen anything like it.

That first day we did not visit the construction site five houses down, but on subsequent visits we did. Almost the entire interior of the place, including almost all the bedrooms, had been torn out and gutted. The name "Chesterton House" would be discarded. It would be called "Dragon's Head." We went into a vast open space where they were papering the walls and where carpenters were banging up new moldings, and where, astonishingly, those Italian workers we had seen earlier were cutting away at some stones.

"We want this done right," Barry said. "We flew them here and are putting them up in trailers on the site, but don't tell anybody."

Only two rooms were complete. One was an exact replica of an old English pub. Actually it was *not* a replica. A pub had been purchased, completely disassembled, flown to America, and reassembled piece by piece. There was the bar, a huge fireplace, a slate floor, and if outside there was no gloaming, there was a pretty good replica of it with the fog from the sea.

The other room that was complete was the salt water aquarium. This was a huge hall, attached to the main house but encased on three sides with leaded French windows, and featuring a main floor where you could take off your shoes and socks and walk around barefoot on rocks and paths, carefully stepping over the water. Around the edge of the aquarium pool, down a flight of stairs to a sub-basement level, you could walk through caves to get to double-paned windows through which you could see the goings-on beneath the water. There were no fish in it when we were there, but very soon, we were promised, there would be big sharks, skates, and other tropical fish swimming around.

Barry showed me a very interesting feature of the aquarium.

"See that spigot?" he asked, pointing through the glass window to a small underwater valve. "If you run out of air

BARRY AND RENEE

(Copy of 'New York' Courtesy of William Hattrick)

in your tank while scuba diving, you don't even have to get out of the water. You just hook up to the spigots. There are five of them. You refill your tanks right then, underwater."

It never even occurred to me there would be scuba diving. And with sharks?

Barry took me up several flights of winding stairs into one of the turrets in the castle. It had a splendid view of all Southampton.

"This will be my prayer room," he said. "I pray every day."

The battle to try to stop this construction raged over the next two years. The members of the Southampton Association wanted to know who had issued these permits to allow Mr. Trupin to build nine feet higher than the legal limit.

Mayor Wines pointed out that it was common practice in the Estate Section for the architects working for that community to bring in plans to the Village Building Department and, if a variance was needed, have them make the proper applications to get it approved; but in the meantime, allow the construction to proceed as if it had already been approved so nobody would be inconvenienced. The WASPS were being buried by their own disregard for the law. If this procedure applied to one person in the Estate Section, the mayor said, it should apply to everybody in the Estate Section.

Articles appeared in the *New York Times,* in national magazines, and in one memorable piece, in the magazine *New York.* The cover featured a smiling Barry Trupin standing in front of his castle under construction, carrying his beloved Renee as if he were about to take her across the threshold.

Inside, there was this quote from a member of the Southampton Association, Charlotte Harris:

"We don't want these people in Southampton."

"Are you saying that because they are Jews?" the author of the article asked.

"You said it, not me."

But then there were other members of the Southampton Association who were disturbed by the behavior of Charlotte Harris and those like her. A rift was appearing in this organization.

One of those disturbed about all of this was Bill Hattrick, a money manager with a brokerage office in town. "You should know," he told me, "that Charlotte put a porch on her house last year without first getting the permit approved."

"Charlotte is a real bitch. Most of us don't think the way she does," another member of the WASP community told me.

I wrote an article about Charlotte's dealings with the building department. She who lives in glass houses and so forth and so on.

One day, in my office, the secretary said there was a man on the phone who wouldn't give his name but who was very insistent on talking to me. I told her I'd take the call. Who could this be?

"I'm calling about this business with Barry Trupin," the man said. "You should stay out of this. It has nothing to do with you. The Southampton Association can get along just fine without you."

I called up Bill Hattrick about this call. He said he wasn't surprised that I had gotten this call, but he said he had no idea who it might have been.

Barry Trupin couldn't understand why everybody hated him. We were having a steak dinner at Barry's favorite dining spot, a restaurant called the Sherlock Holmes Pub on Jobs Lane. They made a big deal over him when he came in. He ate there a lot and he was a big tipper.

"You really want to know?" I asked.

"Yes."

"You have to be invited into their club. Or born into it. You were neither. And you have guards with guns at Dragon's Head. That terrifies them."

"I have a lot of very expensive art and sculpture going in there," Barry said. "What do they expect me to do?"

Barry thought about it for a minute. "I'm going to have a big party for all these people," he said. "We'll make it a costume party. A costume party like they've never had before. We'll see how they feel about us after that."

On another occasion, Renee Trupin took me and my wife up into another of the far reaches of the unfinished castle to show us a bedroom under construction that, inexplicably, had a very luxurious bed made up in it. Adjacent was a bathroom with gold fixtures, all hooked up, a Jacuzzi, a bidet, and so forth.

"Sometimes Barry and I sneak up here and spend the night," she said mischievously. "This is the only room in the house with water."

About a month after Charlotte Harris made her anti-Semitic remarks in *New York* magazine, she had a heart attack and died. We were out on the lawn again sunning ourselves and reading the newspapers after a big lunch under the billowing tent.

"It's God who did that to her," Barry said, turning to me. "She was a bad person and said those things. God struck her down. I know that's a terrible thing to say. But I can't help it."

As planning for the costume party got underway, a lawsuit was filed about the building being too high, and a judge issued a stop-work order. The carpenters put down their hammers. The Italians set down their chisels.

Barry was stunned. But the planning for the party went ahead. It would be held at the house they were renting, not Dragon's Head. The sooner the better.

"I'm thinking of filing a civil rights lawsuit against the village for ten million dollars," Barry told me over the telephone one day. "I have a right to live where I want to live without all these people harassing me."

"Don't do that," I said. "It will tie things up for years. Work it out."

He thought about it. "I don't see how," he said.

The party took place a week later but neither my wife nor I were invited. I was a bit miffed, but I didn't say anything. I did read about it, though. Everyone came as a duke or dutchess or a knight. There was a huge banquet table with a roasted pig with an apple in its mouth, and a quartet played medieval songs from an elevated platform alongside the fireplace. Servants dressed as pages announced King Barry and Queen Renee with trumpet fanfares, and they came down the main staircase into the living room to a throne set up for them, but in the end, none of this did them any good. The guests were polite and happy and then they left. And they never called the Trupins again.

Honestly, I wish I had been there.

A few days later it was revealed that Mayor Wines had the plumbing contract for Dragon's Head. It was for three hundred thousand dollars. And after completing the kitchen in one part of the house, Mrs. Trupin had had the whole thing torn out and rebuilt in another part of the house.

Mayor Wines resigned.

And now Bill Hattrick became Mayor. He offered to allow the project to proceed if Trupin would add nine feet of fill along one side of the house so that the distance from the ground to the top of the turrets would be nine feet less and therefore legal. It was on the order of raising the water when you couldn't lower the bridge. If he did that, all the lawsuits would be dropped.

But then, Trupin, who no longer was seeking my counsel, made a big mistake. He refused the offer. He would proceed with his lawsuit. I tried to call him. He wouldn't take the call. It was over.

Three years later, after depositions were taken from the former mayor, from many members of the Southampton Association, and from others, the jury ruled in favor of Trupin, awarding him so much money that Mayor Hattrick said to pay it would bankrupt the village. The village appealed. And they won the appeal on a technicality and the suit was thrown out. And I never saw Trupin again.

But I did hear from him. Ten years later, he called me on my cell phone—these were the early big boxy cell phones—while I was having a late dinner with my wife at what today is East Hampton Point. Dusk had fallen when he called. We were sitting outdoors on the deck, overlooking the boats, and you could hear the clanking of the lines on the masts in the adjacent marina.

"Renee and I are on our yacht in the Mediterranean," Barry told me. "I just wondered how things are there in fusty old Southampton."

Things were fine, I told him, except that his house, with construction stopped right in the middle, was a complete mess of overgrown foliage, rusting scaffolding and weeds.

"What's going to happen with it?" I asked him.

"Ha," he said.

"How's Renee."

"She's fine. She says hello."

"Then say hello for me. What are you doing these days?" I asked.

I knew that President Reagan had put through a major tax reform that had closed the loophole Trupin had used to get rich. So that was that.

"Well, I've bought some real estate in California. A shopping center. And I'm buying a savings and loan. Things are moving along."

The following year, Trupin was arrested and charged with purchasing stolen property—the paintings, tapestries, and suits of armor that he'd housed in the Radin house. Apparently, he had gotten them cheap because they were hot. Not good. He also got involved in the savings-and-loan scandal. And so he was going down. Soon after that, somebody told me, he and Renee were divorced.

But I truly hoped he wouldn't be going to jail. I really did think he was a nice person, just trying to do something sweet for his wife who wanted to join what passed for high society in America, and for which he fought tooth and nail. He'd been right to at least try to do that. Later, I learned that what Barry Trupin did was basically take people's money, invest it in his various schemes, and sometimes, maybe most of the time, figure out a way for it to wind up in his pocket rather than the pockets of the people who gave it to him. Damn him.

The change in the community that was brought about by the battle over Dragon's Head was swift and dramatic. The WASP community had been brought out of the closet and had been split, largely between the old guard and the younger generation. The younger generation would now join just about everybody else in breaking down many of the barriers in America, even if it amounted to calling the bluff of members of their own family. Things would never be the same.

In the end, Dragon's Head was sold for a song. Today, it is gone. Calvin Klein, the new owner, tore it down and replaced it with a flat-roofed glass-and-stone affair designed by the world-class architect Michael Haverland. In it, he is living happily ever after, apparently.

Shortcuts

~~~~~~

Sometime in the late 1970s, traffic tie-ups began to appear in the Hamptons. This was an alarming development for the locals who had spent all their lives here. Traffic jams? That was for the city. How could this be?

Well, at least they were predictable. They occurred on only one road, the Montauk Highway eastbound, on Friday evenings in the summertime when the tourists and city people drove out. And they appeared again westbound on Sunday evenings on the same highway when they went back. The Montauk Highway was the only way in and out of the Hamptons, of course.

I did write, at that time, that there were all sorts of interesting ways to look at this. It meant that the Hamptons were becoming more and more popular, and that was a good thing. On the other hand, having to wait like this might make people decide that next time they should go somewhere else.

"Of course," I concluded, "we local people know all the back roads to take to avoid these two tie-ups. They happen only twice a week. So if you have to go out on a Friday night

PETER'S POND LANE
(Courtesy of the author)

and suddenly find yourself in one of these traffic jams, just take one of the shortcuts."

The reaction to this last paragraph, in an article distributed in a newspaper distributed in more than fifteen hundred locations in the Hamptons, came as a total surprise to me.

"Why are you telling the visitors to take shortcuts?" someone asked me a few days after the paper came out.

"I didn't tell them to take the shortcuts."

"Yes, you did."

"Well, it's not like they don't see there are roads coming into and out of the Montauk Highway on both the north and south sides of the street," I said.

They glared at me.

As the days went by, more people mentioned this terrible transgression I had committed. And I began to take it more seriously.

"I seem to have struck a nerve," I told my wife one evening when I got home from work. "People want the visitors to come here. But they don't want them driving on all the back roads once they're here. They want them to stay on the Montauk Highway and suffer."

"I want them to stay on the Montauk Highway, too," she said.

After awhile, the furor died down. The new edition came out. The few remaining copies of the old edition got removed from the stores and recycled. Life moved on.

And yet, as the years went by, among the many other things that people thought about me, there was somehow this belief that I was the one who had spilled the beans and told all the visitors about the back road shortcuts from the Montauk Highway. And it would, on occasion, come out.

"I was reading in your paper that people up on David White's Lane in Southampton are complaining about the traffic on Friday nights now," someone told me at a party one night. "That's one of those shortcuts you wrote about, isn't it?"

In 1987, I had had enough. And I decided once and for all to put an end to this. I would write about the shortcuts all right. I'd use fictitious street names. And at the end of every shortcut, everybody would be dead. Wait until the people read *this*.

SHORTCUT AROUND SOUTHAMPTON

From the Montauk Highway in Shinnecock, turn right on Swizzle Tree Lane, go two miles and at the boulder take the left fork. One mile down, past the red barn and the cemetery, there is a dirt road on the left hand side called Breeze Boulevard. Make that left, go half a mile, over the wooden bridge, then right at the big copper beech tree next to the farmstand onto Bending Willow Lane, then left on Sanddune Street, right on Jacob Lester's Way, left on Potato Road, then put the pedal to the metal and on that long straight road speed up to more than eighty-five miles an hour so that when you hit the dune at the end of the road, you are going fast enough to clear all the bathers on the beach before splashing into the ocean.

SHORTCUT AROUND BRIDGEHAMPTON

From the Montauk Highway in Water Mill, turn right on Swizzle Tree Lane, go two miles and at the boulder take the left fork. One mile down, past the red barn and the cemetery, there is a dirt road on the left hand side called Breeze Boulevard. Make that left, go half a mile, over the wooden bridge, then right at the big copper beech tree next to the farmstand onto Bending Willow Lane, then left on Sanddune Street, right on Jacob Lester's Way, left on Potato Road, then put the pedal to the metal and on that long straight road speed

up to more than eighty-five miles an hour so that when
you hit the dune at the end of the road, you are going
fast enough to clear all the bathers on the beach before
splashing into the ocean.

There was also a secret shortcut for getting around East Hampton and for getting around Amagansett. And they were absolutely the same, the same made-up farm stands, Swizzle Tree Lanes, large boulders, and barns. I was here to lay the whole thing out, give away the whole shebang.

I thought this finally and once and for all put an end to my problem. It had absolutely the opposite effect.

"How *dare* you write these shortcuts in your paper!"

"Did you *read* them?"

"I don't have to read them."

"Did you read that at the end of each shortcut, if you follow the instruction exactly, you wind up driving into the ocean? Something which, if followed to the letter, will do away with the problem?"

"I can't believe you did this."

People are so lame, is what I thought.

And so I soldiered on, year after year, as the fellow that gave away the directions to all the back roads to the summer visitors. Traffic backed up on Hayground Road? Blame it on me. Traffic in a three-mile line on Edge of Woods Road? Blame that on me too.

And then, about five years later, as in some great Greek play, a deus-ex-machina figure appeared, lowered on wires from the proscenium above the stage, a heroine to solve this problem and save the day.

Her name was, and is, Jodi Della Femina, the daughter of a prominent multimillionaire advertising man with a home on the beach in East Hampton.

Beginning around 1995, Jodi began publishing a small, glossy booklet called *Jodi's Shortcuts.* In it, among various other secret advice given to the reader, were actual maps of the back roads as they veered off the Montauk Highway to get around the choke points. Her inaugural issue was labeled "1995." She would be publishing it annually.

I was ecstatic.

"You know," someone would say, "if it weren't for you, we wouldn't be having all the visitors using the back roads."

"You've got me confused with Jodi Della Femina," I'd say, nonchalantly. "She started it. Haven't you read *Jodi's Shortcuts?*"

And so, over time, my undeserved reputation faded away.

But it sure was bad there for awhile. And traffic jams were just so miserable. Most cars back then, particularly older ones, had uncomfortable seats, jerky stick-shift transmissions, air-polluting smoke coming out the back, and no air-conditioning. There were flat tires and breakdowns. And radio was just AM and full of static.

Today, cars are a great deal of fun to be in, traffic jam or no. They have two hundred channels of entertainment, flip-down DVD players, lumbar support, captain's chairs, cupholders, climate control, and even navigation systems so you can listen to the nice lady telling you where to turn, where to relax, and where otherwise to get off. They are no longer just a way to get somewhere. They are a nice place to BE while getting somewhere.

About a month ago, the editor of our web site (danshamptons.com) asked me to write a written description of all the shortcuts through the Hamptons as best as I know them.

"You really want me to do that?"

"It goes in the "Getting Here" section," he said.

I sighed, but I did it. There's not been one complaint.

Lance Gumbs

~~~~~~

In 1981, a seventeen-year-old Shinnecock Indian boy from the reservation came to work for me as one of our delivery boys. At the time, the people on the "res" as they called it, pretty much kept to themselves and rarely worked in the regular Hamptons, so this was a pretty unusual thing.

I didn't actually hire him myself. By this time, I had a delivery manager in charge of a four-man delivery staff. So, on occasion, I'd be out back, either watching or helping the men load the newspapers into one of our two delivery vans, and on that particular day, I saw there was this young Indian guy. Although he was dressed in western clothes, there was no mistaking his features. So I asked Mark, the manager, about him.

"He started last week," Mark said. "A hard worker. Actually, he's quite something. He has a terrific attitude. Seems to really enjoy it."

"Name?" I expected it would be Running Fox or something.

"Lance," he said.

LANCE GUMBS
(Courtesy of the Shinnecock Indian Nation)

I'd been running the newspaper for twenty years by this time. The only contact I had had with a tribal member at the reservation was with a woman named Harriet Gumbs. She had this idea that the tribe should build an Indian museum on Hill Street, in Southampton, which was the northern border of the land that was the reservation. I'd met her and we'd talked about it. The museum should be in the shape of a giant turtle, she said. This was an important icon of the Indian nation. I liked the idea of some new contacts between tribe and town. And I liked the idea of a museum. The building in the shape of a turtle, however, didn't appeal to me.

As for the rest of the tribe, I knew no one. The property was a peninsula, and the white men had given it to them—or as the Indians considered it—had confined them to it, in 1850. There were nearly a thousand acres jutting out into

Shinnecock Bay. If you weren't a member, or if you weren't invited, you didn't go in there. KEEP OUT signs were posted at the dirt roads leading into the woods from Hill Street.

I found time to have a conversation with Lance.

"What gave you the idea of working here?"

"My mom," he said. "She knows you."

"Harriet?"

"The turtle lady." He broke out in a broad grin.

I soon found that Lance Gumbs was, at this young age, several cuts above what I ordinarily expected from a delivery boy. The others were local kids for the most part, sons of fishermen or merchants or summer people. I knew what to expect from them. And they saw this for what it was: a summer job.

Lance also intended to be there just for the summer. But he threw himself into the work with enthusiasm. And he was poised, smart, and very sociable. He had almost immediately befriended everybody on the staff, both in the building and out, and soon it became apparent that he had established himself as the leader of the delivery crew, Mark notwithstanding. But he also indicated he would be leaving the area in the fall.

"Where will you be going?" I asked.

"I've applied to Adelphi and they've given me a scholarship," he said. "I want to study accounting. We need a good accountant on the res. Also, I want to open some shops selling tribal goods. And I want to learn about business."

Lance freely told me about how bad things were on the reservation. They needed lots of things there—medical care, day care, a school, and they needed to be recognized as a tribe by the federal government.

"The state recognizes us," he said, "but we need federal recognition. If we can get that, a lot of things will follow." This observation came from a boy of seventeen.

I had noticed, when you drove the three miles down Hill Street, that a lot of the Indian houses on their side of the street had been built with poor building materials and often without regard to building regulations. There were homes with no windows on two sides for example. There were electrical wires that were held up by two-by-fours. I asked him about that.

"We're not part of the United States," he said. "We don't have any building codes. So people build what they want."

About a week later, I happened to be at a cocktail party in the newly refurbished administration building of Southampton College directly across Hill Street from the reservation. Harriet Gumbs, in headband, was there. So I went over to her.

"That's quite a boy you have," I said.

"You take good care of him," she said.

I talked with Harriet for a little while as the party was breaking up. Would the tribe make further application for recognition? We talked about the state police, who had been on the reservation two days earlier because there had been teenagers drinking too much and getting into fights. I told her I had tried to call somebody at the tribe about it, and had been told this was none of my business. It was tribal business. What had happened?

"Just kids with nothing to do," she said. Harriet looked out across the broad lawn of the college to the wooded acreage of the reservation. "Sometimes I think they just ought to break up the whole reservation and have everybody go their own way," she said softly.

Four days later, a Monday, Lance simply failed to show up for work. It was the oddest thing. And very much out of character. I worried about him. Perhaps he was sick. But later that day, I got a call from his mother.

"Lance is in jail," Harriet said. "Can you help him? I need to get him a lawyer."

I knew a very good lawyer, John Jiras, who had an office right down the street. I told her she should call him.

"Is he expensive?"

"I'll talk to him," I said. "I believe he will do this for nothing. What's happened? Where is he? Can I visit him?"

"He's in Riverhead and asked if you'd visit him. He didn't do anything. He was just standing there."

Within an hour, I was in the Riverhead Jail, a grim, awful place surrounded by high walls with razor wire on top. I stated my name and who I wanted to see and was led through two steel doors, searched, and then told to sit on a wooden bench. After twenty minutes, I was told visiting hours were now over and I should come back tomorrow. I wrote Lance a long note, gave it to a guard, and asked him if he could please give this to Lance just to let him know I had been there, and he said he would. But he could only show him the note and not leave it with him. If I wanted him to have it I would have to *mail* it to him. I said that was not necessary. And then I left.

"Lance didn't do anything," Harriet told me again that evening over the telephone. "There had been another big altercation with the teenagers. The police came and they broke it up and arrested several of them. Lance wasn't with them. He was with me. We were right at the front door of our house, just watching everything. But then, a policeman came over and told Lance to move along. Lance said he was in front of his house and wasn't doing anything. So they arrested him."

"What's the charge?"

"Resisting arrest. And disobeying a police command."

"Is he still in jail?"

"After you left, John Jiras came and bailed him out. He's at home. I won't let him out. But there's a court appearance tomorrow. And I wanted to ask if you could be there and speak to the judge about Lance. We simply have got to keep him out of trouble."

"I'll be there."

It occurred to me that somebody in jail, or even with an arrest record, would not be going to Adelphi this September. I did not want that to happen.

We sat in the first row, me, Harriet, and the lawyer, John Jiras, and we waited as several of the other Indian boys were brought in handcuffs before the judge and charged. One of them was one of Harriet's older sons. Harriet had told me about him. He was just a bad kid. She wished it were different, but there was nothing she could do. A clerk read the charge against him. The judge asked a few questions. Prior arrests were noted. He was taken away.

And then they brought in Lance, and John Jiras stood up, walked forward, and told the judge he was there to speak in Lance's defense. He asked that in this case the charges be dropped. And he told him why. Then he asked the judge if I could speak. And so I did.

"My name is Dan Rattiner and I own *Dan's Papers* in Bridgehampton," I said. "Lance works for me. He's worked for me for a month and a half now. He's an extraordinary young man in my opinion, and he intends to go to Adelphi this fall because he has won a scholarship to go there. I strongly believe in Lance. And I want you to drop the charges and let him get on with his life, which will surely not happen if these charges are pursued. I can vouch for him. And I will keep an eye on him. I feel like a father to him."

There were about forty people in that courtroom, and I was told later the whole town heard about how I had spoken up for this young Indian boy. It seemed to have been a very remarkable thing to have done, although I certainly didn't think so. The charges were dropped.

In 1999, which was nearly twenty years later, we were both still in the Hamptons—well, I was in the Hamptons and he was still in the Shinnecock Indian Nation—and we had dinner together at Gurney's Inn. We had maintained contact with one another as the years had passed. Lance had gotten his degree from Adelphi and was running the Shinnecock Indian Outpost on Hill Street, an establishment that was founded by the tribe over half a century earlier. He also had opened and was running an Indian curio shop in a shopping center in Hempstead.

Now, in addition, he had been elected to the tribal council. Seven people were running for four posts. It had been the first time that the council had not been selected in secret by other tribal council members. Everyone on the res had been given the names of who was running. And the results, with the top four vote-getters joining the council, were also made public. Lance had finished fourth, winning over number five by just ten votes.

That, however, was not why we were having dinner in Montauk at Gurney's. We were having dinner just for the fun of it. And to keep up with what we were doing.

"It's good that you caught up with me," Lance said. "I've been traveling all over, visiting other tribes around the country. I came back to the res last Thursday, and will be off again on Wednesday."

Lance openly flirted with our waitress. He told her that she was beautiful, which she was, and asked her what time she got off, or if she was free before he took off in the middle of the next week. She acted flustered and flushed, but she was also flattered by the attention. Lance left it at that. It could either be a serious offer or just something in passing, whichever she wished. In the end, she gave him her name and phone number on a slip of paper and said he could call her sometime, maybe when he was back in town.

"Are you going to do it?" I asked.

"Nah," he said.

"What's your marital status?" I asked. "I thought you were married."

"I've never been married. You think I'm married because I have lots of kids, some of whom you've met."

"That's true. How many kids do you have?"

"Eleven."

Over dessert, he told me he wanted my opinion about an idea that the tribe was kicking around.

"What's that?"

"A gambling casino."

"Where would you put a gambling casino?"

"We haven't got that far yet. There's a man who has offered to back us. And he's backed several other tribes to help them get casinos. But right now we're in the talking stage."

"I think it's a bad idea," I said. "I know the reservation needs money, but there must be other ways."

"It would be just a little casino. Just a bingo hall at first."

"Maybe that would work."

I had very mixed feelings about what he was saying. I liked Lance, even *loved* him. But a gambling casino in the Hamptons? What I thought was that maybe the idea would just go away.

"Think about it, Lance. All those people, bad elements associated with gambling. It wouldn't be good in the Hamptons. Think about all of the ramifications."

Six months later, the community was electrified by the announcement that the Shinnecocks had plans to build a gambling casino on some land they owned in Hampton Bays. An arrangement had been made with a Japanese developer from California, Ivy K. Ong, who was putting up millions of dollars. The plans were in place. It was going forward.

And now Lance was the leader of the Shinnecock Nation. The town supervisors opposed the idea. Our local congressman said he would fight it. The Suffolk County legislature said they would fight it. And I and my newspaper stood around flatfooted. I didn't know which way to go.

"There's a large hundred-square-mile area of vacant land just to the west of Riverhead," I wrote, "that is a very rural, very depressed area with those living there in great need of jobs. A gambling casino might make sense *there*."

Lance sent bulldozers into the wooded property in Hampton Bays and cleared a five-acre site. The police came and gave Lance a summons. Lance stood in front of the stilled bulldozer with his arms folded and made a ringing speech about what the white men had done to his people.

Five years went by. The developer, Ong, having donated a hundred thousand dollars to the tribe up front, which the tribe used to build a health center, had now had enough. He walked off into the sunset.

But then, five years after that, in 2009, the federal government suddenly bestowed federal recognition on the tribe. Today, officials have announced they hope to bring the Shinnecock's proposed casino either to the vacant lot near Riverhead, or to Belmont Park, the site of the Belmont Stakes. It should—and will—make hundreds of millions of dollars a year for the tribe. And inasmuch as in either case it is less than a two-hour drive west of the peaceful Hamptons, I am all for it.

Three years ago, I got invited, for the first time, to be a guest at the Shinnecock's Thanksgiving feast on the reservation, which takes place annually the week before the white man's Thanksgiving, in the great meeting hall on that property. I was flattered to have been invited, and I went.

Last year I went again, bringing my son David, who is now twenty-six, and he and I sat with Lance at his table. After awhile, I was brought over to pay my respects to Harriet Gumbs, now ninety, who was sitting at another table.

"That's quite a boy you have there," I said to her as I leaned down to give her a kiss on the cheek.

"Yup," she said.

Norman Jaffe

~~~~~~

In the summer of 1984, I bought an acre of land on the top of a hill overlooking Three Mile Harbor in East Hampton. The newspaper was prospering. I was raising a family. I thought I should spend the money I was making to build us a big house.

In my spare time in my office in Bridgehampton, I would sometimes take out a pen and paper and make sketches of this house I wanted to build. It should have a deck across the entire front from which to enjoy this great view. It should have a grand living room with sliders going out to this deck. And, if I could afford it, I intended to build into it an indoor swimming pool.

I had made the design myself. Having studied architecture at Harvard twenty years earlier, I felt I should be able to do this. I had never gone into business as an architect. I had become a newspaperman. Up in my newspaper office, I would make a sketch of the house, then erase it because I didn't like it, then make a different sketch and erase that. I was going around and around. It was very frustrating. Meanwhile, my

NORMAN JAFFE
(Courtesy of the Evan Frankel Foundation)

kids were growing. My money was in the bank. And nothing was happening.

One day, at lunchtime, I walked down Main Street from the office to have a hamburger at the Candy Kitchen. This was an old-fashioned soda fountain and ice cream parlor, very cheerful inside, with stools and a marble counter, soft banquette booths, and a jovial Greek man named George Stavropoulos running the place. Early every morning for years and years, just as the sun was coming up, the farmers of Bridgehampton would congregate there to talk, read the papers and have coffee before going out to work their fields. And when they left at seven, most of the shop owners would stop in, either for coffee, or for a breakfast of omelettes and

French toast, talking about politics and the state of the local economy. After that, tourists and high school kids took the place over. And occasionally there would be a group of artists or writers in to discuss the events of the day.

The place was very busy that day. There were no stools to be had at the counter. And there was just one booth vacant. The rule was that when the place was crowded, booths would be for two or more, but in situations where there was nowhere else for anyone coming in to sit, it was allowed that one person could take a booth. And so I did.

Cookie, the waitress, came over and set me up with the paper placemat, silverware, and menu. Then she left, and she didn't come back for a long time. It was clear they were way behind in getting out the food.

And so, I took out a pen, turned the placemat over, and began still another drawing of what my house ought to look like. And then I sensed somebody standing over me.

"Hi, Dan. Mind if I join you? Seems like they've run out of places to sit."

It was the architect, Norman Jaffe. He was small and slender and strikingly handsome. He had a studio somewhere in town and I'd met up with him from time to time. He was usually deep in thought and very distracted. As a matter of fact, I would sometimes come into the Candy Kitchen in the middle of an afternoon to find Jaffe sitting alone in a booth, doodling on a placemat. I considered him a very exotic figure.

He sat down.

"What are you drawing?" he asked.

"I'm trying to design a new house for my family. But I'm getting nowhere. You know I went to architectural school. But I can't design worth a damn."

"Could I have a look?"

He turned it around and stared at it.

"Where is this?"

"On the hill overlooking the boats that back up to the road on Three Mile Harbor, right at the head of the harbor."

"That's a beautiful spot."

Cookie came over and set out another placemat in front of Jaffe.

I had once written a story in the paper about Jaffe. He had designed a remarkable house on a hill overlooking the ocean in Montauk that looked like some sort of soaring bird. It had won numerous national awards. He was soon featured on the cover of several architectural magazines. I wanted to tour the house and had called the owner who told me that he was sorry, but so many people wanted to tour the house he had stopped allowing it because it was interfering with his living in it. I wrote the article without the tour. But I did get to meet Jaffe.

Now, a thrill went through me, watching Norman Jaffe make his own sketches after looking at what I had done.

"I think, with this view, this needs to be an upside down house," he said. "Take it down a little from the brow of the hill. Park at the top. Then walk in at the second floor from the back. Have the whole house open up before you as you go in. Maybe make it all glass. You could see all the way through to the water."

He was now making lines all over his own placemat.

"I can't believe you're helping me with this," I said.

"I just want to give you a rough idea," he said. And then he smiled, pushed the placemat aside, and picked up a menu.

"You do it," he said.

As the weeks rolled by, I continued struggling with the design of the house. I was now clinging to the rough design that Norman had given me as if it were gold. I could not do better. But I could not seem to finish it. Peaked roof? A soaring roof like his house in Montauk? Could I afford it? Maybe a flat roof would work.

In one sense, I was really glad that Norman had not taken this sketch any further. I might have felt obligated to build it. And it might have bankrupted me.

There were so many stories about Norman Jaffe and the houses he designed. There was one story about a house he'd designed where he had come out to see how the construction was going and didn't like what he saw. It needed to be changed. The owner was there. He walked over and said the stone wall just built needed to be three feet further away from the opposite wall. Jaffe then and there had the entire stone wall torn down and then rebuilt three feet further away. That he liked. Then they proceeded to finish the house. The owner, I was told, was happy to spend the extra money to get the house just right. He was a rich man. If this was what Jaffe, the great architect, wanted, then this is what he would get.

Once, about ten years earlier, I took a nasty fall because of Norman Jaffe. I was having dinner in an oceanfront house in Bridgehampton belonging to Steve Perlbinder and his wife, and we were sitting upstairs in this aerie of a dining room. Both the kitchen and the living room were downstairs, which made serving the dinner an awkward thing indeed, but a maid was managing. At one point, I excused myself to go find the men's room.

"Straight downstairs then the first left," Steve said.

I'd had a bit of wine. I took three steps down this steep, winding, slate staircase and tripped, then tumbled all the way down the rest of the stairs. I suffered a bleeding arm, and Norman was not my favorite person at that particular moment. Why had he done that?

If my first meeting with Norman Jaffe had come because of his soaring Montauk house, the next meeting I had with him was not a meeting at all. Out on the sidewalk, I saw him walking across the street in front of the Candy Kitchen about to get hit by a car.

There was a lot of honking and cursing. But Jaffe, lost in his own world, seemed not even to notice. He made it across the street without looking up, then continued on and walked right past, without seeing me, into the restaurant.

Frankly, I was in awe of Norman Jaffe, not so much because of his designs, but because of the unbelievable focus he brought to bear on his work. It reminded me of the sort of intellectual focus that people brought to the game of chess, or, in my college days, of the time I spent in coffee houses making drawings, reading Plato, and drinking cappuccino by candlelight as we listened to the folksingers. Whatever accolades and awards Norman Jaffe was getting, he deserved them. And so, here in Bridgehampton, people let him alone in the Candy Kitchen and elsewhere, and ran around hysterically trying to keep him from getting killed. He was a god.

One day, about three months after our meeting in the Candy Kitchen, I learned that Norman Jaffe had been given the assignment of building a chapel for the Jewish Center of the Hamptons on Woods Lane in East Hampton. Evan Frankel, the wealthy founder of the Jewish Center solemnly announced it to the congregation on one of the High Holy Days, which I had attended with my parents. The chapel would be totally unique and special, Evan said. And Norman would be the man to design it.

The next day, I called up Norman and asked him about it.

"Why don't you come by and have a look at some of the preliminary designs?" he asked. "We've actually been working on this, on speculation, for about a year."

Norman's studio, to my surprise, was not in some big converted barn sort of space, but just two blocks from my office, inside one of the little houses that sit in a row on the east side of Corwith Lane, looking out across a potato field.

I knocked on the door and a young woman answered. Norman was expecting me, she said.

The interior was not much changed from its function as a house. There was a front porch, a kitchen, a parlor. The rooms were small and dark. We walked through them all to a large family-room sort of space in the back where, on a table, was the model of the Jewish Center chapel.

"This is very preliminary," Norman said. "But it will give you the idea."

The model was unlike anything I had ever seen before. It appeared to be in its entirety a wall of six free-standing wood-shingled buttresses, separated from one another by enormous panes of glass. The buttresses also supported the roof.

"It's a pretty small space," Norman said. "A hundred feet wide, three hundred long, one story, twenty feet high. And it attaches to the main house of the Jewish Center over here."

The main house was an early-twentieth-century Victorian summer mansion with gables, porches, and turrets. It was covered entirely with dark cedar shingles. The chapel was in bright, smooth, shiny wood—light ash, Norman told me.

"One of the most important design elements here," he told me, "is this magnificent copper beech tree that is on the property. I'm sure you're familiar with it. It will be directly in front of the chapel and it will tower over it."

The copper beech stood forty feet high and had a trunk that was fourteen feet around. I had measured it once.

"As for the chapel itself," he said, "we're carving the interior walls in the manner in which Jewish chapels were carved a thousand years ago in Mesopotamia."

When Norman finished explaining the building, he asked how the plans for my house on the hill were coming along.

"I've finished the plans. In another week or two I'm going to send it out to bid."

"Bring it by," Norman said. "I'll have another look."

One month later, on a snowy day in January, I stood on the brow of the hill overlooking Three Mile Harbor and waited for Norman Jaffe to get out of his car on the street below and come up.

He had an old, blue Chevrolet. The door thumped closed. I waved.

Under my arm, I held the folded-up drawing of the plans I had shown to Norman one month earlier. In ten seconds, back then in his office, he had made a few strokes to show me how I could get the design to the next stage. My drawing, detailed down to the fireplaces and staircases, looked awkward and clumsy beside his, and so I postponed sending it out to bid. But I had not been able to find a way to incorporate his new ideas in my old design.

Now, there on that hill, I stood next to a Christmas tree I had planted up there just two weeks before. It was one of those trees you get with the roots all balled up. In our living room down the road, we had decorated it the day before Christmas, put presents under it, and had gone to bed just before midnight. My kids were fourteen, eleven, four, and two. Two days after Christmas, my wife and I and the kids had carried the tree, together with a shovel, out to my car and up the big hill to the land I now owned at the top. It still had pieces of tinsel stuck to its branches. And there, in a strong wind, we planted it, said a blessing over it, wished it well, and left. At the rate this is going, I had thought at the time, there won't be a house up here for years and years.

But now Norman was climbing the hill. And when he arrived, we shook hands, and he turned to stare out at the scene.

"What I want you to do," Norman said, "is set your plans aside for awhile. They're just plans. But this place is magic. Concentrate on this scene. Imagine yourself up here, sitting in a chair, in a warm living room, the fire going, the sun setting over there on the far shore. The magic of this place will overtake you. It has to. And then you will know what you have to do. You won't have to ask me."

We paced around up there for awhile, and he gave me more specific advice. This should go here, that should go there. The indoor pool should go on the south side to catch the sun. Here's where there ought to be a deck.

And all I kept thinking was, well, we could do this, but not over here by this Christmas tree. It would have to be at least twenty feet off to the left. I told Norman that.

"Why is that?" he asked.

"I don't want to harm the sacred Christmas tree."

The years went by and Norman Jaffe continued sketching things on paper placemats in the Candy Kitchen. Bridgehampton, it seemed to me, was his inspiration. The Candy Kitchen was his second home, a block away from his studio.

My house got built. You could never declare it a Norman Jaffe house. It was boxy, it had a cheap flat roof, it had vertical wooden siding. Whatever it was, it did not contain any magic that I could see. But it became our home. And the Christmas tree, miraculously, was spared.

I would see Norman from time to time. As the years passed, he seemed to get thinner and thinner. His pace slowed. One day I saw him and felt shocked at how he looked. He was wasting away. Something was wrong. But he continued on as always and it was not something you felt comfortable talking about with him. He was now building a skyscraper on Wall Street.

At seven o'clock in the morning on July 14, 1993, a Thursday, Norman Jaffe drove down to a house on the beach, went into the garage, changed into a bathing suit, and walked down to the ocean and dove in. It was something, the woman who owned the house said that Norman did almost every day. She was only out on weekends. During the week, she was happy to accommodate Norman for his morning swim. On the weekends, she'd have coffee for him when he came out. But this time, she said to the police on Friday evening, when she came out, she saw his car was still in her driveway, his clothes were in the car, and Norman was nowhere to be found.

One week later, I got a phone call from Arnie Pastor, a friend of Norman's, asking if I would attend a burial. There needed to be twelve men to form a minyan. They had eleven. Would I accommodate them? I said of course I would.

Norman Jaffe's remains were buried in a simple pine box in the Accabonac Grove Shaarey Pardes Cemetery on Old Stone Highway in East Hampton. They consisted of a single bone, a pelvic bone, that had washed up on the beach. It had been identified by an injury to it that years before had required minor reconstructive surgery. It was Norman all right.

It was an emotional internment. His widow and small children cried. I cried, not only for him, but for them. Norman had been just sixty years old. He'd married a much younger woman only five years ago. And there she was, with her two babies. What would they do?

Norman never did see the completion of his masterpiece, the chapel for the Jewish Center of the Hamptons. It took nearly five years to finish. Evan Frankel, who was old enough to be his father, also never lived to see it. But the rest of us did.

Shortly after the chapel opened, it was declared that the huge one-hundred-year-old copper beech tree was in trouble. The landscaping company taking care of it had noticed it had not bloomed properly. No one knew exactly why. A rope was put up around the great tree to keep people off it. Various chemicals and sprays were tried on it. But in 2004, it was very carefully, at great expense, and over a considerable length of time, cut down.

And once again, people wept.

Marilyn Dunn

~~~~~~

"Would you have time for me to talk to you about something?" Marilyn Dunn asked.

We were standing on that particular morning in 1985 in the production room of *Dan's Papers,* where, on Tuesdays and Wednesdays, a team of production workers would prepare the newspaper flats for printing. This, however, was Thursday. And as we had stayed up late on Wednesday night, there was now nobody else around.

"What's on your mind?"

"Well, I wanted to ask you about a ten percent raise."

"I guess we could talk about it," I said. "But you've only been here for a couple of months. It's not usual for somebody to get a raise after just a couple of months."

"It's not for me," Marilyn said.

"Then who is it for?" I asked.

"It's for the poor."

I sat down on one of the stools we have in the production room. She continued to stand.

STAFF IN FRONT OF *DAN'S PAPERS,* 1981
(Photo by Ron Ziel)

"You know, I just moved here from Minnesota. I've joined a church. And the pastor says I have to give my tithe for the poor. It's ten percent of what I earn. They pass the plate."

I thought about this. "Why didn't you think of this before you applied for this job?" I asked.

"I didn't know if I'd be staying in the area," she said. "Then the Lord brought you into my life with this job. And then I joined the church."

Marilyn Dunn was about forty years old, soft spoken, a little overweight and very motherly-looking. When she had first come into my office in response to the ad in the paper for a salesperson, I hadn't thought she would be a good person for the job. She was so sincere, often lacing her speech with references to the Lord. What would the customers think? Well, she was from the Midwest. The staff liked her. And when I called the publisher in St. Paul, Minnesota she had given me as a reference and he told me she had a heart of gold, I decided to hire her. So far, she'd not produced much.

I decided we ought to go to my office. We sat down, she in this very comfortable railroad parlor-car chair that Ron Ziel, a railroad buff, had given me years before, me in a swivel chair behind a desk.

"You know," I said, "I'm starting you out with the same weekly salary as I started all the other sales people."

"I know."

"It wouldn't be fair to them if I gave you a ten percent raise."

"It would if they had to pay a tithe too."

"I know what tithing is. But I thought it was optional."

"It was in Minnesota. I paid what I could. But Pastor Havrilla says that at his church it is what God orders us to do."

"Why don't you go to another church?"

"It's the only Pentecostal Church in the Hamptons. There isn't another one."

"Well, in the Jewish religion, we don't tithe," I said. "But we do pay money to the synagogue from time to time. I guess everybody pays money to their house of worship. But nobody says you *have* to pay it."

"It's in the Bible," she said.

"No, it's not."

Marilyn opened her purse and took out a little well-thumbed Bible.

"The Reverend wrote this note that's tucked into it."

She handed the Bible and the note to me. On the note, in pencil, was Malachi 3:10.

I was out of my league.

"Would you mind if I call my religious leader?" I asked.

"Of course not."

I picked up the phone, called information, and asked for the Jewish Center of the Hamptons in East Hampton. In a few moments, I was connected.

"Hello?"

"Is Rabbi Greenberg there?"

"Just a minute."

I put my hand over the mouthpiece. "I'll put us on speakerphone when I get him," I said.

"Hello?"

"Rabbi? This is Dan Rattiner over at *Dan's Papers*. I'm sitting in my office with Marilyn Dunn who works for me, and she has asked me for a raise of ten percent so she can make a tithe at her church. I wanted to ask you a question. Could I put you on speakerphone?"

"Sure."

I pressed the button. "Can you hear me?"

"Shoot."

"Marilyn Dunn, this is Rabbi Greenberg. Rabbi Greenberg, this is Marilyn Dunn."

"Hi."

"Hi."

I looked at the piece of paper. "She says that her pastor told her that there is a passage in the Old Testament which requires that every one of his churchgoers gives ten percent of what they earn to the church as a tithe. It's in Malachi 3:10. Is this true?"

"Well, it's true in its context."

"What do you mean?"

"Let me open to it. Okay. Here is what it says. 'Bring ye all the tithes into the storehouse, that there may be meat in mine house, and prove me now herewith, saith the LORD of hosts, if I will not open you the windows of heaven, and pour you out a blessing, that there shall not be room enough to receive it.' "

"So it says you are required to give this tithe."

"Yes, but as I've said, you've got to consider the context. This isn't the word of God. All that comes earlier in the Bible. Later on in the Bible, there are all these affirmations made by religious leaders as to the truth of the Bible. And this one is by Malachi, a leader at the time, in a speech he is making to one of the tribes of Israel known as the Levites."

"Okay."

"He's urging them to give to the poor. They're a rich tribe. They have a lot. In his speech to them he very forcefully says they must give ten percent of whatever they own to the poor. And he backs it up by saying it's God's will. But it's just a speech."

"So it's Malachi saying it's God's will."

"Yes. But is he saying it or is God saying this through him? It's in the Bible. So you have to interpret it."

"I see."

"Have I been helpful?"

"You have. I think. Thank you very much."

I hung up the phone.

"So there you are," I said to Marilyn. "It's subject to interpretation."

"And Reverend Havrilla's interpretation is that it is the will of God."

She's a very good salesperson, I thought. I tried one more tack.

"If I give you this raise, and you give it to Reverend Havrilla, isn't it *me* giving the tithe to Reverend Havrilla?"

"Reverend Havrilla gives it to the poor."

In the end, it worked out very well. I gave Marilyn the raise. She stayed at the paper for about a year and nearly doubled the advertising revenue in the territory where I assigned her.

But at the end of the year, she moved on. I had seen it coming. As the year came to an end, she started talking to me quite a lot about an apartment house in Vienna that she had quite suddenly inherited from a recently deceased aunt. She showed me a picture of it. It was six stories high and was on a street corner in that city.

"But the building is in very bad shape," she told me. "And some of the tenants have stopped paying rent. I might have to go over there."

And as it turned out, she did.

For the next two or three years, she sent me occasional handwritten letters about how things were in Vienna. She was staying with a cousin. In the last letter I got from her, she told me that the apartment house was not the only reason she had left; the other was that she had secretly fallen in love with me and that wasn't right for her to do.

I don't know what became of her after that.

The Montauk Project

~~~~~~

In the winter of 1992, a book arrived in my morning mail at *Dan's Papers* called *The Montauk Project*. At first, I didn't notice anything unusual about it. We were a big regional newspaper by that time and were getting about three hard-cover books every week from authors and publishers hoping for a review.

I turned this one over and over. It was a paperback. Big print. Not particularly thick. It seemed to be some sort of self-published vanity book. But what was the Montauk Project? I turned to the first page and began to read. And pretty soon I went to the door to my office and closed it, and pushed the DO NOT DISTURB button on my phone.

The authors of the book were revealing for the first time that the old Montauk Air Force base, which had closed in the late 1960s after a twenty-year run, had not been an Air Force base at all, but a top secret Army project involving time travel, experiments in teleportation, and possible encounters with aliens.

THE RADAR TOWER AT MONTAUK
(Courtesy of the author)

Why I even continued reading this book—it was the biggest crock of crap I had ever read—was because it was branding Montauk with the same sort of nonsense that has branded Lubbock, Texas—where flying saucers landed in the late 1940s—and Roswell, New Mexico—where the army had secretly captured a creature from outer space in the 1950s and performed an autopsy on him.

Why would anyone want to do this? I turned to the back cover and read a little about the authors. I'd never heard of them before. And they seemed to be from somewhere in the suburban middle of Long Island, near Bay Shore or Patchogue, about sixty miles up the island.

I read on. There had been a grisly experiment. Local people had volunteered to be experimented upon and many of them were never heard from again. There had been an attempt to teleport a destroyer located at a naval base in Philadelphia to Montauk four years earlier, and then back to Philadelphia; but when the x-rays were turned on at the base in Montauk something went terribly wrong. The destroyer, with the crew, completely vanished. And nothing they did could bring them back. There was a cover-up.

One of the authors said he had been in Montauk at the time. It had been in 1963. And he had gotten around the entry guards at the "Air Force base" and was hiding in the woods. An eerie green glow had begun throbbing on and off in the tall "radar tower." There was something going on there, that was for sure.

"I had to leave town the very next day," the author wrote, "but the next year, I talked to some of the Montaukers I knew and they told me that in August, after I left, all the animals up in the woods surrounding the town had one day come out and wandered down to Main Street. Everybody knew about it. It was reported in the local paper. But the authorities were telling them never to tell anybody about it."

I can't believe I'm still reading this, I thought. And I closed the book and put it up on one of the shelves in my office.

I took the phone off DO NOT DISTURB, and I opened my door. Enough of this. There was a paper to put out. But I could not get all this crap out of my mind. There were no animals wandering out into the streets in August of 1963. I was there. At least I don't *think* there were animals wandering around downtown in the streets in 1963. I do remember something. Snatches of memory came back.

I had walked into the store. My dad was in the prescription room. My mother was up front and she had a big grin on her face.

"Did you see all the traffic tied up on Main Street down by Vinnie's gas station?"

I told her I hadn't.

"The tide is very high, and Fort Pond has overflowed almost to the road. The swans are on the highway. The big white swans. And they've confronted the cars trying to come into town. They're not letting them through. It's the funniest thing you've ever seen."

I went back out to my car, and I drove down there. You couldn't miss this scene. There were police and fire vehicles, a lot of flashing lights, traffic tied up for about a quarter mile in either direction. I parked and walked toward the commotion. Cars were being directed into one lane because these two beautiful white swans—you never messed with swans if you knew what was good for you—had set up shop on the westbound lane and weren't letting anybody use it. And nobody was doing anything about it, except for some flagmen from the highway department who at least had the good sense to let the traffic down the eastbound lane one way for awhile and then westbound down the same lane the other way.

"Don't stop, don't get out of the car," one of them would shout to the motorists as they went by.

I talked to one of the volunteer firemen. He wore a hard hat. "We tried shooing them. They won't budge," he said.

"We're just going to wait them out." These were the town swans. There was no talk of shooting them.

I remembered when the Air Force radar tower started up for the first time. They had built it in 1960, the year I started the newspaper. Before that, in the evenings, I would come home from working for my father in the store, and as often as not there was classical music playing in the living room, coming from an old hi-fi console my father had brought out from New Jersey. He had tuned the radio to a classical music station in Connecticut he had found.

One evening, in 1960, I came home to hear the music—it was Mozart—and every twelve seconds there was a buzzing sound, bzzzzzt, then a pause with more music then bzzzzzt again.

Dad was in the living room reading the *New York Times*. He hadn't had time to read it during the work day. Mom was cooking dinner in the kitchen.

"What's that buzzing sound?" I asked.

He looked at me brightly. "Oh," he said happily, "they've turned on the radar tower. Look."

Out the window, six miles away, over the trees, there it was, this marvel of the military, slowly turning around and then around again. It was taller even than the Montauk Lighthouse. And every time it turned around to a certain point, there was a buzz in our living room.

"Oh," I said.

Dad seemed rather proud of it. Montauk, in the front lines against the Soviet menace. Imagine that.

"Does the buzzing bother you?" I asked.

THE SECOND
BOOK ABOUT THE
MONTAUK PROJECT
(Courtesy of the author)

"We'll get used to it," he said. He assumed that if any harm could come to us from that buzzing the government would have told us about it. He lit his pipe.

If it didn't bother him, it wasn't going to bother me.

Down at the store, many of the Air Force officers who used to come in—you couldn't miss them, they wore uniforms—seemed rather proud of the new radar tower. They couldn't talk about it, though. We all understood.

On the other hand, it wasn't too hard to get in. In the earlier years, when I had been a teenager just getting to know Montauk, I found other teenagers in town to spend time with—at the Montauk Manor where they worked as waiters and waitresses, at the Montauk Playhouse where they worked as stagehands or actors, or out at the Air Force base—where some of them were soldiers not much older than me. Off duty, they'd be in town going to one of these three hangouts to meet girls, and sometimes I'd get invited out to the base as their guests, to the officers' club. At its peak, I think there were probably a hundred and fifty Air Force personnel on the base.

Of course, there were parts of the base that were off limits. Everybody knew that. But you could get in to the rest of the place by the sentry at the main gate if you were with someone, and go not only to the officers' club but to the rec hall, where there was a bowling alley, or to the PX, where you could buy lots of interesting military stuff cheap.

What was really going on at the Air Force base? There was no airport runway, no airplanes, and no anti-aircraft guns. Adjacent to the Air Force base was the old abandoned Army base from World War II, with its big 16" guns, its barracks and mess halls, and so forth, all lined up on a "main street," so if the Germans flew over in their Messerschmitts they'd just think it was an old fishing village. Now, in the late 1950s, that was in ruins. And because it was abandoned and unguarded, it was open to anyone who wanted to wander in and look around. Around 1959, the Montauk Volunteer Fire Department went up there, and as an exercise, deliberately set the buildings on fire and then controlled the burn so it wouldn't set fire to the surrounding woods as the buildings burned to the ground.

In 1966, as the Vietnam War heated up, money for the funding of the Montauk Air Force Base dried up, men were transferred out, and finally, one day, the commander came into the store to see my father. He was in tears. I was there.

"We've gotten the order to close," he said. "We have six months. You've been wonderful to us. I just wanted you to know how much we appreciated it, your getting up in the middle of the night to fill a prescription for us."

"It's part of the job," Dad said. He really believed that.

"I want us to stay in touch," the commander said.

"I'd like that, too," Dad said.

But the Air Force base did not close, really. All the people had left, and they had closed the gate and left as they had done at the Army base, but you could climb over the fence or dig under it and wander in there. When the military abandons a base they don't clean up after themselves.

It's my belief that it was then, shortly after the base closed, that the people who eventually wrote *The Montauk Project* first came to Montauk to have a look around. They'd go there at night. I know that's what I did. Both with girl friends looking for one kind of adventure, or with guys looking for another.

"Ever climb the big lookout tower?" John Keeshan said one day. We were comparing notes. It was 1985 and John was on his way to becoming one of the town's most prominent businessmen. We were both in our mid-forties.

"Never did," I said.

"Neither did I," he said.

He picked me up on his motorcycle around ten that night. We drove out there, parked in the woods, looked around to

ONE OF THE BIG 16-INCH GUNS AT THE ARMY BASE, 1944
(Photo courtesy of the author)

make sure nobody was watching us, and by flashlight, ducked through a hole in the fence.

What a mess. It was just as it had been left when I was last there, but the walls inside the old rec room were peeling, the PX had a hole in the roof, and there was trash everywhere. We jimmied open a heavy steel door to get inside the base of the radar tower. It indeed looked like something out of a science fiction movie. There were rusted gauges and meters on the walls, big machines with vacuum tubes in them, coils of wires attached to the walls that went up and up, various motors and engines with wheels and gears. There was even a room within a room, thick concrete walls making it apparently shrapnel-proof from any kind of enemy attack. Inside this room were rows and rows of green-screened video monitors, used for something—I could not tell you what. The place stank of mold, rotted wires, and dripping water from the concrete walls. We got the hell out of there.

Alongside the concrete radar tower, there was a tall lookout tower, a steel structure with a wooden platform a hundred feet up.

"Dare me to go up there?" John asked.

"I'll give you ten bucks to go up there," I said. "But I'll watch. I'm afraid of heights."

He took his time. But it was the night of a full moon and he went all the way up. He let out a huge war whoop when he got to the top, and I was just so sure someone would come and arrest us. But no one did.

I completely underestimated what would happen after the publication of *The Montauk Project.* The authors were interviewed in the newspapers. They were on television. Expeditions were organized by groups from afar to go through the old Air Force base. Why had this secret been kept all these years? Tens of thousands of copies of this book must have been sold. Maybe a hundred thousand.

In 1993, I actually went to the trouble of looking through the back issues of the paper to read what was published during those early years in the 1960s. Maybe there was something more than just those two bossy white swans in the road. There weren't.

I wrote the authors of *The Montauk Project* a letter. It was easy enough to do. Because they had self-published their book, their address was right on the flyleaf. I told them I published the newspaper of record in the town back then, I still did, and there was no time when all the animals came out of the woods to walk around downtown. I had been there.

The following year, the authors published *Montauk Revisited.* And there, amidst more fantastic findings about the mad science that went on at the old Montauk Air Force Base, was half a page about me. They were publishing my denial. "But of course he would deny it," they wrote. "He is part of the cover up."

Major Bill Cruickshank

~~~~~~

In 1989, two airlines began a regularly scheduled, twice-daily service between East Hampton Airport and LaGuardia. The planes were twin engine, had two rows of six seats with an aisle in the middle, and you could see right up to the two pilots in the front. There was no stewardess.

And it was cheap. The cost was $49 each way—I suppose the owners avoided a price war by having a brief telephone call between them, probably illegally—and it seemed to me at the time to be the greatest bargain imaginable. It was not only a quick way in and out of the city—the whole flight took fifty-five minutes—but it was also a grand tour of our community. The planes flew over beaches and harbors, ponds and farms, and then soon enough were circling around over the tops of the tallest buildings in the world—the World Trade Center, the Empire State Building, and the Chrysler Building—waiting for a spot in the lineup to make the final approach to the landing at LaGuardia.

When we arrived, there was an even further treat. Our terminal was the original Marine Air Terminal, the very first

HC-130 FROM WESTHAMPTON AIRPORT

terminal at LaGuardia, a domed building designed in the same art-deco style as the Chrysler Building in Manhattan. It had been the waiting room where passengers gathered for the eighteen-hour seaplane flights across the Atlantic, courtesy of Juan Trippe's Pan Am airways in the 1930s. And as it was located in a remote corner of the airport, it was getting very limited use. It was very special for us to be there.

At the time, my wife worked two days a week in Manhattan as a therapist at Mt. Sinai Hospital. She had an apartment in Manhattan nearby. Often we both took the flight aboard one or the other of the airlines. Other than their school colors, they were really pretty much the same.

In the third year of this rivalry, Donald Trump started a helicopter service to make it an even more intense competition. And now that three of them were losing money on every flight, all three services shut down by the end of that year. After that, it was back to the charter business, which is what we have at that airport today.

During those three glory years, though, there were some very interesting airplane stories for the paper.

Once, my wife came home to East Hampton to tell me about a delay on the flight she had taken to the city the day before.

"We circled over Manhattan for about twenty minutes," she said. "And then this woman behind me got up and strode right up the aisle to the two pilots. They were flying the plane. She tapped one of them on the shoulder.

" 'What do you think you're doing?' she said. 'I have an appointment. I'm late. I have to be on the ground in five minutes.' "

"What did you do?" I asked.

She laughed. "I did nothing. And the pilots just ignored her. They had earphones on. She kept this up for a while, and when she tapped this fellow again, he took his earphones off, turned around, and glared at her. Then she went back to her seat."

On another occasion, with the aircraft full, my wife and I wound up sitting in different parts of the airplane. My seat was next to that of a military officer. About ten minutes into the flight, I struck up a conversation with him. Down below, slowly moving by, was the Westhampton Airport, a massive affair with runways that could accommodate 747s.

"There's talk about making Westhampton the fourth major commercial airport in New York," I said.

"I don't think it could happen very easily," he said. "It's still our Air Force base. We fly cargo planes out of there, we have rescue choppers, we do fighter jet training. Not in my lifetime."

I introduced myself to the officer. He was, he said, Major Bill Cruickshank, the second in command of the Westhampton Air Force Base. He lived in the small housing project just to the west of the base. He'd been there three years.

I told him I ran *Dan's Papers* and he said he was an avid reader of it. He even told me the lead story in that week's issue, just out the day before.

"I particularly like your hoaxes," he said.

But I wanted to talk more about Westhampton.

"I've always wondered about the history of the place. I know it was in use during World War II. I suppose the Army built it then. Or maybe before?"

"The Army, or the Army Air Force, as that branch of the service was known at the time, had nothing to do with the building of Westhampton," the Major told me. "It was originally built in 1937 for the Saudi royal family."

"The Saudis?"

"Yes. You know, they were as wealthy then as they are today. And they used to import the very finest filet mignon from here. The country could not support the raising of cattle over there, you know, not in that desert."

"I guess not."

"So the cattle were raised here on Long Island."

"I didn't know that."

"They raised cattle in Calverton, in Riverhead, and in Quogue, in those low scrub areas just north of where the airport is now. And then, in 1937, an entrepreneur got the idea to build a runway, and actually ship the cattle live, in transport planes, right to Riyadh, the capital. They had to make stops along the way back then of course. Madeira. Gibralter. Beirut."

"How do you know all this?" I asked.

"I made a study of the history of the Westhampton Air Force Base. It's really quite fascinating."

I asked him what he was doing flying out of East Hampton to Manhattan, and he told me he had met with the Coast Guard chief out in Montauk about coordinating some project or other. And so he flew out of East Hampton Airport, and was taking a few days off in the city.

"You know, East Hampton Airport itself has quite a history," I told him. "Or at least the terminal does."

"It's pretty run down," he said.

"The original terminal was a World War I Army barracks towed to East Hampton from Camp Upton, the training base in Yaphank."

"I never knew that."

"Well, it's true. I did a story in the paper about it because there's been talk in town about building a new terminal. Maybe have an architectural competition for it. That's the history."

"Isn't that something," the major said.

Soon after that, we made the approach into LaGuardia. I never saw this man again.

But you know, as an editor, particularly a newspaper editor, goes about his day, he gathers up what people tell him and sometimes makes it into a story. I had already written about the East Hampton Airport. This story about the Westhampton Air Force Base was even more fascinating. And so I wrote it up, and I ran it as the lead in the paper the following week.

Eighteen years later, on a cold day in early November, 2007, I went to a sod farm on the North Fork of Long Island to witness an extraordinary event. A ninety-four-year-old man named Bill Schwenk was going to take off in an antique biplane from a sod farm, circle around for fifteen minutes over the town of Riverhead, and then come in for a landing. This biplane had been built in 1927, had crashed into a tree just prior to takeoff when two teenagers tried to fly it in 1930, and had been bought for fifty dollars that year from the Southampton dump by Bill Schwenk, then a seventeen-year-old flier. It was in need of restoration. Schwenk thought he could do it.

As it turned out, however, he never did. For the next seventy-five years, it remained in a barn on this sod farm in Riverhead, still owned by him, still all in pieces.

And then a rich collector saw it and asked Bill Schwenk if he could buy it for a tidy sum. But Bill said no. He was still vigorous at ninety-four.

"I want to fix it up and fly it," he said.

A bargain was made. The collector would buy it and fix it up, and Bill Schwenk, at this advanced age, would fly it from the front cockpit while a second pilot, sitting just behind him, would take over if Schwenk got in trouble.

After his flight, when Schwenk climbed down from the cockpit, I talked to him. He said the flight was worth the wait.

I asked him how he had come to be a flier in the first place. He told me that when Charles Lindbergh flew from Roosevelt Field on the western end of Long Island to Orly Field in Paris in 1927, it electrified the nation and made potential fliers out of just about every young man on Long Island. He had a friend back then named "Slim" Heinecke, and he had been the mechanic for Lindbergh at Roosevelt Field, then soon thereafter moved to Hampton Bays.

"He built this little airstrip here," he said, pointing in the direction of Westhampton. "We had one dirt runway then. And that's where we flew our biplanes from all the time. Who knew that the Army would take it over and it would grow into such a big airport today."

I thought about telling him about the Saudi royal family and the cattle in the flying boxcars in the 1930s, and I decided against it. Instead I asked him this:

"Anybody ever fly across the Atlantic back then before the Army bought the place?"

He laughed. I must be kidding, he said.

I write hoaxes all the time for the newspaper. I figure they are fun and fantastic and people sit up and take notice, particularly of the fact that you shouldn't believe everything you read. Reporters and editors have axes to grind too. So you better watch it.

And I better watch what I write, too. I took in that business about the flying cows out of Westhampton hook, line, and sinker.

The weird thing is that at the time I published this amazing history of Westhampton, I guess those in the know about the real history of the place must have read it and just said, well, there's Dan fooling around again. So nobody ever mentioned it to me. And it wouldn't be until twenty years had gone by that I learned I'd been had.

Alan Lomax

~~~~~~

In 1993, I read that a man named Alan Lomax was going to be holding a booksigning at a bookstore on Main Street in East Hampton. The book was called *The Land Where the Blues Began,* and was about the early folk and blues musicians that lived in the South back in the 1930s.

To most people, this would be considered just one more obscure book signing among many.

But for me, it was amazing. I have always loved music, and this man, if this is who it was, had been one of the two men, father and son, that brought folk music and blues into the consciousness of America. He was a legend.

I went to the book signing. And it was him. Lomax, at seventy-five years old, was a large, vigorous man with broad shoulders and big hands, a suit jacket that was too small, and a soft childlike voice. I stood in the back amidst an overflow crowd as he told his story.

"In 1933, at the bottom of the Depression, my dad was given a grant by the WPA to drive through the south and

ALAN LOMAX

record the indigenous folk music of the people who lived in the mountains of Appalachia," he said. "He asked me to come along. I was eighteen."

Lomax told how they had gotten an old beat up Model T Ford, and with the government money had purchased a huge contraption called a wire recorder. You sang into a microphone and it recorded whatever got sung into it onto a wire. The quality was awful, but at the time they did not know what lay ahead so it sounded just fine to them. What they also knew was this contraption weighed over three hundred pounds, and it took the both of them to lift it and strap it into the trunk of the Model T, where it remained, with occasional changes of the wire, for the next six months. With it, astonishingly, they could record native American folk music.

Without John and his son Alan Lomax, America would never know there had been a Woody Guthrie, or a Huddie Ledbetter, or a Muddy Waters, or a Memphis Slim. But the Lomaxes got them all, with one leading them to another, throughout the hills of Appalachia and on through the rest of the South. Unannounced, they visited hundreds of musicians from West Virginia to the Mississippi Delta to the Brazos bottoms of Texas. They ate with them, they drank with them, they interviewed them, and they either slept in their car or slept in their shacks with them. Today the recordings they made are preserved in a special room in the Smithsonian.

"We had no idea at the time, of course, that our pioneer work would launch an entire field of music that would sweep the nation," he said.

After he spoke, I walked over to the table near the door and bought his book and, as he signed it, told him how much I had admired what he and his dad had done. I also told him that on Saturday nights, I had people over for once-a-week jam sessions. For years we had done this. We played old Woody Guthrie favorites such as "This Land Is Your Land," and others such as "Nashville Rag" and "The Erie Canal."

"What time do you do that?" he asked. "I ought to come over."

"You live out here?"

"My sister and I share a house on Gann Road half a block from Three Mile Harbor in the summertime."

"You live less than a mile from me."

Thus began a friendship between the two of us that lasted for the next eight years.

Alan Lomax, I found out, had an apartment on the West Side of Manhattan, headed up a whole musicology research department at Hunter College where he kept his vast record collection, and came out weekends with his girl friend, a quiet woman about forty years his junior, named Ellen. She was also his assistant.

I had a meal with him at his cottage, which Ellen cooked. It was nothing fancy but the conversation was fascinating. He and his father had lured Woody Guthrie to a recording studio in New York City in 1940. Guthrie had stayed at the Lomax apartment, but on the morning set aside for the session, he overslept and said they ought to forget it, he'd had too much to drink the night before. They almost had to carry him to the studio.

Lomax had done so much collecting of folk music around the world that he had developed theories about it.

"My kids at Hunter are using computers to measure patterns in the music from different tribes and from different eras. We've been able to track population migrations. People didn't believe it, but the music proved it.

"We discovered similarities in music from different parts of the world that had to do with climate. We found that up north, in Russia and Finland and northern Canada, the songs largely were about a single man's efforts against the elements. He would be a brave man, and he would sing about girding for battle, strapping on a club or dagger or sword and shield or whatever he had, and then going out to overpower a bear or something.

"Meanwhile, down near the equator, songs from Africa and South America were often work songs sung in unison by large groups. Think of harvest songs, or mining songs. Harry Belafonte's 'Day-Oh' comes to mind."

In the city one day, Alan took me through his department at Hunter. There were students and assistant professors cataloging albums. There were people restoring old records, making copies of records. Everyone greeted Lomax with great deference as we walked from room to room.

My wife and I went to the movies with Alan and Ellen. We'd go to the beach together. And when we didn't call them, they'd call us.

One day, we went swimming for an afternoon at Louse Point, which is a long, narrow peninsula in East Hampton that ends at the inlet to Accabonac Harbor. The outside of this peninsula has a beach made largely of clam shells and stones facing out on Gardiner's Bay. But that day, we lay on the finer sand of the beach on the other side of the road that borders the harbor.

After about half an hour of baking in the warm sun, I waded into the bay for a swim. The water was cold but refreshing, and when I got out not much further than about twenty feet, suddenly the sand beneath my feet dropped away, and I found myself way over my head and caught in the pull of the tide heading out of the inlet.

My first thought was—how could this be? I was just thirty feet from shore. I'd swim in and regain my footing. But I could not. I splashed around, and more and more I found myself dragged away and down toward the inlet.

Suddenly, out of nowhere, I was in the strong arms of someone holding my shoulders up and my head back so I could catch a breath above the water. It was Alan. He had seen me, swum out, and was rescuing me. The man was eighty years old.

"You'll be fine," he said, as he dragged me back toward shore.

We got to the sand and I lay there face down on it, catching my breath. "This is goddamn embarrassing," I said, referring to the fact that I was fifty-five years old. But there was little doubt of what had happened. And I never forgot it.

About a year later, Alan called me up to invite me to go sailing with him and his sister, Bess, who was out for the weekend. Alan owned a twenty-eight-foot ketch that he docked at a marina at the end of Gann Road. We had been out in Gardiner's Bay together before, he the captain and me the mate, as I did know how to sail, and had been sailing since I was a teenager. On this day, however, though the sun was shining, the wind was blowing about twenty-five knots. Heavy sailing weather.

"We'll be fine," he said. "Come on along. I want you to meet Bess."

And so we went.

"You just sit back and relax," he said to me after we had all been introduced. "My sister is an even better sailor than I am."

His sister, perfectly fit, was in her seventies.

Things went fine as long as we were in Three Mile Harbor, but once we got out into Gardiner's Bay all hell broke loose. The winds picked up even worse, the vessel heeled over, and these two together, one an octogenarian and the other a septuagenarian, were not dealing with it the way they should. They were too slow. But they apparently did not realize it.

"Just lower the spinnaker, Alan," Bess yelled at Alan, and he crawled forward and found himself fouled up in the lines. A wave crashed over the bow, drenching him.

"Is there anything I can do?" I asked. I was getting alarmed.

"We're just fine," Alan said.

At another point, a wind shift sent the boom flying across the deck with a crash, nearly ripping the mast right out of its socket. Lines were flapping everywhere now. And I'd seen enough.

"All right everybody," I said, "I'm taking over."

They stared at me. But they made no objection as, for one time in my life, I stepped up to the plate and did what I had to do to get us back into the harbor to safety. I truly felt at the time that I had saved this ship, and perhaps some of those in it. And as it turned out, they saw it that way too.

Soaking wet and still breathing hard, as I finally sailed us into the slip and tied her up to the pilings in what were now gale force winds, Alan said one word.

"Thanks," he said.

"We're even," I said.

In 1996, Alan suffered a serious stroke and was hospitalized in New York City. Ellen had called to tell me about it.

"I want to see him," I said.

"Don't," she said. "He won't recognize you. Just wait."

But she never called back.

Several weeks later, I called the apartment and there was no answer. And he was no longer at the hospital. I feared the worst. But no. According to Hunter College, which I also called, he was on a sabbatical, vacationing in North Carolina.

"How is he?" I asked. "I know he's been ill."

"He's just fine. Nothing wrong with him at all."

They were covering for him. The professors and assistant professors were in shut-down mode, not telling anyone, pretending it never happened, hoping for a miracle. All that brilliance, all that intellect, all that knowledge and history, on hold, as Alan struggled to recover in a hospital down there.

Lomax called me from North Carolina. His speech was detached and occasionally garbled. At one point, he did not remember who he was talking to.

"We've got to get together the next time I get out there," he said.

"We've got to," I said.

When he died, in 2002, a two-page obituary about him appeared in the *New York Times*. He was widely mourned. Prizes were set up in his honor. I miss him.

Nicholas

~~~~~~

"There's a woman from Kennedy Airport on the phone," my secretary said over the intercom. "She works at Travelers Aid. Could you speak to her?"

"Sure. I guess."

I was editing a piece for the paper about Steven Spielberg, one of our more prominent residents. I set it down.

"Hello?"

"Hi. Dan Rattiner?"

"Yes."

"I've got two Russian men here who have just flown in from the Soviet Union. They say they know you. They don't speak English very well."

"What?"

"They want to talk to you."

"Who are you?"

"Travelers Aid. This is where people come who are lost or confused arriving at Kennedy. We often deal with people from foreign countries. Can I put them on?"

"Sure."

NICHOLAS (SANS BERET) WITH WIFE IN THE SOVIET UNION, 1988
(Photo by the author)

"Hi, Dan, it's me. Nicholas. From Leningrad. We have come to America, me and my brother. Could you pick us up?"

I knew Nicholas. "Where do you need to go?"

"To you." There was a pause. "You will like my brother Vladimir. Come get us please?"

On my way to Kennedy, which is a two-hour drive from Bridgehampton, I marveled at how things sometimes work out. Two years earlier, in 1988, my wife and I spent three weeks in January visiting Moscow and Leningrad. The Soviet Union was still intact, and still the sworn enemy of the United States, ready to fire a thousand nuclear missiles at us at a moment's provocation, but cracks were appearing in Russian society. Something was happening.

Friends we knew had managed to visit there. Billy Joel, who lived in East Hampton, had toured there.

And then, three weeks before we were scheduled to go, we went to a Christmas party in North Haven and met Kaylie Jones, the daughter of the great novelist James Jones. Kaylie told us that she had gone to graduate school in Moscow. She knew lots of people and there, at the party, she wrote down on a paper the names of a dozen people, all dissidents, with whom she still corresponded, and whom we could look up. "Make phone calls from pay phones," she told us. "And be careful. All foreigners are watched."

It had been an amazing trip, and on that trip we had met Nicholas, not through Kaylie but through my optician, Dr. Alan York, who owned the building right in the center of downtown East Hampton, on the northwest corner of the intersection of Newtown Lane and Main Street. It was my annual eye examination, and it was a few weeks before we left.

"I've had a pen pal I've been corresponding with in English for many years in Leningrad," he told me, as he peered through the machinery at my irises. "His name is Nicholas Graszny. I can write him you are coming, and I can give you his name and address. He'd show you around Leningrad."

Nicholas did just that. We met him on the stone steps outside the front entrance of the Library of Russia in Ostrovsky Square late one morning. He was a slender man of about forty, wore horn-rimmed glasses, a black beret, and a black overcoat. He was soft spoken, and he knew English well enough.

He spent the day with us. He took us through part of the Winter Palace, in one room of which was a beautiful young woman guard, his wife. Just say hello, he said. And quietly. She's working. She nodded and smiled. Unlike her husband, she knew no English.

He took us on a walking tour—sometimes we took trollies—through this ancient and beautiful city that seemed to have been frozen in time at about 1910. We visited museums. We visited and toured the gunboat in the river where the Soviet revolution had begun.

People trudged along the frozen streets. Few people spoke. There was nothing in the stores. There were long lines of people everywhere waiting to get things.

At the end of the day we went to what passed for his apartment. His wife was home. She had made tea. Two little children were running around. The family only had one room. We sat in a kitchen shared with other families, and his wife Marita served us what was surely her prized possession, an utter rarity in that city in those days, blueberries. We demurred. She insisted. We ate.

As my wife and I left their apartment, so sweet and so sad, with our hearts out to them, we said the only thing we could possibly say, which was that if you are ever in America, please come see us.

I found them easily enough in the International Arrivals Hall in Terminal 3. They had big, battered, leather suitcases which we hauled into the trunk of my car. Vladimir looked nothing like Nicholas. He had a blond crew cut, a square jaw, and bright blue eyes. He looked like a cosmonaut. And he spoke no English.

"My brother Vladimir is a soldier," Nicholas said by way of introduction. Vladimir nodded once and clicked his heels. He smiled. He looked about twenty-five.

Of course, I had called Alan York before coming into the city to pick up Nicholas. He seemed put off by my call, which surprised me. Yes, he would want to see Nicholas if he was coming out here, that is, if he had the time. He'd have to see.

I also told my wife I was going, and who I was coming back with. She thought this was great.

The conversation on the way back was fairly strained. They had absolutely no ideas, no plan. It had been a long plane ride. They stank of sweat. Mostly they looked out the window in amazement. Vladimir slept for a time.

"How is your wife and family?" I asked. "Is your coming here all right with them?" I was now beginning to talk like Nicholas.

"They come later, I hope. First though, is Vladimir."

I didn't follow up on this at that particular time.

Fifteen minutes from my house, I made a left onto Steven Hand's Path, taking me deep into Northwest Woods. This area had, for many years, been undergoing a slow transformation into a secluded vacation home community. Nicholas looked out at it and said the following:

"Berries good to eat in this forest?"

I thought about it. I told him I wasn't sure.

We arrived at my house, overlooking the harbor, and my wife came out to greet us and help us unload all the

AUTHOR IN MOSCOW
(Photo by Susyn Reeve)

stuff. We showed them to a bedroom, showed them where the bathroom was, gave them something to drink, and left them alone. Forty minutes later, the two of them came out, showered, in fresh clothes and looking much more presentable. We had a meal prepared for them in the kitchen. They ate voraciously. Then we repaired to the living room, which overlooks the water.

Nicholas clapped his hands together. "So," he said. "Let's get down to business. We are here," he said, "to get Vladimir married."

"Who is he marrying?"

"That's the thing," Nicholas said. "We will find him an American wife. After that, everything else will fall into place."

It turned out they did have a plan. Nicholas knew I had a newspaper. And therefore we could put an ad in that newspaper, looking for a wife for Vladimir. There would be applicants, there would be interviews, there would be a wedding; and then he, Nicholas, would return to Leningrad, and Vladimir would stay here and things would go from there. Soon Nicholas and his family would be here.

They were adamant about this wedding businesss. I tried to talk them out of it. I told them this was not the way to go about things, I told them that nobody would answer the ad, I told them that perhaps it would be better for them to go to New York City, and maybe to Brighton Beach where there was a large Russian community. I offered to find them contacts there.

Vladimir, at this point, had as yet to speak one word. He spoke to Nicholas in Russian, of course. But those were brief, quiet exchanges. It occurred to me we had no idea what he was like.

I was wrong about there being nobody to answer the ad.

Two weeks later, on a Sunday morning, we began a two-hour project to clean up the house in anticipation of the arrival of the prospective bride and her mother and father. They would be at the house at 11:30, after breakfast, but before lunch. Perhaps we'd make a little tea, Nicholas said.

The teapot got put on. The sofa cushions got plumped, the rugs got vacuumed, the kid's toys got put away, the jackets got hung, the tables got cleared. At 11:15, the dogs got put out and the kids stashed in front of the TV in the playroom.

And at 11:30, with all of us spiffed up and dressed for the occasion, the front doorbell rang.

The girl's name, I had been told, was Linda. Last name was Stackowski or Stanislovski. Nicholas had made all the arrangements. They came in, we all got introduced, with nods and a shaking of hands and so forth, and we briefly all sat down awkwardly in the living room. We have three sofas in the shape of a U in the living room. We were me and my wife and Nicholas on one sofa, the mother and the father on another sofa, and alone on the third sofa, Vladimir and Linda—who sat at opposite ends of it staring down at their feet and occasionally glancing up anxiously at the other. Everybody was holding tea cups.

Linda was clearly older than Nicholas, possibly in her late thirties. She was big-boned, but very beautiful. I never did find out, but it seemed to me I was sitting with a Polish-American farming family from Bridgehampton who had a daughter who, perhaps, had gotten herself through the marrying years unscathed and was now, as the phrase goes, left with her clock ticking.

"I think we should all go into the kitchen," I said to everybody but Linda and Vladimir. "Leave them alone. Don't you think?"

I got up and my wife got up. The parents looked up and smiled, but didn't get up. And Nicholas looked up and smiled and didn't get up.

In the kitchen, my wife and I whispered to one another.

"This is crazy," I said. "Did you ever see such a thing?"

She shrugged. "Who knows? Maybe it will work out."

We peeked into the living room. The two were now looking at one another. And they were saying things, neither in the language that the other could understand, but Nicholas was bravely translating.

"They're smiling at each other," I whispered.

After about twenty minutes of this, the interview ended. There was the rustling of chairs being pushed back, people talking. We went into the living room, and everybody was shaking hands and preparing to leave. Soon, they were gone.

"So how did it go?" I asked Nicholas.

"Maybe yes, maybe no. They will call. So I don't think so."

And indeed, they didn't call. And indeed, there were no other takers. Ten days later, Vladimir and Nicholas, tired of hanging around our house, but appreciative of all we had done, said that they would be leaving the next day because they knew someone who had an apartment in New York City that they could use for awhile.

"We have better luck there, maybe," Nicholas told me. The next day I took them down to the bus stop, packed them up onto the Hampton Jitney, and they were gone.

I never heard from them again, except once, three months later, I got a letter from Nicholas that both he and Vladimir were back in Leningrad, and they still hoped to come to America some other way and were working on that, and they would let me know.

As far as I know, they are still there.

For about five years after our visit to Moscow and Leningrad, we acted as a way station for many other people fleeing the collapsing Soviet Union, putting up a total of seven of them if you count Nicholas and Vladimir, for periods of up to two months, at our home in East Hampton.

Russians also stayed at our apartment on the Upper East Side. I recall one day coming to our apartment to find four Russian people I did not know playing cards in the living room. One of them spoke broken English and told me that they were friends of so and so, who I knew at Columbia University, and that it was okay with my wife they were there. They were just there overnight.

A while later, I went into our kitchen to see one of the Russians, a bearded intellectual fellow, sitting at the table, struggling to figure out how to open one slice of individually wrapped Kraft sliced cheese. He looked at it. He turned it over and over. He bit at it, which just made a dent of toothmarks in the plastic.

So I held out my hand to indicate he should give it to me, and when he did, I showed him the edge of the plastic and proceeded to peel it back a half inch. Then I handed it back to him.

He looked at it, looked at me, and then we both started laughing hysterically. And he said two words.

"Me Gorilla."

Then he bit another dent in the plastic, and we laughed some more.

Out in East Hampton, we hosted Benjamin and Julia for a month. Benjamin was a theatre director in Moscow. We put an ad in the paper that he did landscaping, mowed lawns, and pruned bushes, and I wound up driving him to where he had to go and then picking him up at the end of the day. Julia had been a psychologist in Moscow. We had a sewing machine. She took in sewing.

After a month, they did an amazing thing. They got the American equivalent of a Eurail Pass and, with just fifty dollars in their pockets for spending money, toured the United States for two weeks from New York to Chicago to Seattle to New Orleans and back. They came back with ten dollars. Amazing. A month after that, they emigrated to Australia and they are there today.

Natasha, a therapist from Moscow, came with her eight-year-old daughter Masha, later to be joined by her husband, Mischa. Mischa arrived bearing gifts. He had a piece of Siberian marble, a bottle of vodka, several military medals, and, astonishingly, a piece of orange fabric which, because of the inscription in English on it, had to be from some sort of American-made lifejacket. He explained that he had been in the Soviet Navy and was a seaman aboard the Russian rescue ship that pulled up pieces of wreckage off the bottom of the Pacific Ocean where a South Korean Airways 747 had gone down. It had been shot down by a Russian fighter plane after the pilots had failed to respond to a warning that they were invading Soviet airspace.

Today, twenty years later, this couple lives in Manhattan. Mischa works doing business strategy and planning for Fortune 500 companies. Natasha is a lawyer. And Masha graduated from the University of Michigan and is now working in Washington as a journalist.

Last fall, as a special treat, Mischa and Natasha took me and my wife out for an evening of entertainment at a nightclub on the boardwalk in Brighton Beach. What a special night. Menus were in Russian. Entertainment was in Russian. We ate blintzes and caviar and Russian borscht.

Over vodka, which we were belting down straight, Mischa told us this wonderful story that was making the rounds in that community.

An American physician of Russian extraction named Boris Kazamov was at a conference in Moscow discussing some of the latest developments in medicine. There he met and befriended a Russian physician, and invited him, whenever he might come to America, to come visit him either at his apartment in Manhattan or at his home in the Northwest Woods of East Hampton where he vacationed sometimes.

When the day came, the two physicians drove out to East Hampton for what they expected would be a quiet week in the country. But on the second day, the American was called in for an emergency in the city.

Before leaving, he said he'd be back in a few days, that there was plenty of food in the refrigerator, and his Russian friend should feel free to do anything he liked—watch TV, read, write, or take walks in the woods.

On the second day the American doctor was in the city, he received a phone call from the East Hampton Town police. They had a Russian man they were detaining there at headquarters. He spoke almost no English. They wanted to talk to him about him.

It turned out that during the first day he was gone, the police had received two phone calls about a crazy man in Northwest who had been seen stealing roadkill. He'd dart out from the side of the road to snatch it up, and then run off into the woods with it.

They had finally done a sting, leaving roadkill in the road, and then catching him when he ran out to get it. They had detained him, and he led them to a house where he had skinned and had hung out to dry various furs from the roadkill. He said he was making a hat for the upcoming winter.

Did the American physician in New York know anything about this?

He sure did. With a promise that the Russian would not be stealing any more roadkill, the police released him into Dr. Kazamov's custody.

Alger Hiss

~~~~~~

As more and more people came out to visit the Hamptons, I found I could save time driving to work in Bridgehampton if I took the back roads to get around busy downtown East Hampton. It was a longer ride. But with the new traffic lights they had put in downtown, in 1990, it was faster.

One day in 1991, at work in Bridgehampton, I got a call from a friend of my mother.

"Did you know that Alger Hiss is living in East Hampton?" she asked. I was surprised. I told her I did not. "Well, he is. And he's a wonderful man. A lot of people in town are helping him. He's nearly blind. He doesn't get around much. I read books to him from time to time."

"You go to his *house?*"

"Yes."

"He must be close to ninety," I said.

"Eighty-nine. Your mother thought you'd like to know."

"Where does he live?" I asked.

"On Osborne Lane."

ALGER HISS, 1948

Osborne Lane was one of the narrow, tree-lined residential back streets I was now taking to get to work. I had been going by his house every day. Well, what do you know.

"Would you like me to ask him if you could come over to interview him?"

"Absolutely."

"I'll set it up."

At the appointed hour, less than a week later, I walked up the slate walkway from the sidewalk to Hiss's little ranch house on Osborne Lane. Directly across from it was the fifty-acre Oakland Cemetery, where generations of local people lay buried beneath rows of small tombstones. It seemed an odd place for an eighty-nine-year-old man to want to live, across from an occasional group of grieving relatives.

The slate walk curved around large landscaped bushes and continued across a lawn. The front door was on the side, under a little overhang. I rang the bell. After a long while, an elderly woman answered it.

"Is Alger Hiss home?" I asked. "I'm Dan Rattiner. I think he's expecting me."

"Oh yes. Come on in. I'm Isabel, his wife."

I walked into a plain kitchen. There were women fussing around, talking to one another.

"He'll be about five minutes, I think," Isabel said. "He's being read the newspaper. Please have a seat. Would you like a drink of some kind?" She motioned me to a chair at a metal kitchen table in the middle of the room. I declined the offer of a drink, but sat down.

It did make perfect sense that my mother would want me to know that Alger Hiss was living in town. In Millburn, New Jersey, when I was a little boy of six or seven, Hiss was a major topic of conversation in our house and, in fact, the country.

Hiss had been, in the early 1940s, one of the most highly regarded diplomats in the American government. Many people thought he would be president of the country some day. He was from a good family, Harvard-educated, handsome and well-mannered to a fault. At the age of twenty-nine, he was assigned by President Franklin Roosevelt to organize the international conference in San Francisco where delegates from around the world would create the United Nations. At that pivotal conference, at that young age, he introduced the keynote speaker.

The year before, at twenty-eight, he had served as a State Department aide when the president flew to Yalta on the Black Sea inside the Soviet Union to meet with Winston Churchill and Joseph Stalin. World War II was winding down. It was 1944. The three leaders were going to meet to decide how the future of the world would look. Pictures of the Yalta conference show the three leaders, sitting on chairs, with some of their aides behind them. Directly behind Franklin D. Roosevelt stood Alger Hiss, a tall, elegant-looking young man holding a note pad. It was Hiss who would take notes about the conference for the president and advise him about the proposed United Nations.

Just a year after the war ended, however, with Hiss occupying the post of Director of the Office of Special Political Affairs, a *Time* magazine reporter named Whittaker Chambers accused him of being a spy for the Soviet Union. At meetings of the House Un-American Activities Committee, the prosecution was led by a young California congressman named Richard Nixon. Chambers, under oath, claimed that he had hidden microfilm given him by Hiss inside a pumpkin in a pumpkin patch in his backyard.

At our house in Millburn in those years, I often heard my parents talking with some of their friends about Alger Hiss. Most of their friends agreed that Hiss was innocent, that Chambers was jealous of Hiss's success and determined to ruin his career. What an injustice.

"It's terrible that a man with such a bright future should have to suffer through this," my father said one evening at the dinner table.

In the end, Hiss was not convicted of being a spy, but *was* convicted of lying to a congressional committee about some small point he later said he had been unable to remember correctly. He went to jail for five years. And during those years, America suffered through the darkest time imaginable. Senator Joe McCarthy was conducting tyrranical hearings designed to discover and smoke out communist spies. People were terrified, and the accusations were leading right up to the steps of the White House. On McCarthy's say-so, thousands of innocent people, many of them famous people, were either blacklisted or sent off to jail. I can still remember my mom and dad packing up half a dozen books about communism that my dad had in a bookcase and shipping them off somewhere.

"This is a sad day to be an American," he said, as he taped the box closed.

It was only in a dramatic confrontation, and on President Dwight Eisenhower's say-so, that in 1954 Senator McCarthy was brought down by an attorney for the Secretary of the Army who confronted this maniac on national TV. It was the first time the medium had been used for this remarkable purpose.

So what was Alger Hiss doing in East Hampton?

"You can come in now," Isabel Hiss said. She motioned for me to follow her into the living room.

And there he was. An elderly man in a suit, slender and elegant, sitting on a sofa. He smiled and motioned for me to sit in an easy chair near to him.

"I hope you won't mind that I don't get up," he said. "I read your paper every week, that is, I have it read to me. I'm glad to meet you."

He looked right at me with sparkling eyes. I hoped he could still see, at least a little.

I took out a pad and asked him if it would be okay for me to interview him.

"Go right ahead," he said.

"How did you first come to the Hamptons?" I asked.

"I have always had many friends at the *New Yorker*. One of them was A. J. Liebling, who had a summer house here on Springs Fireplace Road years ago. We'd come out and visit him. I believe the first year was 1960. Then we bought a house on Old Stone Highway in Amagansett, and not so long ago we sold that one and bought this house nearer to town."

"What do you like about being out here?"

"Both Isabel and I are originally from the eastern shore. She's from southern New Jersey and I'm from Maryland. I'm accustomed to sand, low-lying land, estuaries with the sea not too far away. This place beckoned childhood memories. And it's near to New York. I can take the Friday train out and spend the weekend. And every sport is here. I used to play tennis a lot. And my wife and I did a lot of bicycling. This is wonderful land for bicycling, it's so flat. And of course we're a short walk to town."

I learned that Hiss attended Harvard, then Harvard Law School, and then worked briefly for Supreme Court Justice Felix Frankfurter. At twenty-seven, he joined the Roosevelt administration as one of the president's "whiz kids," as they were called.

"I became an aide to a committee instructed to determine if private enterprise had cheated the government in making military weapons. One day, I met a strange young journalist named George Crosley. Crosley was covering the hearings for a paper, and I invited him to a cafeteria for lunch on several occasions. He was low on funds. It was the Depression. So I lent him money, even gave him an old car after a dealer had offered me only twenty-five dollars for it as a trade-in. Crosley, it turned out, was a very sick and tormented man, and that wasn't his real name. His real name was Whittaker Chambers. And it was he who accused me of being a communist spy."

I decided to skip over the unpleasant parts. "That must have been a terrible time for you."

"It was. But I knew what I had done and not done. And it got me through. I have no regrets."

"What did you do after your time in jail?"

"I became a salesman for a printing company in New Jersey. I visited shops and stores and took orders for stationery and things. I stayed with that one firm until I retired. And then Isabel and I decided to move out here."

I left Alger Hiss believing I had met a very remarkable man. And every day afterwards, when I would drive by his house, I would imagine him inside, surrounded by friends and family.

One year later, which was 1992, Alger Hiss's son, Tony, invited the media to a press conference at the Algonquin Hotel in Manhattan. The Soviet Union had collapsed. The doors of the secret police, the KGB, had swung wide open. Now it could be determined if his father Alger really was a spy.

Along with Tony Hiss at this press conference was his father, who had been brought in from East Hampton, and a heavyset Russian man who had been a general in the Soviet Army. The general, in full uniform, speaking through an interpreter, said he had looked through the files in the old KGB headquarters to see if Alger Hiss had really been a spy. He wasn't. The whole episode with Whittaker Chambers, who had long since died, had been a huge and tragic mistake.

Back in East Hampton, there were now even more cars and more people at the little house on Osborne Lane. Alger Hiss was now giving interviews to anybody who came along. He was soon on NBC, CBS, and ABC, and in the *New York Times* and *Wall Street Journal,* sometimes with Isabel, sometimes with his grown son, Tony. Yes, it was all a mistake.

I went to see Alger Hiss one more time after this. My mother's friend had arranged for me to be there for a particular two-hour stretch while Isabel went shopping. I sat and enjoyed another talk with Mr. Hiss.

My mother, in particular, was delighted that I was seeing Alger Hiss. My dad, who was about the same age as Alger, but quite ill, concurred. They had known it all along, mom said, smiling. "Now Alger can go to the end of his life with everybody knowing the truth," she said.

Six months later, Alger died. And then, after all was said and done, it was discovered that this general had only looked through about half a dozen documents in files at the old KGB office. As for the rest, the name of Alger Hiss was all over them. He had done exactly what he had been accused of. His work, had it continued, would have compromised the United States of America as it fought to win the Cold War.

Sometimes, I wonder what Tony Hiss, who is about my age and surely sincere in his efforts to clear his father's name, thinks of all of this. But I've never asked.

I still do take this shortcut to work and eighteen years later, still imagine myself seeing Alger Hiss in his house there.

Martha Stewart

~~~~~~

I met Martha Stewart through a mutual friend. At the time, which was in the early 1990s, I was on a quest to meet and interview for the paper all of the dazzling movie stars and TV celebrities who had moved into the community.

The theme of these interviews was always the same. What was the seminal moment in your life—that moment usually came around age eighteen—when you decided to do what you have come to do? What happened before? And what happened after? It usually took me two hours to complete one of these interviews. But if pressed, I could do it in an hour and a half. Often, people would comment that I had got them talking about things they hadn't thought of in years, things such as the name of their first-grade teacher and the class play they were in, and they liked that very much. I'm Dr. Dan, I thought with amusement after one such interview.

"Martha's agreed to meet with you for one hour," my friend said. I started to object. "And you are lucky to get it. Be on time. She can be very difficult."

There were no house numbers on Lily Pond Lane in 1993. (The village changed that in 1997. Before that it was just "the

MARTHA STEWART IN AMAGANSETT
(Courtesy of the author)

yellow house next to Martha Stewart's is on fire." But in 1997 that was no longer thought to be good enough.)

I drove down the street, past one mansion after another, trying to find the house, trying not to be late. Perhaps this house with all the flowers and gardens. No, that's not it.

I arrived just four minutes late by my watch. The house was neither the largest nor the smallest on this upper-class lane. And it also appeared to be in disarray. I soon found out why. I knocked on the door. And after awhile, this most beautiful, gentle, and charming woman let me in. It sure was her.

She held out her hand and introduced herself. I shook it briefly, and she led me through a house that was clearly in the process of being redecorated and refurnished. She had, as it turned out, just bought it.

We sat down at opposite ends of a sofa in the unfinished living room and talked. I would have, as I knew, not quite enough time to accomplish my mission.

She had been born and raised in the well-to-do community of Nutley, New Jersey, the daughter of a Polish immigrant who had served in the Polish cavalry in World War II, she said. She had gone to Barnard, had married the preppy son of a wealthy Wall Streeter named Stewart, and had settled in to have babies in Westport, Connecticut. Her maiden name had been Martha Kostyra.

I tried to talk a bit about her mother, but she kept steering me back to her father, who she said was the major influence in her life.

"He belonged to a riding club, mostly made up of former officers from the Polish army," she told me. "He would come back from his early morning ride in his beautiful military uniform, and I would be asked to clean and polish his boots, which were covered with mud. I remember that so well."

Martha, so beautiful, had become a part-time fashion model, and later, during her marriage, had opened a catering business for the parties of their wealthy socialite friends in Connecticut. She had a daughter. And then, her marriage unraveled.

As things sometimes happen when these sorts of marriages come apart, she remained close to her husband, and in fact, they did not officially divorce until 1989. He had gone into the book publishing business, and it was through his efforts that she made contact with a publishing house that produced her first beautiful coffee-table book on food and entertaining, and then, a bit later, on weddings and Christmas. There was one on the coffee table in front of us. I flipped through it.

"I found that I was really interested in this sort of thing," she said. "I connected up with Time-Warner. They have begun publishing a magazine with my name on the front. It has been quite successful. Now I have a TV show."

At this point in our conversation, with the interview a little less than half over, her cell phone rang.

Now, a cell phone in 1993 was an unusual thing. They were fairly large. Not many people had them. But there she was now, on the cell phone. She got up and she began to pace as she spoke. I sat there.

The call went on and on. I riffled through the heavy coffee-table book looking at cakes and Christmas gifts. The call ended, and she made a call of her own, and I riffled through more of the book.

We've all had this happen, I suppose.

Should I just get up and leave? Should I wait? Should I read some more? Should I get up and walk around her, and get in front of her face and point to my watch with my eyebrows raised questioningly? I did nothing.

After awhile, the second of the calls ended and, without explanation, she sat down once again on the sofa. I shifted my weight and took a deep breath to pick up where we had left off, and suddenly it rang again.

Now, she was up again. No "excuse me" or "sorry about this," just back up and pacing, talking in measured, soft tones. She really was just so beautiful, her blond hair swept

back the way Princess Di's was. Now she had begun gesturing as she talked.

And so the one hour ended. I do not recall if she ended
the call to usher me out, or just pointed me to the door
with her free hand, or what, but soon I was back in her
driveway, looking at the scraggly remains of a garden put in
by a former owner of the place. It annoyed me that she had
treated me this way. On the other hand, I could be that way
myself, people had told me, and so maybe she didn't even
know she was doing it. In any case, I had enough for my
"Who's Here" profile. And I would leave out the part about
how I had been treated.

Two years later, I sent Martha Stewart, along with about
two hundred other people, an invitation to my Thirty-fifth
Dan's Papers Anniversary Party, an event to be held at the
oceanfront home of advertising legend Jerry Della Femina
and his wife, TV commentator Judy Licht. They had not only
donated their house for the occasion, but had picked up the
bill from the caterer. It was an enormous success, and with
Roy Scheider and Bianca Jagger there, and Peter Jennings and
Billy Joel standing around the pool, I hadn't noticed that Martha had not attended until late in the party when, just about
at the point when people were thinking about going home,
she did arrive, accompanied by two identical white Alaskan
Malamute dogs that each weighed more than she did.

With her dogs, she made a stunning entrance into the
party—no one else had brought dogs, or had even thought
of bringing dogs—and they trotted along with her obedi-
ently on their leashes as she swept right by me to find Joe
Heller, Warner LeRoy, and Elaine Benson. I could not have

done something more perfectly timed if I had thought of it myself.

In any case, she stayed about fifteen minutes, said hello to everybody important, and then left, still without saying anything to me. Oh, well.

We walked back to the car, my wife and I. "Wasn't Martha amazing?" she asked me.

"Yup," I said.

Soon thereafter, with Martha's magazine a huge success and her TV show a huge success, I learned that Martha was insisting to the executives of Time-Warner that they sell her both the show and the magazine, as she had much bigger plans for them than they did.

My immediate reaction upon hearing this was, well, no contest. The suits at Time-Warner didn't stand a chance. And of course, I was right.

I also learned at this point that Martha had bought a *second* home in East Hampton, not far from the first. I'd never heard of anybody buying two homes so close together like this, particularly when that person lived alone, and my first thought was that perhaps she planned to just go from one to the other and do her decorating skills at each, perhaps in different styles, to see what was what.

As a matter of fact, that seems to be exactly what she had in mind. This second house, on Georgica Pond, was an architectural gem, built in the minimalist modern style by architect Gordon Bunshaft as his own personal summer home in the 1960s. Upon his death, the house passed to the Museum of Modern Art, which in turn had now sold it to Martha.

Soon, Martha Stewart had gotten herself into a bitter battle with her immediate next door neighbor on Georgica Pond, a Manhattan real-estate developer named Harry Macklowe. At the time, she was in the middle of renovating this house, with practically the entire interior gutted on the orders of a British architect she had hired.

Apparently, there was a dividing line between their properties that was disputed. And though this might have just simmered along at some low level, it instead exploded into lawsuits when Macklowe planted some bushes on this property.

Martha had not been consulted. They were horrible bushes, bushes that were in the worst of taste and, besides everything else, were not indigenous to the area. Macklowe may have known everything there was to know about sixty-story office towers, but he knew nothing about design. Martha ordered her gardeners to remove them. Macklowe had them replanted and, soon, there was an injunction against planting anything on this land which, apparently, both parties could look out at when seated in certain spots inside their fifty-million-dollar oceanfront mansions.

An interesting sidelight to this was that Macklowe began a campaign of simply ignoring all summonses that came from an East Hampton Town Court about the matter. He was supposed to show up. He didn't. He was supposed to show up again and he didn't again. After about five of these summonses, he was subject to penalties. But he wouldn't show up to receive them either. The town didn't know what to do. Arrest him? They did nothing.

Then something very dangerous happened. Martha drove home to her Georgica Pond house one afternoon in her Land Rover to find gardeners once again planting stuff where they were not supposed to. In addition, they were building a fence. Wild with emotion, she yelled at them to get out, and when they did not respond because, apparently, they did not understand English, she got even wilder. At one point, she backed up, pinning one of the gardeners between her car and the fence, before putting the car in forward gear and racing off. It had been a close call indeed.

In the end, Martha stopped the rebuilding project in mid-renovation. Her house, open to the elements in several places, now sagged and, in a few years, filled with mold and vines. In one room, a floor collapsed into the basement. It fell into seriously decrepit condition.

Martha was criticized for how she had let the Bunshaft property fall into ruin. Eventually, when she had further legal troubles, and went to jail for five months for having lied about insider information in a stock transaction, the Bunshaft house finally got torn down. Martha's empire, as it was now referred to, was in serious disarray. She might have not had either the will or the way to save the Bunshaft.

Martha advertised her magazine, and later some of the apparel that bore her name, in *Dan's Papers*. But how it was done was unlike any other advertising that we've ever had.

With most advertising that comes from New York City, you run the ad as a result of an insertion order, then send a tearsheet of the ad to an ad agency so they can see that it was done.

With Martha Stewart, there were twelve different people, each of whom had a different job and each of whom had to be sent a copy, so they could approve of it from their different perspective. One would check the color quality, another the registration, another the page upon which it ran to be sure it matched up to where they had ordered it, another to read the magazine and see if there was any negative story in it about Martha, and so on and so forth.

I noticed that my staff was sending these out by overnight mail, which when you added it all up was pretty expensive.

"They require that it be sent to them overnight," one of my staff members told me. "And they have deadlines that must be met as to when they receive this material."

I was told that if any one of these dozen people, all young women as near as I could figure, found anything objectionable about the ad, or if we were just one day late in getting them their tearsheets—correct that: they each required the *entire* magazine, with a sticker noting where the ad was—then we would not be paid.

At this point, I had come to the conclusion that Martha Stewart was just plain brilliant. And I would forgive her everything. She had single-handedly transformed the entire country, bringing pride and expertise to women who wanted to follow a traditional lifestyle. And, in the process, if she had made herself a household name and a fortune—it briefly exceeded a billion dollars according to *Forbes* magazine—and if she busted everybody's chops, had no personal life, was totally focused and wildly successful—wasn't that what America was all about? And wasn't that what I was celebrating in my "Who's Here" interviews?

I thought maybe she'd like to have a weekly column in *Dan's Papers* at that point. I tried. I called her up. Sorry. Not at this time. Oh, well.

All through this, I continued to mention her just about every two or three weeks in our "South of the Highway" boldface names column. She had bought a home in Westchester and so now had at least four residences that I knew of, but whenever we wrote about her, we referred to her as "Martha Stewart of East Hampton."

Hey, if you were famous and bought here, you were one of us. Fair is fair. So that's what I can tell you about my good friend Martha Stewart.

Kurt Vonnegut

~~~~~~

In the autumn of 1993, I had a standing date to have dinner on Tuesday night with Kurt Vonnegut at Bobby Van's restaurant in Bridgehampton. It was always just the two of us. These dinners ended abruptly on a frightening note which I will get to later, but during these ten weeks or so we had a very nice time.

After the fifth week of these dinners, it occurred to me I ought to write some of what we talked about down. I felt guilty about doing this. The dinners were just the two of us, and surely it was a private thing. On the other hand, there was nothing that we talked about that might be privileged. And since he was, at the time, one of the greatest writers in the English language in the world, I thought that I ought to do this just for posterity. I never intended to sell this story or publish it, and until today—seventeen years later—never have. I just thought maybe some future biographer might want to know what we talked about during those dinners, particularly the parts where we talked about literary things.

THE KURT VONNEGUTS

The part I felt guilty about was that he did not know I was doing this. After all, who writes about dinner conversation? Well, maybe Boswell. Here is what I wrote:

CONVERSATIONS WITH KURT VONNEGUT, 1993

I do not recall how the conversation turned to Ruth Kligman. But it did.

"Now here's a woman who has been the mistress of six or seven of the best abstract expressionist painters in the world," Kurt Vonnegut said. "She wrote a book about it. Or at least she wrote a book about her affair with Jackson Pollock. And she was only with him for maybe a month and a half."

"I spoke to her on the phone once," I said. "I thought she was very uncooperative and nasty and full of herself."

"Well, like I said, she was only his mistress for a month and a half."

Both of us knew the spectacular and fiery car crash she was in with Pollock. She and Pollock were in an open convertible in East Hampton on their way to a homecoming party for Alfonso Ossorio who had just returned from the Philippines. Pollock was drunk. He and Ruth argued. Pollock turned the car around again and headed back to his studio in Springs. Then he turned the car around and headed back to Ossorio's house in Wainscott. Then he turned the car around a third time, put his foot to the floor and, on Springs-Fireplace Road, lost control, turned the car over, and smashed into a tree. Kligman survived. Pollock was, among other things, beheaded.

"Reviews of her book said it was very sappy," I said. "I haven't read it."

Vonnegut shrugged. "I once asked Syd Solomon how Ruth Kligman came to be the mistress of so many abstract expressionists. He said, well, we'd be out there painting in our studios and there'd be a knock on the door. There would be Ruth Kligman. 'I'd like to be your woman,' she'd say. And we'd say 'okay,' and we'd motion her toward the kitchen. Then we'd go back to our painting."

We are sitting, Kurt Vonnegut and I, in Bobby Van's restaurant in Bridgehampton, New York. This place is about eight miles from where, almost thirty years ago, Jackson Pollock lost his head. We have kept, off and on for two months now, a sort of standing appointment to have Tuesday dinner together at exactly six-thirty.

Usually, I am quite prompt. Today, however, I am three minutes late according to the clock on the far wall. Vonnegut is already seated at this square table in the middle of the room. It is always this table. I hurry over.

"I'm just finishing up," he says, sarcastically.

For the record, this is mid-November of 1993. We've talked about wives, about children, about where we have grown up. At the present time I am fifty-four. Kurt is seventy-one.

"Syd Solomon was involved in something resembling a scandal, you know," Kurt said. "He signed on with this company called the Great Writers Series. It also was the Great Artists Series. People would send in their work and supposedly the Great Artists or the Great Writers would review it. Everybody was paid in stock in the company. I don't think they actually did anything."

"They must have done *some*thing," I said.

"Well, I guess they did. I don't know. Anyway, Syd had all this stock and a lot of other people had all this stock and the stock went up. People wanted to sell. But Solomon said no, no, hang on to it. Years went by. And then there was a scandal and the stock dropped like a stone. Everybody lost everything."

"There's a bright side," I said. "Think of all those years where everybody thought they were so rich. Walking around, thinking they had all this money if they ever sold the stock. It's something."

I couldn't tell if Kurt liked this or not. I tried a joke.

"I heard this on the radio this morning," I said. "I didn't know you could tell jokes like this on the radio."

"You can tell *any*thing on the radio."

"Little boy walks into his parent's bedroom at the wrong moment. They are in flagrante delicto. 'What are you doing?' he asks. 'We're making a baby,' father says. 'Well, flip her over,' the boy says, 'I'd rather have a puppy.'"

"I met Imus once," Kurt says. "It was about twenty years ago. He was already well known. A friend brought him over. Nice guy. I remember he brought his own liquor."

The popularity of Imus today, and also that of porno radio personality Howard Stern who, as we are sitting here, is occupying the number one spot on the *New York Times* bestseller list with his book *Private Parts,* made me think of the almost smothering way that the media had come to dominate our lives.

"Back in the 1940s, when I was a little kid," I said, "people had friends. They'd invite them over almost every night. I remember my parents had a

Wednesday night bridge club. People would sit around and talk to one another. This bridge club went on for ten years. My parents *still* see these friends today. I was thinking about this this morning. Now, everybody sits home and watches television. And I'm the worst. We sit and watch television or we rent a movie and watch it on the VCR. Then while this is going on, I go to my desk and I mess around on a laptop computer. The phone rings and I answer that. And I'm still watching the movie."

Kurt leans forward conspiratorially. His eyes twinkle. "I got the whole computer rig," he said. "Apple gave it to me. They took pictures of me at it. So I was upstairs yesterday and I played this game against Sargon. He's an evil son of a bitch, Sargon, and I beat him three times. I couldn't believe it. I wanted to run downstairs and tell everybody, hey, I beat Sargon. They wouldn't have cared."

"Isn't there some way you can list yourself inside the computer as a winner?" I asked. "They do that with video games."

"Maybe. But I haven't got that far yet. I even thought I'd tell Apple. Hey, I beat Sargon. I don't think they want to hear that."

Here is how we have come to have dinner together at Bobby Van's, always on a Tuesday and always punctually at six-thirty.

Before two months ago, I didn't even *know* Kurt Vonnegut. I hadn't even met him. It is true that running this newspaper in a land of famous artists and writers and celebrities, I have come to know about everybody else. But Kurt Vonnegut had escaped me. He had, in fact, intimidated me. I absolutely love his writing and I have loved it for thirty years. I'd see him around and a case of hero worship would come over me. I could talk to everybody else, but I could not talk to him.

And so, our meeting took place by chance. And it took several chance meetings in the same location before we kind of hooked up. Here's the story:

For several years now, I have gone almost every day in my Toyota Previa all-wheel-drive van down to the ocean three miles away from my office. I have a little laptop computer. And I sit there in the afternoon, usually for one-and-a-half to two hours, in the front passenger's seat of the car perched on a sand dune, and I look at the ocean and write the stories for the paper on my laptop. A big black dog comes with me and sits in the back. If anybody I know approaches my van—and I always go to private out-of-the-way beaches where this is pretty unlikely—my dog barks up a storm, making conversation almost impossible. I smile sheepishly, and I hold up my laptop to indicate I am working and my friends walk away.

Incidentally, you would be amazed at how many times I am down at the beach, and somebody I know comes down there with a member of the opposite sex that is not the designated member of the opposite sex I am familiar with. They see me and look away.

Then they trudge down the beach and they trudge back and they drive away in their cars. Amazing.

About a year ago, I found my very "favorite" sand dune. It is at the end of Sagaponack Main Street. I have been coming to this spot regularly ever since.

And then, one day, there he was. He is slender, has this great shock of curly hair and a moustache, and he was apparently down to look at the surf. My immediate reaction was intense and mixed. Perhaps he would see me and come over. I was in the middle of something. I would like that. I wouldn't like that. All sorts of emotions coursed through me. I had just finished reading his latest book, *Hocus Pocus,* and I had loved it. Now there he was. He walked around on the beach for a while and then he went away.

About a week later, on another magnificent autumn day, he was out there again. He was wearing a big, bulky, handknit turtleneck sweater, the same as he had worn the first time. No coat. Again, he walked around and left. Earlier, someone told me his house was in Sagaponack, not far away. This stop at the beach must be part of a walk that he takes.

The third time this happened, we were, already, old friends. Not a word had been spoken. Yet there it was. When I called to him on some pretext, he came over and he leaned on the window and we talked for a considerable time. Yes, he knew who I was and yes, he had noticed me. I showed him my laptop and described for him the story I was writing.

All this time, in the back seat, my dog was barking madly and, as always, no matter what I commanded, would not shut up. We talked loud.

"I kind of go into another place when I write," I said. "I don't know where I am. Could be anywhere. I remember once I was writing about the only witch that the Hamptons have ever had. It was 1680 and John Gardiner was running down to East Hampton Town Pond to rescue this purported witch Goody Garlick from the townspeople who had her tied to a ducking stool and were going to see if she'd drown. And John Gardiner is making this speech about how she is not a witch, and I look up and out the window a woman walks by with a pot on her head. And I remember. It's January and I'm in a rented house in Guatemala. Oh."

Kurt Vonnegut seemed to like this story. We talked more. After awhile, my dog gave up and lay down on the back bench seat and went to sleep. And then Kurt Vonnegut said he had to go and he left.

About a month went by after that and I did not see him. That was it, I figured.

And then one evening I was at Bobby Van's having dinner with some other people and there he was, sitting at a table by himself, eating, reading a newspaper, looking lonely. He looked up and acknowledged me with a nod. Then he cut himself another piece of steak. One of the people I was with said he had heard that Vonnegut and his wife, photographer Jill Krementz, pretty much go their separate ways. But he wasn't sure about that. We went back to our own dinner party.

The next day, a Tuesday, it occurred to me in the morning—why I hadn't thought of this the day before I do not know—that my family had gone off on a trip and I really could use a dinner partner. Otherwise, I too would be eating alone, something I don't like to do. On the other hand, the morning went by at the office busy with telephone calls and I didn't call anybody. And soon it was two in the afternoon and I was down at the beach writing on my laptop.

Well, I thought, why don't I call Kurt Vonnegut? Indeed, there's a pay phone down at the pavilion there at the end of Sagaponack Main Street. Well, I thought, there's a good reason I can't call him. I don't have his phone number. It's unlisted. Oh well, I thought. It was a good idea but I guess it is not to be.

And then, right alongside my car, there he was again. I leaned out the window.

"Hey, Kurt!" I shouted. "Would you like to have dinner with me tonight?"

We made a date for dinner at six-thirty at Bobby Van's restaurant. Then Kurt Vonnegut went for a walk down by the ocean and I went back to my computer. But I was floating on air for the rest of the day.

During that first dinner, we spent much of the time describing our respective backgrounds. Vonnegut, apparently, was under the impression that I was native to the East End. Well, I wasn't. I had grown up in Millburn, New Jersey, "near Newark, the land of Philip Roth," I told him.

Vonnegut told me about his growing up in Indiana.

"I got married very young," he said. "I was nineteen and I was going off to war. It seemed like a good thing to do. Then I came home and we started having kids. I'd have to make a living. I'd been writing short stories for magazines. Now a relative of mine said he could get me a good job working for General Electric in upstate New York. I went to see them. But they didn't offer me quite enough money. If they had, you'd probably be sitting here in Bobby Van's having dinner with a guy who'd been retired from General Electric for the past six years. I'd have a gold watch. You know that picture up there over the bar?"

Above the bar at Bobby Van's is a photograph of Bobby Van's with four of its most famous writer/artist-patrons facing the camera. They are James Jones *(From Here to Eternity)*, Willie Morris (editor of *Harper's* magazine), Truman Capote *(In Cold Blood)*, and Howard Kanovitz, the photorealist painter. It was taken about 1979 by Jill Krementz.

"My wife took that picture," he said.

"I know," I said.

We sat silently, for awhile, then we began talking about the kinds of love we had known. Companionship. Lust. True love. Puppy love.

"I once asked a group of women how many times they had been in love," Kurt said. "I was surprised at the answer. The average was three. I would have thought it would have been more than that. Maybe six."

"How many times have you been in love?" I asked.

"Three."

"Well, if it was good enough for you, then it should be good enough for them. Personally, I think I've been in love about forty times in my life."

Kurt raised an eyebrow.

I told him how I had been married three times, how I had two children from a first marriage and two children from a second marriage, and now I was on my third marriage. And all the women and all the children lived within three miles of me. He raised an eyebrow even further.

"Sounds like you're still in love with all of them," he said.

"Maybe."

"You're making yourself the grand patriarch. Norman Mailer did that. There are a whole slew of women and children he supports."

We talked more about Bobby Van's. For more than twenty years, it had been considered a mecca for some of this country's most famous writers. Now Bobby had gotten into financial troubles and had sold the place. There were new owners. We lamented Bobby together.

"I heard he's playing the piano at a bar in Southampton," Kurt said.

"Yeah. It seems kind of sad. I had thought he would have gone on and done something else, but I guess he only wants to play his piano."

"I once played poker with Bobby Van," Kurt said. "It was quite a group. The others were James Jones and Irwin Shaw. Shaw and Jones were these two big novelists and they were yakking away about their books and arguing about this and arguing about that and Bobby Van was looking down, focusing on the game. His pile of chips got bigger and bigger."

"So much for big egos," I said. "And how did you do?"

"A fair question." He thought about it. "B Plus," he said.

I recalled that it was at Bobby Van's that I got the first inkling that my first wife was about to divorce me.

"I'll never forget it. She and I were sitting at the bar. And Marina Van came over. She had something to tell me and couldn't stop laughing. She says, 'You see those two ladies over in the corner booth?' and we look over and we see them and she says, 'They're tourists. They came in and said they had heard they could see somebody famous at Bobby Van's, and I said well over there in the corner is James Jones and over in that corner is Truman Capote, and at that point they interrupted me and said isn't that guy over at the bar *Dan Rattiner* and I said, indeed, yes, it was. And I thought you'd just have to know about this.' And there at the bar my wife turned to me and she said 'if I hear one more nice thing about you I'm going to throw up.' And that's how I knew my marriage was coming to an end."

"You going away this winter?" Vonnegut asked.

"My wife and I have talked about it. I think we're going to Greece. It's a warm place. And I've never been there."

"Sometimes I wonder why I live in this climate," he said. "You go out to the car and you wait until all the heat comes on."

"They've got remotes now you can use to start your car."

"Sometimes I wonder how they could ever have settled the prairie," he said. "Out in the Midwest, they dug holes in the ground. They lived in them. Can you imagine that? There were no trees to cut down. It must have been so, so hard. I think about it sometimes and I really feel sorry for them."

"Well, everything is relative," I said. "Maybe one winter is not quite as bad as the one before. Or maybe they built fires."

"They did build fires."

"How about you? Are you going away?"

"I just got back from Iceland. Gave a talk there at a literary festival. They don't have trees there either. Until a hundred years ago everybody lived in mud houses. Then the English and the French came and they brought two-by-fours. Have you ever been to Sweden?"

"No."

"I once went with my wife to Sweden. We went to this club and got into the sauna. Then we thought—well, this is what they do here in Sweden—and so we got out and ran naked through the snow and jumped into the swimming pool." Vonnegut's eyes twinkled. "They were shocked. They had never seen anybody do that."

"I think they do that in Finland," I said.

We both laughed so hard and long we almost fell off our chairs.

The accounting of these dinners ends at this point, because the appointment to have these dinners ended very abruptly.

On November 22 of that year, my wife and I—my third wife—were in New York City at the Plaza Hotel for the annual Guild Hall Gala. It was a formal affair. I was in a tuxedo, and Susan was wearing a beautiful dress. Then, through the crowd milling around drinking champagne there in the grand ballroom, I saw Kurt sitting on a chair along the wall, sipping champagne by himself. He did look slightly ridiculous in a tux. But there he was, and so I walked over and sat down next to him.

We immediately picked up with the conversation we had ended with two days before. It was good to see him.

After awhile, I became aware that there was somebody standing behind me, looking down at us. I looked up. It was my wife, her hands on her hips, her head cocked to one side. She did not look happy.

"Um," I said. "Hi. Susan, this is Kurt Vonnegut."

"So you're the guy who is keeping my husband on Tuesday nights," she said. She was completely serious saying this.

Then she walked away.

I looked at Kurt and saw fear in his eyes. And I knew from how I felt that he was looking at me and seeing fear in my eyes as well.

"Well," I said, "I've gotta go."

I got up and walked quickly to Susan's side. Kurt and I both knew what had just happened. There was no need for either of us to call the other about the fact that the dinners could not continue.

On the other hand, I kept getting things in the mail from Kurt every once in awhile. Once it was a poem.

Another time he sent me some drawings. And another time, it was some handwritten comment about something I had written.

I honestly was very flattered to be receiving these things. And I published them, the poem and the letter in the letters-to-the-editor column, the drawings in an article about an upcoming art show of his work.

Almost a year went by. And then I thought perhaps it would be all right to call Kurt up to try to restart our friendship of the year before. He certainly knew I did profiles of prominent people in the newspaper. I'd ask him if I could do one of him.

"Sure," he said.

"Whenever is good for you," I said. "Anytime and anywhere."

I was surely fishing for Bobby Van's.

"Come over here," he said. "To my house. You know where I live?"

I knew that by this time. He lived in a beautiful old shingled saltbox, probably the oldest house in Sagaponack, right on Main Street.

"I sure do."

"Come by on Thursday afternoon at four."

At the appointed time, late in the afternoon of that November day, I knocked on the front door. Nobody was home. But it occurred to me that perhaps he and his wife might be around back and just couldn't hear the knock. And so I peered around the side yard. And there, standing by the swimming pool, which had been covered up for the winter, was Kurt. He was raking the autumn leaves from the bricks. And when I called to him, he turned and smiled and invited me to come over and sit with him at a wooden picnic table by a barbecue that was there.

We chatted briefly, and I soon realized he was the only one home. We were alone.

I took out a pad.

"So you know how I do these things," I said. "I sort of start from the beginning and write it all down. Where were you born and raised?"

And so it went. After about twenty minutes, we had gotten to the time in his life when he had joined the army and gone off to fight in World War II against the Germans.

I sat forward on my bench. This was of considerable interest to me—my hobby was reading books about the Second World War.

"What unit were you in?" I asked him.

He told me. And so we talked for quite some time about the battles in Europe in 1944 and 1945.

"I thought this was supposed to be an interview about me," he said.

"Well it is. You were there."

A little later, we began to talk about how he had been taken prisoner and brought down to a concrete underground slaughterhouse in Cologne. The next day, the city was set on fire by Allied bombers and practically the whole place was destroyed. This led to the writing of what is perhaps Vonnegut's best-known book, *Slaughterhouse-Five*. And yet, at that particular moment, I didn't want to talk about *Slaughterhouse-Five*. I was more interested in the fact that after his rescue from the remains of Cologne, he had gone on to participate in the Battle of the Bulge, which was Hitler's last desperate assault of the war before capitulation. Vonnegut and tens of thousands of other American troops were surrounded in an ever-shrinking pocket in Belgium for nearly a month. Finally, they broke out.

Suddenly, Vonnegut stood up.

"I know why you're asking me all this," he said. "Veteran's Day is next week. You're writing something about Veteran's Day. This interview is over!"

I was stunned. And then he turned, walked over to where he had leaned the rake against the barbecue pit, and began raking leaves once again.

Scrape. Scrape. Scrape. He had his back to me. I got up and, without saying a word, left.

I really did think this was once and for all the end of our friendship. And I did not try to call on him again. Also, for several years, I was no longer receiving things in the mail from him.

But every once in a while, that final conversation would come up in my mind, and I'd think of what I wanted to say and didn't say—that it was just that I was a World War II buff, and no, the questions were really not intended to trick him into providing me the material for an article for Veteran's Day.

About four years later, Kurt was approaching eighty years old. Though I was not in touch with him directly, I did follow his career. He had said he would not write another book, but then he did. It was called *Timequake* and I read it and it was another classic Vonnegut.

At this time, because Vonnegut was getting older, people talked about the fact that he had been passed over when they were handing out the literary awards and it was not right. People said he was perhaps America's very best writer. But the critics disagreed.

And now Kurt once again began to send me stuff, and occasionally write letters about things I had written in the paper.

Around 2000, a man named Ira Rennert bought a fifty-seven-acre oceanfront farm in Sagaponack about a mile from Kurt's home, tore up all the rich potato crops and topsoil, and proceeded to begin construction on what many said was the largest private home ever built in America. It would be more than a hundred thousand square feet in size. It was a disgrace, people said. It would ruin Sagaponack. Kurt Vonnegut said that if this project continued, he personally would leave Sagaponack and never come back. It continued. But Kurt stayed.

Kurt Vonnegut died in April of 2007 at the age of eighty-four. He had taken a fall, banged his head, and had slipped into a coma from which he never recovered.

I have this very strong feeling that Kurt and I had a whole lot of unfinished business we needed to take care of. I still want to call him about the World War II misunderstanding. We'd have dinner. We would make up.

Then, if he wanted, he could go.

Michael Forbes

~~~~~~

The trouble began on the morning of October 26, 1996, at nine o'clock. I had dawdled over breakfast in East Hampton longer than I should have, so, now I was fifteen minutes late for the editorial meeting in Bridgehampton. I hurried inside. And there they all were, seated at the round table in the glass room just to the right of the front door—five annoyed-looking people.

"This is the third week in a row you've been late," Elaine Benson said.

"Sorry," I said, slinking into a chair.

"You know we all have other things we have to do today," Elaine continued.

"I'll try and do better," I said

We had been having this meeting every Friday morning for years, ever since the paper had grown so large that I could no longer write all the stories myself to fit into its pages.

I looked around the table. There was Debbie Tuma, a freelance writer who had grown up in Montauk and wrote features. There was Jan Silver, who wrote a column about

MICHAEL FORBES (RIGHT) AND FRIEND
(AP photo)

cultural events. There was my managing editor, the man who made the trains run on time at the office, Dick Brass. And there was Elaine Benson, the prominent art gallery owner who lived in a house adjacent to her gallery just a block down the street.

Of course, we couldn't just go around the table asking people what they knew about events coming up. People didn't know everything. And so we would read the competition.

The way it worked was that one person, the designated "reader," would read the entire contents of the two competing weekly newspapers that had come out the day before. Then they would give brief summaries of each article in them, from front to back, one at a time, and the rest of the table, following along with their own copies of that paper, would comment about them. After each story was presented, I would decide whether to assign a reporter or not.

Of course, these articles were from the week that had just ended. We were looking for stories that would run a week into the future, so there was a danger we would just be rehashing something that already was in a newspaper. The ideal story read at this meeting would be about a big controversy during the past week that would end with the phrase, "and so there will be a big demonstration in front of town hall this upcoming Saturday. Fireworks are expected. But the police will be on hand."

We'd cover the Saturday demonstration.

It was not lost on anybody at this meeting that we were sitting at a table in a glass room facing right out to the pedestrians and automobiles going by on the Montauk Highway. People could look in at us. And if they did, they could see *Dan's Papers* editors, all holding up copies of the same issue of the competition right there in the *Dan's Papers* offices, talking about what they were reading in the competition.

Once, Channel 12 News, doing a story about the media in the Hamptons, asked if they could video our weekly editorial meeting. No, I had told them. That's private. Sorry.

Anyway, at this particular meeting, Elaine Benson, who had been the designated reader of the papers for the prior ten years, proceeded with the reading. She read about an upcoming film lecture at the college (we'd cover it), a guy who wanted a zoning variance for the house he had inadvertently built too close to his neighbor (pass), and a new leaflet being handed around involving Halloween safety tips (pass again).

"Now here are two-and-a-half pages of coverage on the upcoming election. Interviews with all the candidates," Elaine said.

Pass.

"Why don't you endorse some of these candidates?" she pressed.

"Well, once in a while, I do," I said. "If it seems to be important. But mostly I like to stay independent."

"The last time you endorsed anybody was during the Reagan administration."

"I like to stay out of politics."

There were also two other reasons I didn't do endorsements. One was that I felt that *everything* in the paper was opinion and said what it had to say, so you didn't need endorsements. The other was that we were in a very awkward competitive position as far as local political advertising was concerned. One of our competitors covered Southampton Town. The other covered East Hampton Town. As we covered both towns and then two more towns, it was hard to sell candidates on the idea of advertising with us. Much of what they would spend would go to areas where the people could not vote for them.

That night, after dinner, I got to thinking about what Elaine Benson said. She was one of my best friends. I really ought to listen to her. And so, maybe this one time, I would make endorsements.

There was our state assemblyman running for reelection. Fred Thiele, a Republican, had been an excellent legislator and very responsive to the needs of this community. He'd been in office for six years and had won reelection by ever-increasing margins. Who was he running against? I looked him up in the competing newspapers, both of which I had brought home. Never heard of him. I'll endorse Thiele.

Next there was the run for state senator. And the incumbent from our district was a Democrat named Ken LaValle. LaValle wasn't quite as high profile as Thiele, but it was the same thing. A good man, working hard. I had nothing against him. And again I had never heard of his opponent. I'd endorse LaValle.

Finally, there was the run for the House seat from our district. The encumbent was a Republican named Michael Forbes. If he won, this would be his second term. So he was just getting started. The only thing I knew about him was that he was a member of a prominent family in Riverhead that owned a competing newspaper, the *Riverhead News-Review*, and the previous February, at the annual St. Patrick's Day Parade in Montauk, he had been in the parade line directly in front of me. I drove slowly along in an old red sports car with *Dan's Papers* banners on the side. But Michael Forbes, our congressman, was on foot. He walked, and the whole way he was directly in front of me. I thought he had bad hair—was it a wig? In the wind, it did not fly off. He was about forty, had rosy cheeks from the cold, and a perpetual do-gooder smile on his face. He waved to the crowd as he walked. Not my cup of tea, but on that brisk winter day he had walked the whole route, which was at least three miles. Certainly, he was a man of vigor. I'd endorse him, too. What the hell.

The only thing that struck me about all of this when I wrote up the endorsements into an article later that night was that, gee, everybody seemed to be doing a pretty good job here. They were all incumbents. Good for them.

Thursday, the eighty tons of newspaper arrived at our offices in two moving vans, and the bundles of them were tossed down and sorted into delivery trucks and sent out on their way.

The next day, Friday morning, I was again fifteen minutes late for the editorial meeting. And again, everyone was glaring at me.

"Do you know what you just did?" Elaine asked. I thought, uh oh, I'm late again.

But it was something else. She was looking at *our* paper, not one of the competing newspapers. And it was open to where I had written up the endorsements.

"Michael Forbes is one of the worst people we've ever had in office," she said. "He favors gun control. He's against women. He's weak. And he's in the pocket of Newt Gingrich, the House speaker, who is trying to undue every new social and environmental law passed by the Clinton administration."

Newt Gingrich I had heard of. I hated Newt Gingrich.

"And here the Democrats had selected to run against him one of the strongest candidates ever, an enlightened, liberal, caring, intellectual named Nora Bredes from Sag Harbor."

"I didn't know . . ."

"And we had a real shot. The polls had us even. And here you go—with the biggest circulating newspaper out here—and you endorse *Forbes*."

A long silence settled over the table. Nobody was rising to my defense. This was serious.

"I've got an idea," I said. "I could change the endorsement next week. Say it was a mistake."

"The election is on Tuesday," Elaine said. "Where are you? You're always off in your own world. That's why we have this meeting. But look what you did."

And so there was nothing to be done.

Four days later, around ten o'clock, I was home watching the results on television. Around the country, the Republicans were surging. It looked as if they might seize control of the Senate. And yes, that was happening. The Republicans would hold a one-vote majority in the upcoming Senate. This would make things quite difficult as far as Bill Clinton went. But he would carry on.

And then it flashed on the screen. In New York's first district, Michael Forbes, fighting back a strong challenge from the Democrats, had retained his seat in the House of Representatives by the narrowest of margins. He was the projected winner by less than one-half of one percent.

At the next editorial meeting, I arrived right on time. We discussed the results of the Hamptons Film Festival. We discussed the upcoming plans for a Thanksgiving Day event with the local Shinnecock Indians. We didn't mention one single thing about the elections.

A month later, I received the following letter from Michael Forbes.

Dear Dan:

Your endorsement meant a lot to me. Unlike all the other newspapers, you were able to see through the labels to who I really am. If there is ever anything I could do for you, please let me know.

Sincerely,

Michael Forbes
Congressman

Two months later, one of his aides called to ask if I would like to have lunch with the congressman, just he and I, on a certain date when he would be out east. I told the aide I would be busy.

After this, events in Congress involving Michael Forbes moved very rapidly. There was a scandal in his office where one of his secretaries resigned and accused him of being a miserable person to work for and a little petty dictator. He made impossible demands. He cloaked himself in the trappings of the office. He had her do personal errands for him. He did little work, or so she said.

Two weeks after that, the coalition put together by Newt Gingrich began to come apart, and people began to speak out against him. Perhaps the most vocal of them was

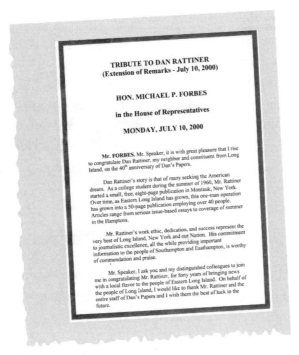

TRIBUTE TO DAN RATTINER
(Extension of Remarks - July 10, 2000)

HON. MICHAEL P. FORBES

in the House of Representatives

MONDAY, JULY 10, 2000

Mr. FORBES. Mr. Speaker, it is with great pleasure that I rise to congratulate Dan Rattiner, my neighbor and constituent from Long Island, on the 40th anniversary of Dan's Papers.

Dan Rattiner's story is that of many seeking the American dream. As a college student during the summer of 1960, Mr. Rattiner started a small, free, eight-page publication in Montauk, New York. Over time, as Eastern Long Island has grown, this one-man operation has grown into a 50-page publication employing over 40 people. Articles range from serious issue-based essays to coverage of summer in the Hamptons.

Mr. Rattiner's work ethic, dedication, and success represent the very best of Long Island, New York and our Nation. His commitment to journalistic excellence, all the while providing important information to the people of Southampton and Easthampton, is worthy of commendation and praise.

Mr. Speaker, I ask you and my distinguished colleagues to join me in congratulating Mr. Rattiner, for forty years of bringing news with a local flavor to the people of Eastern Long Island. On behalf of the people of Long Island, I would like to thank Mr. Rattiner and the entire staff of Dan's Papers and I wish them the best of luck in the future.

Michael Forbes. He was turning on Gingrich. Michael Forbes denounced Gingrich as a danger to society. He said that he, Michael Forbes, would be taking a much more socially responsible position on upcoming bills. He said that he had seen the light.

Two months later, Michael Forbes, arm in arm with Bill Clinton, was out on the White House lawn, standing silently as the president praised him for what he had done, not only speaking out against the newly disgraced Newt Gingrich, but on this day, switching his party affiliation.

"From this day on," Clinton said. "Michael Forbes is to be a Democrat. I would like to thank him for doing what he has just said he would do. It means a lot to me. And it will mean a lot to the Democratic party."

At the run-up to the next election, which was in 1998, the Democrats in our district did everything they could to keep Michael Forbes from running again for his House seat. He was now a member of their party, of course, but he was a turncoat member. They didn't like him when he was a Republican, and they still didn't like him. Forbes decided to run in the primary anyway. Let the voters decide. Running against him in the Democratic primary was a seventy-four-year-old grandmother from Brookhaven named Regina Seltzer, who had been on the local library board. She was a very weak challenger, but she clobbered Michael Forbes.

She then went on to run for the House as a Democrat, where she got clobbered by Felix Grucci, the Brookhaven town supervisor and a popular Republican who owned the Grucci Fireworks Company in that town. The Republicans in our district had the House seat again.

We're running our weekly editorial meetings on Friday mornings to this day, but nothing ever happened as remotely interesting and inadvertent as what happened that October and November in 1996.

Just before Michael Forbes's final run for office, it just so happened to be the occasion of the thirty-fifth anniversary of *Dan's Papers*. As we had done on other important anniversaries, we held a big party and made a big deal out of it. One of the things that we had done, beginning with the twenty-fifth anniversary, was to ask for, and get, an award from our local congressman, praising the longevity of our enterprise, which we would make a big fuss over at a party and then hang on the wall in the editorial room.

A letter requesting such a document was sent out to Michael Forbes. Nothing happened. But about six months later, after the party was over, I did get the award from him, which consisted of a framed copy of a paragraph he had entered into the *Congressional Record* about the paper. It was a nice gesture, late as it was, but it also had in it numerous typographical errors, including a glaring one announcing that after all these years, we had achieved the feat of expanding our newspaper to more than fifty pages in length. In fact, we had passed the fifty-page mark about twenty years earlier. We were now maxing out at three hundred pages a week. He didn't even read *Dan's Papers,* apparently.

I don't know where Michael Forbes is today or what he is doing, but I wish him well. I should say that if he happens to read this book, he will be reading this absolutely true story for the first time. This is the first time I have told it.

Jack Whitaker

~~~~~~

For about thirty years, from the beginning of the 1970s until the late 1990s, Jack Whitaker was one of this country's most beloved TV sportscasters. Tall, blond, and movie-star handsome, he would provide the analysis and commentary during and at the end of a horse race or a tennis match, giving his perspectives from a vast storehouse of knowledge that seemed to say, "Well, now that the excitement is all over, here is what it was all about." In another life, he might have been a governor or president. But we preferred him as our nation's chief sports commentator. And so that is where he made his career.

In July of 1994, he called me up at *Dan's Papers* and invited me to have lunch with him at his golf club, the National, in Southampton. I had never been to the National. If anything, it is even more exclusive than it's more well-known neighbor in Southampton, the Shinnecock Hills Golf Course.

We sat in the main dining room, on uncomfortable chairs at a rickety table. The National was built in 1904 for the wealthy New York City steamship, oil, and railroad barons,

JACK
(Courtesy of Jack Whitaker)

who would go out east to "rough it" in the Hamptons. And it had changed little since.

"I wanted to personally invite you to a new fundraiser that Nancy and I are putting together," he told me over Bloody Marys. "It's quite interesting." Nancy was Nancy Chaffee, his wife, the former tennis star.

"It will take place over Labor Day weekend and will benefit cancer research. It will be called the Cartier Grand Slam, in acknowledgement of the gracious sponsorship provided by that jewelry firm. We hope to raise over a hundred thousand dollars. But it will not be your ordinary fundraiser."

As I looked out the window at the golfers—some of whom were in knickers—Whitaker described a four-day event that would be divided into three parts. During the first two days, a Thursday and Friday, preliminary tennis matches would be held on the private tennis courts of one dozen wealthy people around the Hamptons. About sixty people would participate, each paying five hundred dollars for the privilege, and each would pair off and play matches to determine the semifinalists, who would play on Saturday, with a championship match on Sunday at the East Hampton Tennis Club.

The second part would be a series of parties to celebrate the event, one at the tennis club and the other at the Whitaker's summer home in Bridgehampton on Saturday night.

And the third part would be something Whitaker called "Corporate."

"Nancy has many friends in the tennis community," he said. "She's invited some of the great tennis stars of the past to be on hand. And on Saturday morning, these stars will give lessons to corporate executives at the Tennis Club. Imagine taking a lesson from Pancho Gonzales, for example. Well, he will be there."

"You'd like me to cover all this for the paper?"

"We'd like you to participate in it. As our guest."

Driving home, I considered that this was probably the most extraordinary fundraising event ever to come to the Hamptons. Other fundraisers—and by this time there were more than twenty charities holding fundraisers during each summer season—consisted of a big tent on the lawn of a private home, some speeches, a dinner, an auction, and dancing to a band. At the end of the night, the organizers would count the money.

I looked forward to this weekend with considerable anticipation. A lot of other people did, too. "*This* is a fundraiser!"
I wrote. "It's way, way above the run-of-the mill."

Two weeks before the Cartier Grand Slam, I got a call
from Irwin Hasen, the cartoonist who had made a considerable
fortune drawing a syndicated cartoon panel called "Dondi,"
that ran for years in newspapers around the country. I'd
met Hasen at a fundraiser once, and then met him again at
another. He was a little guy, and for fifty dollars for charity, he'd do a cartoon of you. But I didn't know him other
than that.

"Someone told me you're on the list to play tennis at
the Grand Slam in the novice division," Hasen asked. "Are
you any good?"

"Not at all," I said. "I used to play in high school. But
about fifteen years ago, I broke my ankle and I had to give
it up. My ankle hurts when I swivel. I've given up skiing and
tennis. Other than that I'm fine."

"So what are you going to do?"

"Well, I'll go out there just to fly the flag and help out
the Whitakers. I can move about a little bit. I'll probably
lose real quick."

"Great," Hasen said. What was great about that? "I'm
not particularly good either. So why don't we partner? I can
arrange it. We can play one another."

"Okay," I said. "If you don't mind me limping about."

After I hung up, I figured out what *great* meant. It meant
that this little guy Hasen would beat me and move on into
the semifinals. Then he'd have a shot at the novice division
cup.

At nine o'clock in the morning on the appointed day, I dressed in whites and then realized I did not have a tennis racket.

"Oh, yes you do," my wife said.

"I do?"

She and I went out into the garage and we found an old wooden Wilson tennis racket. Wooden rackets hadn't been used in twenty years. It was an antique.

"All the strings are fine," she said. "Take it."

At eleven o'clock, I was in the leafy backyard of a large mansion on Meadow Lane in Southampton alongside a tennis court with seven other businessmen and their wives, all in white and ready for a go at the novice division. Hasen, who is about five-foot-five, eyed me up and down. He spotted my racquet.

"Hey, look at this!" he shouted. And he took it from me and he passed it around. Everyone marveled at it and laughed. Then they passed it back.

Hasen went out to one end of the court, and I went out to the other, and we lobbed a few balls back and forth. Immediately, I realized that, lo and behold, I could move around on my left ankle without pain. It had, finally and at long last, completely healed. I just had not known.

"Okay, gentlemen," a woman with a clipboard said. "Let's get started."

This was an amazingly exhilarating experience. I served, Hasen hit it back, and then I sent a spinning shot into the corner, and Hasen, on his short legs, could not get to it.

"Fifteen love," I said.

I served again, and this time Hasen hit it back harder, I reached for it and, quite suddenly, I discovered that the old tennis game I had perfected in high school was back. I angled the racquet just perfectly to give it a bit of a cut and spin. It came back directly over the net to Hasen, who charged for it, figured to slam it down my throat, but then watched in amazement as it bounced sideways. He swung and missed.

"Hey," he shouted.

"Thirty love."

I had developed this wonderful game in high school. I was small for my age and not particularly strong. But I was fast. People would hit a line drive at me, and I had developed the skill of hitting it back with a big slice on it. I'd aim for the corners, and it would bounce inside the line and skitter off sideways.

My theory was that if I couldn't beat these big muscular high school guys one way, I'd beat them another. In fact, I could play them almost dead even for awhile, but then as sure as night turns to day, they would wear me out. After that, I would lose. Oh, well. I'd have held my end up for quite a while.

"Forty love," I said, hitting a ball just barely over the net, which Hasen once again could not get to.

Hasen was red in the face. "You call this *tennis?*" he asked. "We're supposed to play *tennis.*"

"Sorry," I said.

I can beat this little guy, I thought. I can easily beat him. But do I really want to do that? It's really pissing him off.

I deliberately double-faulted. "Forty fifteen." I wanted to think about this. But on the next volley, I couldn't help myself. I cut his hardest shot right back at him. He jumped sideways to get out of the way but it hit him anyway. Game.

"God dammit," he shouted. "Play *tennis!*"

Now it occurred to me that if I beat Hasen, I would be going on to the semifinals on Friday, and I might, for example, come up against the vice president of Seagram's, one of the national advertisers in *Dan's Papers.* What would I do with this terrible tennis game? I couldn't help myself. I would play this guy, and if I beat him with my cuts and spins, he'd be in such a rage he'd pull all his ads out of the paper.

I'd have to learn how to lose, and so I might as well start with Hasen. Concentrating with all my might, I forced myself to hit the ball back to Hasen straight and slow. Then I hit one long. Then I hit one into the net. And in the end, he won.

"There," he said, breathlessly. We walked off the court. He was red as a beet, but he was moving on to the semis. And I was going home.

"How did it go," my wife asked when I got home.

"I lost," I said.

Two days later, on the Saturday morning, I arrived at the tennis club at nine o'clock to participate in the corporate lesson. There were about thirty of us, and we went out and volleyed back and forth for a while (I was being careful), and then went off to the sidelines and to the outdoor deck of the club where we met this most dazzling array of tennis stars from years gone by. I met Ken Rosewall, Jack Kramer, Vitas Gerulaitis, Rod Laver, Tony Trabert, and even the promised Pancho Gonzales. Gonzales was a big beefy man about six-four with a great smile and a great way about him. In the 1950s, he had played a long series of matches with Jack Kramer—Kramer beat him more than he beat Kramer—and what they did had been front page on the sports pages, the head-to-head competition of the two greatest tennis players in the world at that time. I talked with Gonzales for awhile, and he just was the nicest guy. I also talked with Vitas Gerulaitis, who told me he had hurt his back and would be teaching only a little. He'd flown in from Seattle for this fundraiser. He was going to get a massage.

There was coffee and breakfast—Jack Whitaker was there and so was Nancy—and then we went out to the four courts, and all us corporate executives, some of whom were captains of industry and all of whom except me had paid quite a bit of money, would be lined up one behind the other to take a turn facing a tennis great on the other side.

I was in a line of eight facing Jack Kramer. The man in the front of the line, a very wealthy older man I knew, stepped forward and asked Jack Kramer if he'd look at his backhand, and Kramer said he would, and hit a soft lob over the net to him. The man hit it back. Then they got into a rhythm of hitting it back and forth maybe five or six times, and then they stopped and Kramer shouted across the net to him.

"Try and do a full follow-through," he said.

"Okay."

"That's a bit better."

They hit a few more and then stopped, and Kramer said "next." And so up stepped the next player for his brief lesson.

What an amazing thing, to be rallying like this with a tennis star, even if it was just for a few moments! As I moved up the line, I wondered what I might say to Kramer. Finally, I was at the front of the line.

Jack Kramer looked at me.

"I have this bad slice," I said.

Kramer bounced the ball and hit it across the net to my forehand, and I sliced it back at him. He'd have to move to get it. And he did. He'd seen it coming, figured it, and there he was, right with it, and he lobbed it back. How easy he made it look.

I hit him another slice, and he moved to get that. Then he stopped.

"Keep it up," Kramer said. "Club players hate that."

And so that was that. The big piece of advice.

"Next."

The following morning, Sunday morning, would be the day of the finals held at the club. A portable grandstand had been built. We saw it there on Saturday morning. I was looking forward to going.

But when I woke up at home on Sunday morning and turned on the radio, I learned that something terrible had happened during the night. Vitas Gerulaitis had died. He was only forty years old.

It had happened this way. In the weeks leading up to the event, the Whitakers not only had to arrange for the tennis stars to come, but also to arrange for where they should stay.

Vitas Gerulaitis was to stay in the guest house of New York City real-estate developer Marty Raynes at his oceanfront mansion on Meadow Lane in Southampton. There, Saturday night, Gerulaitis had gone to bed. And he had not woken up. He was dead.

Whether the finals were played at the club that day I do not know, but the news that day and for days after that was all about the death of this colorful, legendary tennis star with the long blond hair. It apparently never should have happened. It turned out Gerulaitis was not being put up in the guest house. He was being put up in the pool house, a one-story structure directly on the ocean, built over a basement, which housed the pool-heating equipment. Because of a faulty venting system in the pool house, Gerulaitis had died of carbon monoxide poisoning. Because it was odorless, he probably never even knew what was happening to him.

In the months that followed, there was a $65 million lawsuit filed by Gerulaitis' family, and there were trials held to determine if either a handyman or a propane company was guilty of manslaughter.

The Raynes house had seventeen rooms—Gerulaitis certainly could have stayed in the house—designed and built by architect Norman Jaffe for Raynes in 1981. In 1982, Raynes married Patty Davis, the daughter of one of the more unscrupulous billionaires of that era, Marvin Davis.

In 1991, just three years before the Grand Slam, during a slowdown in the real estate market, Raynes went bankrupt, but not before he put the big house in Southampton into the name of his mother-in-law, Barbara Davis. Raynes emerged from bankruptcy two years later. He was just now steadying himself when this death occurred. But now it was his mother-in-law who owned the property.

The pool house, according to the zoning, was supposed to be built on a slab, and was supposed to be used as a changing room for the pool. It had a bathroom and shower. But it was not supposed to be used for sleeping. The pool heater was supposed to be above ground, somewhere else.

It was learned that, two weeks before the event, there was trouble with the pool-heating equipment, and a handyman by the name of Bartholomew G. Torpey tried to fix it. Also called in was the propane gas company servicing the pool heater. They arrived two days later.

When Gerulaitis was found asphyxiated in his bed, police investigaters discovered the faulty heater below, faulty because a plastic venting pipe was five inches too short to vent the carbon monoxide outside. As a result, the pipe vented the carbon monoxide right into the basement, and then up through the gratings and into the room where Gerulaitis slept.

The handyman was tried, and the propane company was tried. But in the end, the jury voted for acquittal. There was no clear evidence about which of these two was at fault, and so you could not convict either. The lawsuit was dropped.

The Cartier Grand Slam raised $120,000 for the American Cancer Society. But the Whitakers decided against ever holding the event again.

Ten years later, in 2004, a friend who lives on Meadow Lane suggested I look into what many said was an absolute monstrosity of a house being built on that lane nearby to Cooper's Beach. I had a look.

Marty Raynes and his wife had sold their oceanfront estate to a man named Jay Sugarman from Palm Beach, Florida, for $12.5 million. The memory of the death of Gerulaitis, the Rayneses said in an account published in the *New York Observer*, had never left them. They just wanted to leave the Hamptons.

Sugarman bulldozed everything. But when he applied to put up three separate buildings on the property—Raynes had built a main house, a pool house, and a garage—he found that new zoning laws now prevented there being three structures. You could only have one.

Sugarman, though, was determined to have three. He hired an architect, who drew up a plan for a concrete basement extending 365 feet underground and parallel to the ocean. It was longer than a football field. But it was underground and so it was legal.

And so, perched on various parts of the basement, Sugarman was building three separate buildings just as he had wanted, but now, because they all sat on one underground football-field-long concrete basement, they were legally just one building.

I wrote a piece about this. The basement was underground, all right, but only because Sugarman had bulldozers piling dirt up to it on all sides to make it so. It was actually mostly above ground, and there were accesses to it and windows in it. The plans said "garage" and "laundry" and "storage," but you know, after it was built and the C.O. delivered, those uses could change to "theatre," "rec room," and "exercise studio." Ah, those tricks of the trade.

More importantly, however, was the fact that this amazing reinforced concrete basement actually was no different than a sea wall, or in this case a concrete coffer dam, that was not only illegal when seen from that perspective, but also totally blocking all access and even a view of the beach from Meadow Lane.

Sugarman wrote me a letter after I wrote the article. It was a basement, he said. And he soldiered on.

To this day, I can see in my mind the bulldozers smashing down the pool house and the propane heater and piping that, ten years earlier, put a tragic end to a wonderful golden-haired tennis star and to the Cartier Grand Slam.

President Bill Clinton

~~~~~~

You might think that the most exclusive place in the Hamptons for the rich would be along the ocean, where the big mansions are. But it's not. The most exclusive place in the Hamptons is inland, along the banks of Georgica Pond, a body of water completely surrounded by millionaires and billionaires. Living there today are such gentle folks as Steven Spielberg, Martha Stewart, Tina Fredericks, and Ron Perelman, all with beautiful and well-cared-for mansions that not only look out onto the pond, but in the back onto beautiful woods a half a mile thick that extend seamlessly in a great horseshoe behind all of the houses, sort of enveloping and uniting them.

Nobody from the general public sees who lives there. Nobody even sees the pond. And those inside only see one another across the pond. On one side of the pond they like that. And on the other side of the pond they like that.

There have been, from time to time, efforts made at placing interesting things into the waters of the pond. For a while, the things were Venetian gondolas, that were owned, most famously, by the great Philippine painter Alfonso Ossorio, who owned a mansion there during the mid-twentieth century.

Most recently, the retired publisher of the *Wall Street Journal,* Warren Phillips, has taken it upon himself to organize a "Georgica Yacht Club," which has consisted, by agreement, of only one kind of very picturesque boat, which is only twelve feet long, has a single daft-masted sail, a mast, a bench, a tiller, and a rudder. It's called a Beetle Cat, and on Saturdays there are displays and races of them, and they make a fine picture postcard indeed for those watching from the mansions along the shore as, on windy days, they tack this way and that.

When you live on Georgica Pond, you are just as snug as a bug in a rug. And that is that.

It was probably for this reason that, in the summer of 1998, when the President of the United States, Bill Clinton, and his wife, Hillary, decided to come to the Hamptons to take a little vacation and do a little fundraising, they allowed themselves to be hosted by filmmaker Steven Spielberg. Spielberg and his wife, Kate Capshaw, live on the pond on the east side.

After the visit was over, I visited my friend Tina Fredericks, who also has a home on the east side of the pond, and we talked a bit about the visit while sitting on the roof deck of her mansion and looking out at what can only be called a disaster. Georgica Pond, during the president's stay and for the entire rest of the summer, was bereft of water. Nothing was there but flies, weeds, and foul-smelling mud.

"Everyone thinks the Secret Service did this," Tina said, waving her hand at the Georgica Flats. "But nobody can prove it."

The president, his wife, and their entourage, came to the pond on July 31, 1998. About a week prior, some Secret Service agents had come to visit Tina.

"They told me he would be coming," she said. "And they asked that, for the duration of his stay, I not come up here on the roof deck. They were these tall men in black suits with earpieces. They said that I could either agree to that or I could have a Secret Service man stationed up there for the duration. I told them I'd agree to not go up there."

Secret Service men stationed themselves everywhere they could around the pond. They were not about to let some sniper sneak in and do something bad to a sitting president.

But in the course of their investigations, they discovered that the pond had a dirty little secret. At its north end, there was a spot where, through some brush and thickets, you could actually carry a kayak from a public parking lot into one of the narrow coves of Georgica Pond. Every once in a while, those living on the pond would encounter some kayakers, usually in pairs, paddling about in the pond alongside the Beetle Cats. The residents would try to shoo them away. But what could you do.

The Secret Service decided that the kayaks posed a threat, not just from possible terrorists, but from overeager paparazzi, who might go out in a kayak to get photos of the president and his wife in compromising positions, such as being in bathing suits on the lawn.

Immediately after making this discovery, the Secret Service arrived at what they believed could be a solution to this problem, although to be fair, it has never been proven that they did act on this solution.

On the south, the edge of Georgica Pond reaches the Atlantic Ocean, only separated from it by about two hundred yards of a sandbar. What the Secret Service learned, by talking with some of the locals, was that every six months or so, when the water in the pond got too high, the locals would go down there and "let" the pond into the sea. They'd do this one night with the aid of a bulldozer that would go out on the sandbar and create a narrow trench from the pond to the ocean. They'd start digging it by the ocean, and then, when they got to the edge of the pond, break through. The high water of the pond would then come rushing out, spilling huge amounts of water into the ocean, until the pond was about three feet lower than it had been a few hours before.

That the locals would do this every six months was really part of a very ancient and remarkable tradition. The woods and the mansions that surround the pond today were not always there. Three hundred years earlier, when the white men first arrived, there was merely swampland surrounding the pond. The pond, with neither an entrance or egress, would get higher and higher as the days went by, until it overflowed its banks. Then, after a while, with some of the water settling into the swamp and the rest of it overflowing into the ocean, it would settle back down. Much of the land surrounding the pond was, therefore, extremely rich and fertile.

Those early settlers saw this as an opportunity. They felt that if the pond could be stabilized, the land surrounding it could be farmed. And so they would tame Georgica Pond. At certain times of the year, a group called the "Trustees" would ring all the church bells in town to call every able-bodied man down to the sea in order to participate in opening up Georgica Pond by digging a trench with shovels. If you didn't come, you could be fined, or even put in the stocks or in jail. The people came, they dug, and the water would flow out until the level was equal in both. Soon, a great bounty of crops was in the ground in neat little rows around Georgica Pond. The local Indians must have shaken their heads in wonder.

Running *Dan's Papers* all these years, I would often get calls from either an employee of one of these wealthy people or from one of the wealthy people themselves, telling me that the Town Trustees were not doing their job, that the waters were getting higher, that the lawns were getting wet, that the basements were getting damp. I should write about it. Get those Trustees down there with their trucks and bulldozers.

The Trustees had their own perspective. The tide needed to be just right. The pond, filled with fresh water seeping in from underground, would become slightly salty when the ocean would be joined. The tide needed to be just the right salinity for the health of the clams and shellfish. It couldn't be too fresh or too salty.

On the evening of July 31, 1998, the Clintons arrived. The *New York Times* reported that several events were planned, including a political fundraiser at the Amagansett estate of Alec Baldwin and Kim Basinger (a thousand guests, each of who had donated up to five thousand dollars) and an "intimate dinner" for sixty people at the home of investment banker Bruce Wasserstein in East Hampton ($25,000-a-plate). There were also rumors of a golfing trip to the Atlantic Golf Club.

The town eagerly awaited the upcoming events. This was just weeks after the revelations about the hanky-panky with Monica Lewinsky in the Oval Office had become public, and so people in town wondered if the Clintons would be seen hand in hand or not speaking to each other. (They were not speaking to each other.)

What a wonderful time this was going to be, with the helicopters hovering overhead and the limos gliding through town and the Clintons moving from place to place.

That first night, when the Clintons went to bed at the Spielbergs, the pond was full. When they awoke in the morning, when everybody around the pond awoke the next morning, the pond was a stinking mess of sticky mud with angry black flies buzzing all over the place.

This had never happened before. Actually two things had never happened before. One was that somebody, other than the Trustees, had let out the pond. The Trustees were in a rage. They posted a ten thousand dollar reward for any information leading to who might have done this. But there were no takers.

The other thing that happened for the first time in memory was that the pond had been entirely let out right down to the mud. It was almost impossible to do this. You'd have to dig six feet deep and you'd have to do it when the tide in the ocean was way, way out.

One man, Donald Petrie, who lives by the pond, and who for many years wrote a four-page quarterly newsletter entitled *The Pond Watchers Almanac,* had this to say in his December 1998 edition:

> [The complete letting of the pond] happened just at the time President Bill Clinton and his family arrived for a summer holiday at the Georgica Cove residence of Steven Spielberg. Some boob started a rumor that the pond had been let by the Secret Service to protect the president.
>
> On the face of it, that suggestion is pretty stupid. If you are guarding a castle, you don't drain the moat. Nevertheless, the zany tale was taken up by the national news media and for a couple of days the Georgica Cut competed with the Monica mania.
>
> The truth is that, for a century or more, adolescents (and sometimes adults) along the beach at night, through pure deviltry, have tried to open Georgica. It's a form of three-dimensional graffiti. Anyone who has tried it, including, I blush to say, your Pond

Watcher many years ago, will tell you that it's a lot more difficult than it looks. It is bad manners, it is shameful conduct, it is inconsiderate to others, but it is a lot of fun. And it wasn't even prohibited by law until very recently.

So much for that. It may be difficult if you are just an ordinary Joe, but if you are the President of the United States and the commander-in-chief of the armed forces, well, I think you get the idea.

In October, finally, the water began to trickle back. By Christmas, with most of the residents gone down to Palm Beach or other places, it had fully restored itself to the good old Georgica Pond everybody knew so well.

Had the people been there, they'd have cheered.

Eleanor Leonard

~~~~~~

In 1995, a wealthy older woman named Eleanor Leonard came to my office to tell me about a music festival she wanted to start in the Hamptons. I thought I knew what she wanted. Free advertising. But we would go broke if we did that. There were two or three charity events every weekend. So I'd do my best to fend off these sorts of requests.

I was right that she wanted free advertising. "If I do it for you, I'd have to do it for *everybody*," I said. My stock answer.

"Well, I'm not *everybody*," she said.

I sized her up. She was a tiny but beautiful woman of about fifty-five with beautiful jewelry, blond hair, and the kind of determination that says, before I leave here you will do exactly what I want.

She described her vision. She'd have a series of white tents in a field with about a thousand people coming to hear Mozart and Handel and Debussy played every evening by pianists and string quartets.

I love classical music, and the thought of it wafting through the Hamptons on a summer evening excited me.

ELEANOR LEONARD

"How many concerts?" I asked.

"For ten days. A different concert every day. I want to do it for my great uncle, Benno Moiseiwitsch, the celebrated Ukrainian-born composer and pianist. I want to dedicate this festival to him."

In the end, she asked—having given up on the free advertising—if I would be on her board of directors. So, taken with the idea, I said I would do that. After that, she said I *had* to give her free advertising.

This festival went on year after year for ten years, staggering about, mostly losing money and with such low attendance that Eleanor, in spite of her wonderful vision, would have to reach into her pocketbook at the end of the year and pay off its debts.

Part of the problem was that although Eleanor could not do everything herself, when she asked others to do something and then saw that whatever was being done did not match her vision, she'd step in and just take over this person's job and do it herself—until she could find somebody new who would like to guess if what they did would match her vision.

"I just have to do this myself," she'd say. Then she'd say something disparaging about the most recent person who had attempted to please her.

That first year, she found an unused horse pasture she could use for the festival for free. But the next year, she was not welcome there anymore.

Then she got someone to volunteer to videotape all the concerts. But when she watched the tapes, he was out.

At the start of that first festival, I saw her tents sitting bare in the middle of the pasture, and so with her permission, I ordered twenty evergreens in big pots brought over from a friend who owned a nursery.

"Do it as a favor," I told the friend. "At the end of the week, you can have it all back. I'll acknowledge your gift in the paper if you'll do this."

He agreed. The landscaping came over, and now the place looked just so elegant. But Eleanor called me up. They were nice, she said, but they were not what she had in mind.

"Next year I want flowers and beach grass around the tents," she told me.

I went to the first concert of that series, through the path defined by the trees which the landscaper had not yet heard were only marginally welcome, and I sat on one of the two hundred folding chairs inside with about thirty other classical music afficionados. The sounds wafted over us. Played by professionals from Manhattan. Conducted by Lukas Foss. Violin solos by Itzhak Perlman. Singing by the Harlem Boys Choir. I loved it.

The next year, the Southampton town supervisor allowed the festival to be held in a small public park. That went well. But at the beginning of the next year, because the neighbors had objected about the park being used for only that purpose for so many days, the town supervisor spoke to her about perhaps reducing the number of concerts from ten, to say seven, for the upcoming year. Instead, Eleanor announced there would be fifteen concerts. As a result, her festival wound up off in a muddy field, and with a large bill from a new printer who had to reprint the glossy fliers to indicate the changed location.

"Why did this happen?" I asked her, as we slogged through the mud that first day.

"I don't know," she said.

I told her all advertising had to be in my office on Monday at noon for the following Friday's edition. She had gotten her ad in, but then on Wednesday called to say I had to simply put a second full page in.

"The paper went to the printer last night," I said.

"You'll have to stop the presses," she said.

"I can't stop the presses," I said. Why did she always have me on the defensive?

After that first year, she called to tell me there would be a board of directors meeting. It would be the first full meeting of her board.

"We are holding it at my house at five o'clock on Friday," she said. So I went on Friday. Only she was there.

"We met last night. Didn't anybody tell you?"

I lingered. Her modern home had such a beautiful view of the sea, with the decks and sliders and the roaring ocean just outside.

"Should I make you some coffee?" she asked.

The next year, she asked me if I knew any famous composers whom she might ask to be the honorary chair of the festival. I did. I was good friends with Richard Adler, the Broadway composer famous for *Damn Yankees* and *The Pajama Game,* and I asked him and he said yes. Eleanor loved him.

The next year I asked him again and he said no.

Why? I asked.

Eleanor, he said.

In 2000, Eleanor had invited a Hamptons celebrity to be the narrator for the orchestral piece *Peter and the Wolf,* as she always did. But although his name was in the program, he forgot to show up. It was one hour before the performance.

"I thought somebody told him," Eleanor said. "Dan, you'll have to read this."

After I declined twice, she persisted and so I accepted. It was great fun, and the kids and their parents had just as good a time as if what's-his-name had shown up.

Thus did the Music Festival of the Hamptons launch itself, in fits and starts, into the twenty-first century.

Then, one day in 2002, with the festival now in a small former farm field, I found myself sitting under the beautiful tent on a folding chair at the back of the audience, listening to a few of the Brandenburg concertos played by the American Festival Orchestra conducted by Lukas Foss, who had now agreed to become the new festival director—a real coup for Eleanor—and I closed my eyes to enjoy the pieces.

At fifteen minutes into the first concerto, some noise began to interrupt my reverie. It was the Long Island Railroad train, thundering along, its wheels clattering, its horns honking, getting louder and louder as it approached—the thin fabric of the tent offering no acoustic resistance at all—and the sound got more and more overpowering as it came nearer and nearer. It was the 8:55. There are only two trains a day to the Hamptons. But the single track of the railroad went right along the side of the venue of that year's festival—a grassy field otherwise used just once a year for the horse show parking-lot in September—and here, right in the middle of a Brandenburg, it was charging through. The ground shook. Foss ignored it. His baton swished this way and that. The musicians played. And the train slowly raced off down the track westbound toward New York City, and I closed my eyes once again. That was that, I thought. Until tomorrow. The 8:55 was every day.

As it happened, I did attend a summing-up board meeting at Eleanor's house the week after the festival ended, and I listened once again with the other board members to Eleanor lament how they'd again lost money and she would have to make it up out of her own pocket.

"Attendance remains poor," she said. "But it's improving. Maybe if we get the word out better for next year, we can pull it up to break-even."

"Some people commented that the train going by was a big distraction," a board member said.

"I don't see why," Eleanor said. "*Nothing* can disturb this wonderful music. My great uncle Benno Moiseiwitsch played in salons in Vienna as a boy, right over the busy Schottenring, where his mentor, Theodor Leschetizky also had a salon. If he can do it, we can do it."

"Next year?"

"Same place," she said. "I signed the papers yesterday."

There was a collective groan.

Then it hit me. "I have an idea," I said. "Why don't we *celebrate* the train going by."

"I don't get it," a board member said.

"We know the train goes by right at 8:55 PM," I said. "It's just out of Montauk so it's not going to be late. Why don't we have a symphony *written* to accompany the train?"

I couldn't believe I had just thought of this.

"There's plenty of precedent for this," I continued. "Consider the 1812 Overture. Cannonfire is written right in. It goes off on cue. It's right there in the score. Why not a train?"

"Who would write such a thing?" Eleanor asked.

"I don't know," I said. "Maybe we could have a contest to get it written."

Eleanor looked skeptical. But then Lukas Foss, the director of the festival and the vice president of the board, spoke up.

"I *love* this idea," he said.

Lukas Foss was among a handful of people, myself included, who had stuck with Eleanor over the years through thick and thin because of her remarkable determination. He was seventy-nine years old. His eyes sparkled.

"What a great idea," Eleanor said. "Lukas, you can judge the submissions from the contest. Dan, you organize it."

"Eleanor, leave me alone with this and I'll get three thousand people to the festival," I said.

Immediately after Labor Day of 2002, I got this project underway. Cajoling some of the staff of *Dan's Papers* to help out, I organized the mailing of a poster to every music conservatory and institute in the country from Julliard on down.

$500 FIRST PRIZE

Student Music Composing Competition

Submit a 12-Minute Piece of Original Music

"Symphony for Train and Orchestra" that includes the sound of a passing railroad train.

Winner receives an award, $500, an invitation to the festival, room and board, and a world premiere of the piece conducted by Lukas Foss at the Music Festival of the Hamptons on August 22, 2003.

Entrants must be full time music students under the age of 30. For further information, send your name and address and a $15 entry fee to the Music Festival of the Hamptons, c/o Dan Rattiner, 2221 Montauk Highway, Bridgehampton, NY, USA. Application must be made before December 31, 2002. Competition entry must be received by April 30, 2003.

RECIPIENT: PLEASE POST THIS ON A PROMINENT BULLETIN BOARD

Fifty-five students around the country applied to enter this competition before the December deadline. I was astonished at this large number. In mid-January, on a freezing cold evening, I took our resident computer techie, Leif Neubauer, up to the railroad tracks next to the grassy parking area, and at 8:55 PM, working with him, made a digital recording of the long, low, moaning sound of the train and its horn as it approached, roared by just twenty feet from the two of us by the side of the rail bed, and then disappeared into the distance.

"Forty seconds," Leif said, looking at his laptop and his stopwatch.

That sound bite, as a CD, was sent out, with an accompanying note, to all fifty-five entries within the week. Put this into your twelve minutes somewhere, I wrote. That's all you have to do.

Then I got another idea. I found out the name of the president of the Long Island Railroad, and I sent him a letter about the "Symphony for Train and Orchestra." In my letter, I asked if the 8:55 could have somebody from the railroad on board, perhaps a marketing person. As the train would come through the old abandoned Wainscott station, he could call one of the festival people inside the tent on his cell phone to tell us the train was now fifteen minutes away. With that information, we could, hopefully, arrange to have the train come in exactly on cue, whenever that would be indicated in the music score.

"Wouldn't this be wonderful public relations for the railroad?" I concluded. "Wouldn't this be great if the railroad helped a music festival like this?"

James Dermody, the president, wrote back to me within a week. He would go one better and deliver us our own personal train! The morning of the concert, he would send twin loco-motives and five cars out for the day. We could have the train wait on a siding, and then on cue come charging through. We could have a rehearsal, with the train present, earlier in the day. Whatever we wanted, he'd make it happen.

"With the two locomotives, it should make a rich, won-derous sound," he wrote. "It just has to happen before the regular train, the 8:55, comes through."

In addition, he himself would attend the performance.

That Saturday of August 22, 2003, was the most highly anticipated day ever held at the festival. I had volun-teered to put up the winning entrant in a guest bedroom at my house for the weekend. And who that was, as selected by Lukas Foss, was Mark Petering, twenty-seven years old, a quiet, slender young man who was a graduate student in music at the University of Minnesota, one year away from receiving his doctorate in composition.

Petering arrived on the day before the beginning of the festival—the train piece would be opening night—and my wife and I took him out to Nick & Toni's restaurant. He was a lanky, polite young man, and he was not surprised that he won.

"I think I completely understood the thrust of how this needed to come out," he said. "I made a CD of my entry, and I have it with me. Want to hear it when we get home?"

"Actually, no," I said. "I want to be surprised."

"Okay."

The next morning, I drove with him, both of us as excited as a couple of kids, from our house in East Hampton to the festival venue next to the railroad tracks in Bridgehampton. We arrived about noon. The members of the orchestra, in full tuxedo dress, were backstage tuning up. Out front, there were reporters from NBC, the *New York Times, Newsday,* and several other newspapers and television stations. Eleanor was there—later she would change into a white evening gown and a gold tiara. Also, there were several people with recording devices.

I got introduced to a marketing man from the railroad. We shook hands.

"When is our train coming?" I asked.

"It's here," he said. "Parked on a siding at the Bridge-hampton Station. Listen."

He picked up a cell phone, poked a few numbers and then said something. Immediately, from a long way off, over the woods by the tracks, there were two short toots of a locomotive horn.

Mark and I squealed with joy. The man laughed delightedly.

I could not sit down. I paced. Around 12:15, the orchestra came out onto the stage, with their instruments, and then got instructions from Foss. Further conversations took place between Foss and the railroad marketing man.

Shortly, with the plucking of some violin strings, the rehearsal for this piece began. It unfolded very softly and mysteriously, a quiet classical piece, staccato at the beginning, then building and building through an andante middle, and then exploding into a triumphant crescendo leading into—nothing.

The orchestra played three final notes. There was a pause. And then the thundering, screaming, rumbling train came roaring by. Late by four seconds, according to Mark.

This was brilliant!

"Okay, okay, okay," a man wearing earphones said. "We do it again."

The rest of the afternoon passed anxiously. This was going to be a nailbiter. At seven, about fifty regulars came to listen to the orchestra, now in informal dress, begin to play Handel's Water Music. As it continued, people came in to sit and listen. This was soon a torrent of people, tiptoeing in, sitting down or standing along the walls of the tent in the back. By seven-thirty, nearly five hundred people were packed into the tent, which was filled to overflowing. Next would be the world premiere of the "Symphony for Train and Orchestra."

Dusk had now settled into darkness. Sitting in the audience I imagined the train rumbling through. On cue? Not on cue? The piece would have to start before eight for the train to be sure to come through and be gone down the tracks before the regular 8:55. As the Handel continued on toward its gentle conclusion, I saw the marketing man, over by the side of the tent, talking quietly on his cell phone.

The Handel ended and the audience applauded politely. Then, the lights came up and after a long interval, a terribly long interval as far as I was concerned, the preparations for the Train piece proceeded once again. The lights remained up.

Roy Scheider, the star of the movie *Jaws,* came in with his wife Brenda, and sat down. Mark Petering waved to me from his seat in the center of the audience, indicating that his mother and father were there with him—a surprise to Mark. They had flown in from Chicago, bearing the largest bouquet of flowers I had ever seen. The president of the Long Island Railroad, James Dermody, arrived with his wife and found a seat, and the marketing man motioned for me to come over and be introduced. I did. He looked about as excited as everybody else did. Mark, and Eleanor in her gown and tiara, came over and shook his hand, too.

And then, in a flash, Eleanor had climbed the stairs to the stage, with Lukas just behind her, and she took the microphone. Everybody applauded. I looked at my watch. 7:53 PM. Off to one side, I could see this guy with the cell phone.

I thought, oh God, she's got five hundred people in front of her. She could talk and talk—I just knew she could—and she could do so until it was absolutely too late.

"I am so pleased to see this wonderful crowd of people tonight here at this festival. If my great uncle Benno Moiseiwitsch were alive today . . ."

Oh, please, oh, please.

"I know you have paid your admission fee and that is a big help to us. But it is only a beginning. As you listen to the winning symphony of this competition, I want you to reach into your pockets . . ."

8:01. Oh, God, oh, God.

Mercifully, just a few minutes later, she stopped, introduced Lukas Foss, then Mark Petering, who came up with his parents and received an award from Eleanor and a huge bouquet of flowers from his parents. People applauded. And then, finally the lights went down.

What was it like? Anybody who was there that night will tell you it was one of the most memorable events of their lives. In the darkness, the orchestra started up, worked its way through the beginning of the piece and then, with the plucking of the violin strings, began to play faster and faster until, there it was, you could hear the locomotive and its horn from far off begin to integrate itself into the music. The piece continued on, got louder and louder, until, with a great almost unbearably thunderous chord by the entire orchestra, reached its climax, with a single cymbal crashing the place BANG, into utter silence. There was a beat of silence. Another. Then the shrill screech of the train whistle, and then the streak of the train, its windows lit up and blurred through the trees, coming alongside the tent, right on cue, streaking through at forty miles an hour with its horn moaning.

People leaped to their feet and screamed. The orchestra, its music having ended three seconds earlier, leaped up and, instruments in hand, jumped around. And Eleanor, her tiara askew, came rushing over and hugged me, and we danced around and jumped up and down deliriously.

The "Symphony for Train and Orchestra" competition was held again the following year. This time, however, the competition was won by a heavyset Chinese student who presented some sort of odd cacophonous modern thing. Our train, once again, was there. But this time it was instructed to move by in the middle of the piece, slowly, and with just a low rumble and no horn. The drama was not there. Honestly, I didn't get it.

The following year, the venue was moved once again, this time by a town supervisor angry at Eleanor about still another thing, to a potato field with rain and more muck, but no train tracks within miles. And so that was that.

Six years later, Eleanor continues to complain to the board that the festival just never was able to match the great draw at the box office in its peak year of 2003, when the first train came through. But she does confess that now the festival is at break-even.

In 2008, once again, the concert was back at the old site by the railroad tracks. And it did make me wonder. There was, however, no further "Symphony for Train and Orchestra" competition. But the week of the concert, I did receive a letter from Mark Petering:

Dear Dan:

I was just thinking about the great time we had five years ago and the hospitality of your home offered me at that time. It was such an honor to win that prize and to have the "Symphony for Train and Orchestra" get its world premiere with Lukas Foss. I can't tell you how much that all meant to me.

I graduated from the University of Minnesota and now have my doctorate. I've taken a post at

Carthage College, in the music department, as an assistant professor, and I will be able to continue to compose. I enclose a clip of my latest piece. I hope all is well with you.

Mark Petering

Demis Gnatiuck

~~~~~~

On an icy cold morning in January, 2004, I got out of bed, dressed warmly, took the basketball out from the front hall closet, and headed out the door to play myself a game of one-on-one. I had a backboard and hoop attached to the garage in back of the house. And out there, I began the forty-minute workout I did every morning.

I hated working out. But if I could make it a game, with one shot for the Knicks and the next shot for the Nets, with three point attempts from far out, occasional foul shots, and a roar from the crowd for a particularly amazing swish from the corner, I could fool myself into working up a sweat and keeping myself in shape. I'd been doing this for years.

After about ten minutes of this that morning, with the Nets in the lead 18 to 15, the young workman from the roofing company who was putting a new roof on my house drove up my long driveway in his truck, got out, and after strapping on his tools, strolled by. I nodded my head in acknowledgement, and stopped to face him with the ball as I always did.

DAN AND DEMIS
(Courtesy of the author)

Care for a shot?

Sometimes he'd smile and I'd bounce it to him for a shot. He did this time. And so I threw it to him and from way in the backcourt, still strolling along, he gave it a heave. As always, he missed. But this time he was close.

"Aww," I said, simulating crowd disappointment. He walked on.

For the prior week, I'd had very little contact with this man other than the occasional single basketball heave. We'd exchanged a few words from time to time. Could he have something to drink? Could he go in and use the bathroom?

He was about thirty, had long curly hair and spoke in a heavy foreign accent, probably Russian, and because I knew he would be around my house for ten days, I introduced myself to him when he first arrived with his ladders and truck. We shook hands. He said his name. Demis.

My main concern with him that week was, frankly, that he might fall off the roof and sue me. He was up there, banging away, doing a very good job as near as I could see, but the building contractor who I had hired to do this job never gave me an assurance that he was sending over a legal worker.

He had given me insurance information about the job and *legal* workers when we signed the deal. But when it came time to begin, there was Demis. Alone.

Well, Demis would only be here for ten days. And apparently he hadn't fallen off a roof yet is how I rationalized it.

Around 11:30, I finished my workout, came in, and took a shower. It had been a fight to the finish, and there had been this icy patch in the backcourt I had to look out for. In the end, as seemed to be happening more and more recently, the Nets won.

One good thing was Demis's big truck. Before Demis, the ball would sometimes bounce away and head down the driveway toward the street at the bottom of the hill. I'd have to run after it and rush to get to it before it bounced across the street and into the harbor. I had briefly thought of parking my own car in the driveway, but decided against it. The run downhill would be part of the game.

With Demis here, though, errant balls would hit the front end of his truck and getting them was easy. I considered asking him not to block the driveway, but in the end, decided to let his truck stay. It did change the game a bit. So that was good for as long as it would be there.

At noon, fully dressed, I went into the living room and built a fire in the fireplace, then walked into the kitchen and made myself a tunafish sandwich. My wife Chris was in the city for a few days, so I was alone in the house. I sat down at the kitchen counter with my sandwich and looked out the slider at the panoramic view of the harbor, all iced over. And then, quite suddenly, there was Demis, standing outside on the deck looking in at me.

He said something and pointed excitedly. But because the door was closed I could not hear him. I got up and opened the slider.

"A woman is in the harbor. She drove her car into it. Call 911."

I looked to where he was pointing. Far off, at Three Mile Harbor Marina, I saw what looked like somebody splashing in the water at the docks. That was too far away for us to do anything about but call the police. But then I realized that what I was looking at was the winter bubble system used by the marinas in the wintertime to keep the ice from the bulkheads.

"No, no," Demis said. "Look *here*."

He motioned for me to look in the water just across the street from the house. Oh, my God. There was a car in the icy water, in one of the boat slips, floating. It was just fifty yards away from us.

Years earlier, I had found an orange circular lifesaving ring on the beach, and had attached it as a decoration to the shingles on the front of the house. I pointed to it.

"Use the ring," I said. "I'll call the police."

He snatched it and ran. I made the quick call, then grabbed the twine we use to bundle newspapers for recycling, and ran after him. We could attach the twine to the ring.

Running across the street, I almost got hit by a pickup truck coming south down Three Mile Harbor Road. It did miss, though, and the driver, alert to what was happening, pulled over, and with the slam of a door was running down to the water too. Moments later, I was standing with Demis at the top of the aluminum boat ladder that, in the summertime, would go down four steps to a boat, but was now going down to a car. We were talking to the woman in the car, which was now beginning to sink. The car window was open.

"Grab this," Demis said offering up the ring so she could see it. She was confused and didn't seem to know what to do.

"My cell phone! My wallet!" she shouted.

"Just take this," Demis said. And he tossed it to her and she caught it. But after catching it, all she did was pull it through the window and clutch it to her chest.

"Get out," I shouted. We had not used the twine.

The car, continuing to lower into the pieces of ice all around, was now low enough so that the icy water was beginning to pour through the open window. And still she continued to sit there, clutching the ring. We all yelled at her, over and over, get out, get out, get out.

And then an interesting thing happened. As the car began to sink faster, the rising water simply floated the ring, with her clutching it, out the window. Now she was next to the car, splashing about trying to get to the ladder. And she was where we could reach her. We grabbed her and struggled with her—in her wet clothing she was very heavy—and we pulled her up the ladder and onto the dock. She was about forty, soaking wet in a heavy winter coat, gloves, and scarf. It was, with the wind chill, about fifteen degrees. She was breathing heavily.

Joined by another man who had also stopped his car, we now half walked and half dragged her to the pickup and bundled her into the passenger seat. The man then climbed into the driver's seat, started the engine, and turned on the heater full blast. It would warm her up quickly, though her teeth were now chattering.

"I'm no trouble. No trouble. I go home now," she said.

"I'm a police officer," the man in the pickup said. He was, I now saw, Tom Miller, a nephew of my nearest neighbors, the Cliffords. He was in plain clothes, off duty, and it was he who had almost run me over.

"No police," she said. She had an accent. "Don't call anybody. I go home now."

I was at the window. "It's not a problem," I said. "You almost drowned. Get warm. We will help you."

By this time, more people had arrived and were crowding around the pickup. "I think she's Hispanic," Miller said. "Maybe the cleaning lady. Any of you speak Spanish?" He asked this in a louder voice. People shook their heads.

"I speak Russian," Demis said. "I could try that."

The woman was now visibly shivering. I told Miller to close the window I was standing at. He raised it halfway.

"How do we know there was nobody else in the car?" somebody in the crowd asked.

I don't speak Spanish either. But I was right by the passenger window, closest to her. I pointed to the water, and tried it in pig latin.

"Otre Personna?" I shouted.

"No, no."

She was really shivering now and so I asked Miller to close the passenger window the rest of the way, and I stepped back. Then I realized I was freezing. I had run across the street without a coat. And one whole side of me was wet.

As the police and firemen had now begun to arrive and were quickly taking over, I headed back across the street to the house, went inside, and warmed myself before the fire in the living room. Then, incredibly, I heard hammering on the roof. I went out on the deck and looked up. Demis was back up there. There was this huge crowd of people across the street now, and he was up there roofing again.

"You just saved a woman's life," I said.

"I know," he said.

"Why don't you come down? The police are going to need a statement."

"You give them the statement. I'm not too happy around police."

"Okay," I said. But then I thought about it. "Because of the old country? Or because of the paperwork?"

"Paperwork."

"But I want to write about this. I want to use your name in the paper."

"What paper?" he asked.

"My paper," I said. "I publish a weekly newspaper."

"Okay," he said. He smiled. "I really did save this woman's life."

"Yes, you did."

I went inside, bundled myself up in my coat, and then returned to the dock. The place was swarming with ambulances, paramedics, fire trucks, town trustees, police, traffic control people and other rescue types. I decided I wanted my life ring back. It had saved a life. It was a lucky charm. It needed to be back on my wall.

"It's still in the water," Miller told me. He was now walking around alongside his pickup, talking to people.

I looked in on the woman. She was still in Miller's pickup truck, but now she was wearing a plastic neck collar, was covered with an aluminum blanket, and was being examined by a paramedic with a small flashlight. She looked fine. Two women were pulling a gurney out from the back of an ambulance. America. What a country.

"Last I saw, it was still floating in the hole in the ice," Miller said.

We went over and looked way down into the water. The car was gone, but there was the ring. Too far down to reach down and pick up. I ran back to my house and got a long aluminum pole with a net on the end that was stored under the deck for cleaning the pool, and I ran back. But the firemen told me to stay away from the water. So instead, I gave it to Miller, the off-duty policeman, and he fished out the ring.

TOWN VOLUNTEERS AFTER THE RESCUE
(Photo by the author)

A woman in a uniform came over and asked me a few questions.

"Did you see the whole thing?" she asked.

"Just the last part," I said. "She had started climbing out the window. Then she didn't know what to do, to jump out or stay in the car, which was filling with water. Then she had the life ring and she just came out the window as the car sank."

"So how long had she been in the water?"

"Total maybe six minutes. Five minutes in the car filling with water maybe, another minute in the water."

"Thanks."

"How is she?" I asked.

"I think she'll be all right."

I noticed the victim's name on the clipboard. Pola Gla-cowitz. A Polish name. She didn't talk or understand much English or Spanish.

At this point, I was standing there holding a life ring under one arm, and a long pole with a net on the end under the other. I was also still carrying the twine. Although I now had a jacket on, I must have looked pretty odd, particularly in the straw hat I defiantly wear all winter. I returned once again to the hero of this adventure, Demis, on the roof. Again I shouted to him.

"Where are you from?" I asked.

"Riverhead," he said.

"No. Before that."

"I'm from Lithuania."

"What town?"

"Why do you want to know?"

"Because the woman is from Poland. Maybe you lived near her."

"My city is Siauliai," he shouted. "It's a three-hour drive to Poland. I should have talked to her in Lithuanian. She'd have understood that. That's a lot like Polish."

"How do you think she drove into the water?" I asked him. He wasn't getting a lot of roofing done.

"I saw it. She was trying to drive up the hill on the ice," he said, pointing to a steep driveway next to my house on the other side from Clifford. "Her wheels were spinning.

I think the transmission blew. It was screaming. Then the car just rolled down backwards, crossed the street and went straight in."

It did not escape my notice that the steep driveway was something that I had personally caused to be built. I had bought that property up the hill, built the house there, and built the driveway. And then later, I sold the property to Al Lewis, a retired New York City state assemblyman.

I looked across the street again. The ambulance was gone and the pickup was gone, and there were new people there along with a tow truck. Also the police scuba team. They were going to go down into the freezing cold water and hook up the tow truck cable to the car bumper to bring it up. Of course, you couldn't leave the car there on the bottom of the harbor.

From inside the house, I watched these proceedings for the next hour, and I photographed the event with a long lens when this big Toyota got hauled up, dripping wet, hanging like a dead fish at the end of the tow truck cable above the water.

The next morning, I was out back again, playing one-on-one. Demis pulled up, I threw him the ball, and from thirty feet out, he arched a long, high throw that came down as a perfect swish, rippling through the cords of the basket.

We whooped, high-fived, and danced around for a bit. And then he went up on the roof and soon I could hear him, once again, banging up there rhythmically on the shingles.

"Can I write about this in the paper? Could I use your full name?" I shouted up to him.

He'd had the night to think about it.

"Demis Gnatiuck," he said.

ACKNOWLEDGMENTS

This book could not have happened without the help and encouragement of the following people. My wife Chris Wasserstein, my agent Scott Miller, Alec Baldwin, SUNY Publisher James Peltz, Diane Ganeles, Marty and Judy Shepherd, David Rattiner, Kelly Merritt Shelley, Andy Sabin, Mark Schneier, Dennis Lynch, Joan Hamburg, Billy Joel, John Roland, Charline Spektor, Susan Isaacs, Betsy Carter, Mercedes Ruehl, Bill Henderson, Jimmy Finkelstein, LeRoy Neiman, Melissa Levis, Mischa Brenner, Natasha Brenner, Rusty and Diane Leaver, John Keeshan, Darielle Watnick, Joan Baum, Cecil Hoge, Jerry Cohen, Henry Hildreth, Joslyn Pine, Richard Gollin, Bob Edelman, Jerry and Adrian Cohen, Alex Boukas, Maya Baker, Matt Cross, the late James Brady, Ted Kheel, Joan Zandell, Geoff Lynch and the Hampton Jitney, Kaylee Jones, Arthur Bloom and the Shelter Island Bridge and Tunnel Authority, Adelaide de Menil and Ted Carpenter, Richard Lewin, Tim Gilmartin, Mary Guillen, Paul "P. J." Jeffers, Will Frank, Ralph George, Jim Monaco, Kaitlin Gallagher, Elizabeth Graziose, Ambassador Carl Spielvogel and Barbaralee Diamonstein-Spielvogel, Bill Hattrick, Pia Lindstrom, John

White, Jeff White, Red White, Stewart Lane, E. L. Doctorow, Leif Hope, Bonnie Gitlin, Sandi Mendelsohn, Eric Cohen, Gabriel Rattiner, Solange and Rhone Baker and Joan Gray.